Symphony of
REDEMPTION

L. LEAH PHOENIX

authorHOUSE®

AuthorHouse™
1663 Liberty Drive
Bloomington, IN 47403
www.authorhouse.com
Phone: 1 (800) 839-8640

Published by AuthorHouse 08/11/2015

ISBN: 978-1-5049-0530-5 (sc)
ISBN: 978-1-5049-2898-4 (e)

Library of Congress Control Number: 2015912935

Print information available on the last page.

Scripture quotations marked NIV are taken from the Holy Bible, New
International Version. NIV. Copyright © 1973, 1978, 1984 by International
Bible Society. Used by permission of Zondervan. All rights reserved.

For my daughters.
Each one of you is my teacher.
You deepened the capacity of my heart just by being born.
On my own, I am selfish and ugly.
Because of you, I can try to do better.
I love you with everything that I am.
Always and forever …

PREFACE

This is my life. I am an ordinary girl with an extraordinary journey. These are my memories, opinions and ideas. Some of them may seem silly, naïve, or flat-out wrong. A smart person once said that you can't argue with opinion. I'm not smart enough to remember who that was. I don't claim perfection. Please forgive my shortcomings, and bear with me. Maybe we have something in common.

About seven years went into the writing of this book. It started as a journal and developed into a memoir. I forced myself to reveal things that I would have rather kept private. It is raw, gritty, and bleak at times, but it's also honest and full of heart. It is the path that I had to walk in order to find peace, learn who I am, and eventually love myself despite my many flaws. And so, I am grateful.

My hope is to shine a light in the darkness for those who struggle with grief, sexual abuse, posttraumatic stress disorder, or addiction. Something within these pages may ease that vague yet tangible feeling of aloneness in this world.

Despite the darkness, my life is filled with happiness. My wish is to share that happiness with you. For me, it is all about perspective and never giving up. It isn't despite profound despair but because of it that I have found joy.

The End ... But Not Really

"Be kind; everyone you meet is fighting a hard battle."
—Plato

February 2004

Lying in a bathtub full of warm water, I sink down and think about what's gone wrong. *What did I do to deserve this?* There's no way out, and even if there were, I don't have the energy to go on. I'm sure some of my tedious depression is rooted in the fact that I can't sober up; I read somewhere that Prozac doesn't work when you take it with a drink. My routine is to take it in the morning with a nice big swig from the vodka hidden in my water bottle. I feel the edges round off as the pills hit my brain. I took a lot of different kinds. I bet Walter will be irritated that I took all of them—mine and his—but who cares? I won't be around to hear his criticism.

Walter is my boyfriend. He's at the movies with friends tonight. I was invited, but I had other plans. I knew I'd end up here. Calling him my boyfriend feels ridiculous. It sounds trite and silly to call a fifty-one-year-old man anything with the word *boy* in it. I can identify with the word *girlfriend* though, because I'm only twenty-five. I'm also immature. I don't feel like a grown-up. Walter and I get along pretty well, considering we work and live together. He's my boss, both at work and at home, but I don't mind. Someone has to be the boss of me. I recently went through a divorce, which was my idea. My life was out of control, and Walter seemed to be just the guy to step in and take the reins. Maybe he realizes that trying to control me is biting off more than he can chew. He tries, though; gotta give him that much. I love him, I really do. It just isn't enough to make me want to live. I feel alone in every possible way.

When it comes to bathtubs, this is definitely the best one ever. Walter's entire house was custom built, and the bath is one of my favorite spots. Behind my head is the shower, which is enclosed on the tub side by a wall of glass bricks. All around me are slate tiles that were hand-picked by Walter and his ex-wife. The entire house was built and designed by Walter and his ex, but their marriage didn't survive long enough for her to live in it. This is something I have come to appreciate, as I am the first woman to ever make this house a home. I have lived here about a month. Under different circumstances, I might have wanted to continue living here. Instead, I have decided that it's a nice place to die. My sorrow has taken on a life of its own. It actually has a physical weight, pulling the skin down all over my face, especially around my eyes. The heaviness causes me to be unbearably exhausted all day long. It feels nearly impossible to keep my eyes open, even without the vodka and pills.

I've tried this before, but I've never really had the nerve to follow through. This time it's different.

I'm not about to chicken out. My life is in the toilet, and I despise the process of waking up each day. My self-loathing finally has outgrown my fear of committing suicide. Carefully, I disassemble the razor on the side of the tub, slowly so I don't cut my fingers. Yes, I know it makes no sense, but that's me.

Envisioning my little girl, I start to cry. Once the floodgates open, it's impossible to stop. *Rose, I'm sorry.* The only thing that quiets me is the onslaught of sleep. Rose is six years old. She has the bluest eyes I've ever seen, clearer and brighter than her father's. She is the person who taught me how to be a mother. I promised myself I'd never fail her. We all make mistakes, and I have allowed myself plenty, but I haven't seen her in months. This is an unforgivable thing, the sting from which I cannot escape, day or night. She is a pawn, used by my ex in the divorce, the one tool he knows he can annihilate me with. *Mission accomplished, d-bag.* She probably thinks I left her alone on purpose. I understand the pain I've caused her in the divorce, yet I can't fathom the disgust I would have felt staying with her dad one more day. When I left, I asked her with whom she would rather live—her dad or me. Maybe it wasn't fair to pose such a question to someone so young. No one asked me that question when I was a kid, and I wanted to give her a choice instead of making one for her. In my heart, I knew she would choose him. She was always a daddy's girl. It's nothing I've ever taken personally or felt resentful about; I had been a daddy's girl too.

With as much strength as I can muster, I gouge the soft side of my arm with the razor blade and drag it from wrist to elbow. Staring at my skin, I think my body is broken or my skin is too thick or maybe I'm dead already, because nothing is happening. It's gross. There's just a big, gaping, bloodless gash. Oh, wait … here it comes. Dark, thick blood pours out of my arm and begins to drip off my elbow, mixing with the water in the tub. Quickly, before I lose my nerve, I manage the same thing with my left arm. I'm mad now, so I take three swipes at it before I submerge both arms so the cuts won't coagulate. *Well,* I think, *congratulations on finally doing something to end the incessant passing of day into night and night into morning, the constant waking up and thinking. Just bring me peace and quiet,* I pray. I want darkness … no more longing, no more loving, no more tears, and no more pain. *Oh, Rose, I'm sorry for all of it, including this.* I hope she'll learn to forgive me. Hopefully, somehow, some day she will understand that I had no options left. Without her to give me something to look forward to, there's no way I can make it through. She has probably already forgotten what my face looks like. It happens faster than you'd think. *Just look in the mirror, my love, and you'll see me. There you are, still innocent, a prettier version of me, looking so similar that I feel pity for you.*

I open my eyes. It hurts. It's bright. I try to focus, but it's hard. I am flattened out, completely exhausted. My eyelids flutter, and my eyeballs roll around in my head. There's a man sitting next to me. It's Walter. Oh, God. He looks both deeply concerned and stiffly perturbed. *Oh no! A hospital. This is not supposed to be happening.* I glance down and notice that my arms are stitched; the sliced parts look like railroad tracks. *Ew! I bet that will leave a scar.* I groan pathetically but say nothing. Walter looks at me. He also has nothing to say. He's got his poker face on, and I am unable to tell what he is thinking. He gets up to go to the restroom, leaving me in the cold brightly lit room by myself. If only the door were shut, I'd cry or curl up in a ball and wallow. But

I don't want to wallow without privacy. *This sucks.* Suddenly a friendly faced nurse is at my side; she quietly asks if I'm aware that I am pregnant. My eyes grow wide with disbelief. Silently, I shake my head. She grins slightly and nods so subtly that I almost don't register the movement. Then she walks out into the hallway, leaving me alone again, except I'm not.

A good friend once told me that the definition of a miracle is a change in consciousness. Based on this definition, I have experienced many miracles in life. One occurs in that room at that very moment. The weight falls away from my shoulders, from my gut, and from around my eyes. Each cell in my body lets go of the darkness it had been carrying around like a cancer. My whole outlook flips. It's true that perception is everything. Suddenly I have the energy to go on. The sadness leaves me so quickly and completely, it feels as though it hadn't been there at all. Unfortunately, my therapist isn't buying it, not with my arms looking that way. He recommends "a little time to rest and relax" at the mental hospital. I was prepared for that. It won't be my first time to rest and relax in the hospital.

Depression is a constant nagging feeling inside me; it has always been there, like my own shadow. When Rose was a year old, they called my depression postpartum, but it felt pretty much the same, only slightly more exaggerated and pitiful. With the encouragement of my then husband, I checked into a hospital for the first time. The time went by as slowly as time can go by, and I was already used to days dragging into oblivion. The time at the hospital seemed to stretch into a hundred years.

It's amazing to think back on it all, to remember the pain and the heartache I felt. *Treacherous* is the word that comes to mind. Now I'm in my thirties, and I've learned how to be content. I love being alive and to be present in the moment every day. But it sure was a long road to get here. Let me rewind things a bit.

Part 1

THE REAL BEGINNING

"I want my history to be your legacy.
Go ahead and show this world what you've done
in me ..."
— Francesca Battistelli, "Write Your Story"

1978

Things were not always depressing or chaotic. Growing up, I had many opportunities that other kids didn't. I was adopted by a couple who was unable to have children the old-fashioned way. (I'll say Mom and Dad a lot through these pages; unless I specify otherwise, I'll mean the parents who raised me.) My mom got pregnant a few times and then suffered miscarriages. Through a childhood friend, she met my biological mother, Mary, who was at the end of her pregnancy. Back then, women had a harder time being single and pregnant, and I had not been planned.

I grew up wondering and fantasizing a lot about my biological mother. I knew basically nothing about her or her circumstances. I loved guessing. *Is she pretty? Did she die? Is she a bad person? Did she ever love me? Was I born ugly? Was it hard to give me away?* I wondered if I had seen her around town and not recognized her.

I found out the answers to some of my questions as I got older. I don't know that it is exactly what happened, but this is what I have pieced together. Mary had married young and did not have any children with her husband. She was nineteen and employed by a woman named Gwendolyn as an in-home elder caregiver. Gwendolyn had a good-looking son named Harold. I imagine he had to have more than good looks to get my bio-mom to break her vows. Maybe it was his fun personality; maybe it was his sense of humor. After a short affair, she found out that she was pregnant with me. Her husband told her that she had to terminate the pregnancy or give me up for adoption, and threatened divorce if she refused. Mary considered keeping me until very late in her pregnancy, but everyone close to her encouraged her to give me up. In the end, she relented. After she met my mom, who was married and so desperately wanted a baby, Mary figured my mom would do a better job of raising me than she could. Her husband divorced her anyway.

From then on, I had a new mom, one who was overjoyed to have a little baby, even though I was a fussy and underweight preemie. I've heard the story told and retold by my mom, my dad, and my maternal grandmother, Mae. On a hot day in late August, I was born jaundiced and significantly early to a girl who saw me only for a moment before they put me into the arms of my mom. I can imagine the look of overwhelmed awe and joy on my mom's face. I saw her like that in the delivery room after she saw me deliver my own daughters. It was priceless.

From the beginning, my mom took a unique approach to raising a child. Soon after I was born, she became involved with a Chinese church in Santa Barbara, so she could get some help taking care of me. She wanted me to learn the culture and felt very strongly about giving me the gift of other languages early on. She knew that it would be easier for a baby to learn more than one language from the beginning. Soon she heard about a woman who had just moved to our city from Taiwan. Her name was Mrs. Xin, but she became Xin Mama to me, and she ended up being very much like another grandmother.

Every day, since before I could speak any language, I went to her home, and she treated me like I was her own grandchild. I learned her language, her culture, her humor, her cooking, and most important, I learned her way. Xin Mama was very poor, but she never complained. Standing less than five feet tall, she walked everywhere. She smiled a lot. She made most of her own clothes and never changed the furniture in her little apartment. She raised two good kids of her own (a son and daughter who are both older than I am) and never fought with her husband in front of me. With her quiet and patient ways, she drew out a side of me that only existed around her. She gently commanded respect, and the love that grew between us was absolute and unconditional. I knew I could tell her anything, and most of the time I did. Xin Mama and I spent at least an hour or two together every single day for thirteen years. In all that time, I did not have one unhappy memory in her home. Totally immersed in an environment where everyone spoke only Chinese, I picked up the language simultaneously with English.

Some of my fondest childhood memories are with Xin Mama. She cooked a lot. The prep work seemed to take forever. She'd bring the cutting board into the living room so we could hang out together. I watched as she painstakingly cut all the fat off of the meat or prepared vegetables. I can still see her sitting on that old brown couch, watching the soap opera *Santa Barbara*, trying to understand what was going on. Sometimes I just showed up and lay down in her living room, my home away from home, knowing that even if I fell asleep while she was talking, she would still love me and smile when I woke up.

When I was sixteen, Xin Mama moved down south, near Los Angeles, somewhere with her daughter. I visited her once, and she died not too long after that. At the funeral, her family treated me as though I were family. At that age, I was desperate to have a sense of acceptance and belonging and it meant very much to me. During the service, there was a spot reserved for me up front, next to her adult children. It warmed my heart to realize that they felt the same way about me as I did about them. It was my first experience with an open casket, and it stunned me to see her in there with makeup on her face. I'd never seen her wear makeup a day in her life. It was so surreal, I put my hand out to touch her skin. I still remember how she felt—like candle wax that had melted and hardened again on a cold glass table. After the service, I asked if I could have her green sweater. She'd knitted it with variegated yarn, and she wore it so often, it was all I could remember her in. It surprised me when they said I could keep it. At the time, I believed that asking for anything owned by a woman who possessed so little was asking too much. I have owned and lost many material possessions in my life, but this is one of the few I still have.

Throughout the first few years of my life, my mom worked hard to give me a good foundation. Knowing the benefits of breast milk, she acquired what she could for me. She made her own baby food and even squeezed fresh fruit and vegetable juices for me. When it was time for me to start preschool, she enrolled me in a Spanish- and English-speaking school where I would learn a third language.

My first memory is being in the driveway, watching my dad work on something in the garage. What he was doing didn't make sense to me at the time. He had a picture I'd made for him, with melted crayon designs all over it. It was framed so there was glass over it. He had a razor blade in one hand and a straw in the other. At the time, it looked like he just had a strange way of cleaning the dust off my picture. *My dad must think I'm a really good artist to take such great care of my art work!* For whatever reason, that image stuck with me. Of course, years later I realized my dad was snorting dope.

Around the same time, my great-grandmother on my mother's side came to live with us, if "live" is what you want to call it. She was struggling from Alzheimer's and had lost the ability to take care of herself. My mother got us bunk beds, and all of a sudden I had a new roommate. It was fun for me, because I liked being on the top bunk. My mom also hired a lady from Guatemala to help take care of both Great-grandma and me. She spoke only Spanish to me.

When I was four, my mother had me start taking piano lessons. I've heard lots of stories about little kids who are thrown into musical lessons, where the child is forced to take time to practice, and eventually they are allowed to quit. This was not the case with me. The piano is not an instrument to me but an extension of who I am. There were neighbor girls to the left of us and behind us, but I preferred to be alone. In retrospect, I'm not sure if it was their choice or mine. Maybe it was a little of both. I took to playing the piano, because it made my own little world more fun and interesting. I felt the music inside. It gave me a new voice. Music is one of the greatest gifts my mother ever gave me. It lives inside my heart and soul.

There are countless examples of how my mother worked hard to provide me with every advantage she could think of. She is innovative and had unique and creative ideas of how to help me learn, even though she'd graduated from high school without knowing how to read. We learned to read together. Something I've noticed is that the love of reading tends to be learned at a young age. She read to me at night-time, usually drifting off while I stayed awake, wanting more. When I was old enough to be able to follow a longer story, she found books like *Anne of Green Gables* to read to me. I remember lots of days lying on a blanket at the park, in the partial shade of an oak tree, listening to the cadence of her voice while she ignited my imagination. We were inseparable back then.

The Early 1980s

Dinner is over, and pretty soon it'll be bath time. I like taking a bath and taking a long time to do it. I like feeling the water get cool. I wish I could play with bubbles, but my skin gets all itchy and it hurts, so Mom says I can't have any. She starts the water running, and I try to go pee in the toilet before getting in. My pee takes a long time to come out, and it burns. It happens all the time now, and I cry a little bit and complain about it to my mom.

"I'll get you some more cranberry juice," she assures. She's used to this, and so am I, but that doesn't make it hurt any less right now. It burns really bad, and the pee just drips out little by little. I complain a little more before giving up on it and standing up. It will feel better once I get in the bath.

"You need to drink more water," she says.

Water is boring, I think, but say nothing. She gives me a toy and a washcloth to play with. I like to get the washcloth warm and place it across my tummy until it gets cold. My favorite is lying down in the water all the way, until my head is underwater and the only thing sticking up is my nose. I used to think I could breathe underwater, but I really can't. When I'm under there, I can hardly hear anything at all, except the water running and my own breathing. It is my world under the water, and I am a mermaid. I move my head back and forth under the water, side to side, and feel my long hair swishing around my face. The higher the water gets, the deeper I let myself go, and I see my hair floating around me. My hair is prettier under water than anywhere else. That's because it's mermaid hair.

My dad comes in to shut off the water and to check on me. This is my least favorite part of bath time. He wants to make sure I'm nice and clean and helps me do the things I forget to do.

"Stand up," he says. He looks at me and at the water.

"It's too clear. You didn't use enough soap or that water wouldn't look like that," he tells me. But putting the soap in the water is what makes my skin feel yucky. *Doesn't he know that?*

"Here, let me help you." He is always very helpful at bath time. I hardly ever do it right, but he is smiling at me, and I can tell he isn't mad that I've done it wrong again. He quickly goes over my body with his hands, and the last thing he touches is my privates.

"It's important to make sure you're nice and clean," he reminds me, and I agree. I'm glad he pays so much attention to me. He takes a long time here, and puts his fingers all around that part and his soapy fingers go inside my privates. His fingers go all the way inside, and it stings. This is why I don't like this part of bath time. Maybe we need a different kind of soap, because it always makes my privates burn so bad. It makes me feel like I have to go pee again or something, but I'm afraid to because that will make it hurt even more. He's done now, and I know that bad feeling will go away after a little bit. It always does.

Soon my mom comes back in to get me out. She helps me dry off, and I decide to tell her about Dad and the hurting thing he does.

"When Dad puts the soap in my privates, it hurts. I wish he would stop putting the soap in there. Maybe we need different soap." I say it just like that, matter-of-fact, but she doesn't seem to hear what I am saying. She is looking at me like she is confused.

"Your dad puts soap in your privates?" She asks me this very slowly.

"Yeah, and it makes it burn."

"He shouldn't be putting it in there," she says, pushing her eyebrows together. "All you need to wash that part of your body is water. You never want to have soap in it."

"Okay," I reply, but in my head I'm wondering, *why doesn't he know that?* Maybe boys don't know about girls' privates.

"I'll tell him," she assures, and it makes me feel better. *Poor Dad. He just tries to do too good of a job taking care of me.* He doesn't always do things that make sense, like when he drinks the apple juice that tastes like fire or cleans his picture in the garage. He's nice to me, though, way nicer than Mom. He is definitely my favorite.

Summer 1985

We went to Asia for three months the summer I turned seven. It was just me and my mom. We stayed with people who treated us like we were a part of their family. We flew, we bused, we drove, and we rode on trains. We went to Taiwan, Thailand, Singapore, and Malaysia. I learned all kinds of cool things. I learned how to make my way through a big busy airport and catch a plane. I learned about going through customs. I even learned how to pee in a hole on a moving train while I watched the ground fly by underneath me. We ate things most Americans will never experience. (Some of those things I ate to be polite but swallowed whole. Sometimes chewing is the worst part. Once in a while I was able to discreetly cough my food into a napkin.) After a couple of weeks, I was speaking Chinese like a real Chinese person.

I thought I was Chinese back then. Since my dad was half-Chinese, all of my cousins have beautiful olive skin and almond-shaped eyes. I just figured I was one of them. Then one day when I was around nine or ten, I grew taller than nearly everyone in my family on his side. Embarrassingly, my feet also grew way too large for a Chinese girl. I started to bind my feet in the only way that I could think of, which was to wear way-too-tight shoes. This is why, before having children, I was about five feet ten inches tall and only wore a size 7.5 shoe. I still remember the day I looked at myself in the mirror and realized something was definitely different. I had always known I was adopted, but it became obvious that I was apparently a white person!

Our trip overseas was really great. It is the last time that I can really remember being close to my mother as a child. We had fun learning things together. We knew each other so well, we didn't have to speak to communicate with one another. We could just look at each other in a certain way and *know*. Being together was fun. My closest friend growing up was definitely my mother. I loved the company of my dad and felt we had more in common, but my mom and I were always together, and we had good times.

Christmas Eve, 1985

I was lying down on my parents' bed, watching the same children's Christmas special they still air today, with Rudolph and the elf and the storm at the North Pole. The animation is clunky, but it's a cute story. It looked a lot more cool and high tech through my seven-year-old eyes. All the lights were out except for what was coming from the TV. I wasn't snuggled in for the night, just lying on top of the covers. It had been a weird day. Dad didn't come home, so Mom and I had to put up the tree alone. We were both sad about it, but we still made it happen. I don't remember what my dad said he had been doing, but he finally came home, and he and Mom were in the living room, fighting. Dad spent a lot of his time away in those days, and when he was home, they spent most of their time fighting, which was getting louder and scarier all the time. This fight wasn't as bad as some of the others. The worst one so far was the one where Dad had Mom backed into a corner in the kitchen with a knife held all the way up to her neck. That was definitely the scariest. Usually, I liked to lurk outside the door listening to every word of their fights, but this night was different because I really liked the TV show.

Over the last couple of years, my mom and I had been drifting apart. We'd both changed, but in different ways. We didn't understand each other anymore. Soon, it felt like we didn't know each other at all. After a while, I stopped asking her to do anything about Dad coming in the bathroom. I stopped thinking she cared about me in some ways. I started doing really weird things like stealing my great-grandmother's adult diapers and going to the bathroom in them. I felt weird about the toilet and about my poo. I knew what I was doing was weird so I would hide the dirty diapers in my closet. I couldn't stop sucking my thumb, even though I was too old to do that anymore. I still had no friends and lived in a world all alone with my books and my music.

Those days, the phone rang a lot and if my mom answered, the line went dead. One day my mom left to go run errands. My babysitter, Elaine, came over. She was also a secretary at my dad's office. She had her one-year-old baby, Michelle, with her. She and my dad said they had some things to talk about in the other room, (my parents' bedroom), so Michelle and I hung out in the living room. I was young but I knew what was up. If Mom found out she would be really upset and hurt, so I knew that I'd better do what dad said, and keep it between just us.

After a while I couldn't stand it, so I told my mom. It was just like with the other stuff, and she didn't hear me. She didn't want to believe the things I told her sometimes. She couldn't or wouldn't accept the truth. No one ever really found out how many years Dad and Elaine had their secret affair, but I think it was from the time I was maybe three or four. I don't know. Depending on how drunk they were, the story changed, and after a while it stopped mattering to me how long it had gone on. It became old news, and nobody cared anymore.

Back to Christmas Eve. Around the time when Rudolph became an outcast and tried to cover up his glowing nose, my dad stormed in the room, holding a navy-blue suitcase with tan piping. He put the suitcase on the bed and opened their big wooden armoire and started packing.

Seeing he was upset, I asked him what was wrong and what he was doing. I don't remember the exact words he used, but he said something like, "Your mom wants me to leave, so I'm leaving."

I was confused, because I knew that all she'd wanted was for him to come home all day long. We both had. Why would she want him to leave now? I guessed maybe it was another one of the games he played, so I said nothing. I just watched as he tossed more clothes in his suitcase and huffed and puffed, making a huge production out of it. Usually my dad didn't show his anger around me, so this was different. It was always my mom who acted out and yelled. He would get her angry to the point of exploding, and then he would sit back calmly and watch her blow up. Later, he would laugh at her and tell me, "Look at her going crazy again." And of course, I always agreed with him, because it was true. She *was* going crazy all the time. She raged and yelled and threw things, not caring if I accidentally got caught in the crossfire. I led a nervous and unpredictable life as their child during the last few years of their marriage.

There was no way for me to know how betrayal can shatter a wife's heart, so I could neither sympathize nor understand my mom, let alone try to be there for her. I had no idea what she was going through. Like any child, all I knew was my own limited experience. I was self-absorbed and confused. All I knew to do was try to make logic from my little-kid point of view. *Mom acts like a raving lunatic. Dad lets me have chocolate. Dad wins!*

11

When I could see that Dad was really and truly leaving us, all I could think was that I wanted to go with him. Yes, I wanted him to stay, but if he had to go, then he had to take me too. (Sorry, Mom, I wish I were more loyal back then. I know I made things harder on you by taking his side.) I prayed a lot for God to keep them together, because they were the only family I knew.

My mom never came in the room while he packed his things. Once his bag was packed, she begged him not to leave us. We both pleaded with him. I wrapped my arms around his leg, holding onto him, yelling "don't go" while he made his way to the door. He was bound and determined to leave, and there was no talking him out of it. Out he went, stone-faced into the night, without a tear in his eyes. I retreated under my piano to cry. My whole world and everything I knew ended in that moment.

I could see him wanting to leave her, I mean, she was bananas. But why me? We had a special relationship. How could he walk out on both of us? What was more important than us? If he ever loved me, how could he leave me with her? It was the worst hurt in the world for me at the time. It was my very first heartbreak. It may sound twisted (because it is), but to me that was the one positive physical relationship I had. Nobody else paid me that kind of attention. I wasn't important to anyone in that way. My mom was proud of me, because I was smart. I scored high on IQ tests, which impressed grown-ups, and that pleased her. I could order Chinese food in Chinese. She liked that too; everyone did. She came to all my school things and was happy for me when I won a poetry contest or spelling bee. She was proud that I took home straight A's. She always had a huge smile on her face when I played in a piano recital. I always played my piece just right—no mistakes. She gave me a lot of time and energy and helped me learn. Even I knew I was smart.

In my world though, smart was lonely, and my mom was scary. My dad made me feel special, and not just because of the one secret thing. There were so many reasons. He was awesome, and I loved everything about him! It felt impossible that he could leave me. I was sure Christmas wouldn't happen after he left. My mom crawled under the piano and cried with me for a while. We eventually packed up some things and went out to her sister Carol's house. I liked Auntie Carol a lot, but I was pretty sure that Santa Claus would not find us over there. Auntie Carol is my mother's only sister. She and her husband, Frank, lived in Goleta, a little north of Santa Barbara, with their kids, Aaron (a couple of years older than I was) and Sophia (a few years younger). As much as I liked spending time with them, Christmas was ruined.

In fact, as time would tell, it was ruined forever. It became such a forced issue. *We* will *enjoy our Christmas! We love gingerbread men! Decorating a tree is such fun!* Yuck. Then it became artificially sweet. We all knew what we were thinking, but nobody dared to admit how crummy we felt inside. *So, how is your father?* (Thin-lipped smile, nibble on this, sip on that …) *Oh fine, I guess, um, yeah, he's good.* (Cross legs, shift in seat, attempt a smile, check the time …) So awkward.

My dad never came back. He went to live in an apartment at a building my parents owned on the other side of town. My mother and I stayed in our house for a while. Crazy turned insane. My poor mother went out of control, and her anger was deep and violent. She hoped they would work it out and that he would come back home. She was still in love with him. They had known each other since junior-high school. Understandably, she had a hard time letting go. My dad continued to lie, telling her he wasn't seeing Elaine anymore. I know it made him feel badly to see what he was doing to his wife. He was stuck, and he didn't know what he really wanted. He was emotionally invested in both women by that time.

He couldn't and wouldn't stop seeing Elaine. He'd already fallen in love with her. She'd left her marriage to be with my dad by that time too. My mother finally gave up and remarried a doctor named Stewart. They wed on the day that her divorce was final. He was a decent man who tried to make us into a family. At the time, I didn't like him simply because he wasn't my dad. No matter how moody or sullen I was, he was nice to me. My mom found out that he cheated on her with a nurse and wasn't willing to go through it all over again. The marriage only lasted about three months.

Soon after their divorce, we went to live in a trailer behind Grandma Mae's house. The trailer was about eight feet wide and thirty feet long, with a bed at the back, a futon in the middle, and a stove and sink at the front. My dad got a lot of money in the divorce. My mom kept the properties and bought him out. Suddenly, we had no money, and we needed to rent out our home to have money to live on. We still had my great-grandmother with us and her caretaker, Armida. We couldn't all fit in the trailer comfortably, so I set up a two-person tent outside on the gravel. Armida slept on a mattress in the old wooden horse barn nearby. Great-grandma got the bed, and Mom took the futon.

That year, I started going to Laguna Blanca School. This was the kind of school where the older students drove BMWs or Porsches. It was my sixth-grade year, and I was unhappy. I hardly saw my dad and I missed him a lot. Sometimes he pulled up to my school in his blue work truck, and was so happy to see him. He'd bring lunch, and we'd eat together. When that happened, it was the best part of my week.

Otherwise, my life at school was miserable. They knew I was poor, and it put me on the outside of every social group. Nobody liked me. To make matters worse, I hadn't been able to stop sucking my thumb and my teeth were hideous. I had a mouth crammed full of big, gangly teeth that jutted straight out. I looked like I could eat an apple through a hole in the fence. They also made fun of me for being adopted. I got called names like Trailer Trash, Bucky Beaver, and Test-Tube Baby.

I rarely ate outside with the other kids. Instead, I chose to stay inside, alone. I had my first crush that year, on a boy named Benjamin. One lunch, I sat at his desk just to see how it felt. I wanted to have his cooties on me. In a rare moment of courage, I opened his desk just to see what he had in there. Inside was the usual stuff ... books, binders, pencils, etc. He also had some Halloween candy. I was hungry, so I took a little tiny box of Milk Duds. He had other candy, and I didn't think he would miss it. Of course, he did notice it was missing, and they knew I was the only nerd in the whole class who ate lunch alone inside. After that, they also called me Milk Duds. Stupid.

My whole life I'd gotten top grades, and now I was failing. That year went by very slowly. For seventh grade, I went to La Colina Junior High School and did equally poorly. I left mid-year to live with my dad. He was living at Hollister Ranch with Elaine and Michelle. I went to a very small public school in Gaviota called Vista del Mar. It was a good school, and I liked it there. The next year, I went back to live with my mom. Somehow, I got a scholarship to go to Laguna Blanca again based on high IQ test scores (Mom's idea). I went there with a bad attitude fueled with resentment over my sixth grade year. I was determined to payback the bullies. If nobody liked me and I was friendless, it would be my choice, not theirs. I was a girl with thick walls and something to prove. Halfway through that school year, I got expelled. But before that happened, I kissed that same boy, Benjamin, I'd had a crush on all through sixth grade. I still think about him sometimes. Strangely, I even have dreams about him once in a while, although I think those dreams are less about him and more about liking boys that are mean to me.

After the expulsion, I went back to my dad's and Vista del Mar. The year that I graduated eighth grade was pretty fun. Two things happened that year that stand out in my mind: the first was getting chicken pox from Michelle, and the second was running away from my dad's house. I got mad over something small. I didn't want to have to do the dishes after dinner, so I walked away with the family dog,

Coho. It wouldn't have been such a big deal except that we lived on the last parcel of a private ranch, totally isolated from everyone. At one point, I heard people call my name, but I kept on walking down the side of the mountain toward the ocean. We lived right up a steep cliff side from Point Conception, which is where California sticks out the farthest on the coastline. I was tired of their drunken fights, and I wanted to make a statement, so I just kept going. I knew that if I could make it down to the ocean, I would find railroad tracks that went along the entire coastline.

By dark, I had made it to the tracks. That night was pretty scary. I hadn't planned on being gone all night long when I walked down our driveway, but that's exactly what I was doing. My pride and anger wouldn't let me turn around. Earlier that year, a little boy had been killed by a mountain lion in that area. Before the sun set, I saw a herd of wild boars, but I didn't see any mountain lions. It was a dark and moonless night, cold but not freezing. I heard the waves crashing to the right of me as I walked in the dark. At one point, Coho started barking, and I stopped walking. I stood as still as I could, staring into the darkness in front of me. I saw a large shadow move out of the way and off the tracks. That did it. I was nearly paralyzed with fear.

I decided to make my way down the mound of rocks surrounding the tracks and sit down near the base. I never put my head down that night. I just pulled my sweatshirt over my knees (I was in shorts!) and tucked my head inside when I got really cold. The train went by a few times. The sound of it rushing by was both terrifying and exhilarating. At one point, I thought my dog had been hit by the train, but after a while she came back to me. The next day I was in big trouble with my dad. By the summer, he was ready to send me back to my mom's house.

Things felt very alien back at my mom's. I had outgrown the tent, and slept in a camper shell that was parked right next to the cemetery fence. She worked at Robinson's Department Store. She was unhappy in life and complained about being tired a lot. We disagreed about everything. I was scared of her. More and more, her anger was directed at me. One morning she found a dirty fork in the sink, and she dumped a pot full of cold water on my face while I was asleep. That made me really mad. One night I wanted to call my dad. When I picked the phone up, she grabbed it out of my hand, ripped the mount off the wall, and hit me repeatedly with the phone. She was still very angry with my father. We had many fights and I lived in constant fear of her moods. Her rage changed her into someone I didn't recognize. The last physical fight we had was out at my aunt's house. It was over my shoes. She started hitting, shoving, and smacking me and then she got down on her knees to force the shoes off my feet. I'd had enough. She had my leg in her hands, pulling at my shoe, and I jabbed her in the back with my elbow. She rolled to the ground with a stunned look on her face. It was the first time I had ever hit her, and it was the last time she ever physically attacked me. Not only did I feel like she had stopped loving me, I began to think she didn't like me anymore either. Sometimes I would overhear her talking to family members about me. The things she said about me when she didn't know I was listening confirmed my fears. I felt totally betrayed, and I started to question whether she had ever loved me to begin with. I felt alone no matter where I went or whom I was with.

Summer 1991

The year I turned thirteen, my mom sent me to Guatemala for the summer. It's fun to think back about this incredible trip, because it was so strange and amazing. Why in the world would a mom send her kid off on her own to a different country? She knew the family of someone down there, and she thought it would be a good thing. She was right. It was also a great way to polish up on my Spanish. When I think back about my life, that summer was one of the most empowering and exciting experiences I've ever had.

The people I lived with were generous in every way that people can be. They treated me like family. They threw me a birthday party even though they could barely afford to eat. The town was totally rural, and there was no bathroom inside the house. There was only one telephone, and I don't mean in the house. There was one telephone in the town. It was wonderful. I found my independence that summer.

One day, giant, dark storm clouds covered the sun, and everything got dark. It started to rain. All of a sudden a gorgeous lightning storm happened all around me. I had never seen anything like that growing up in Southern California. I couldn't stay inside. It was still a warm day, and I wanted to be part of the storm. I was the only person in the middle of the dirt road looking up toward the sky, transfixed by the electric beauty. I could feel the storm inside me, and that feeling is indescribable.

Most days were muggy and hot. We went to the corner store often. They didn't serve sodas in bottles. For some reason, they poured the cold soda into a plastic baggie and wrapped it around a straw. I'd down it in a matter of seconds. I always ordered orange, and it tasted like pure heaven. At times, I would look at the mountains in the direction of home and try to imagine all the miles between my family and me. It gave me a feeling of incredible personal power, like I could do anything, go anywhere, be anyone.

I don't remember the flight there, but I sure do remember the flight back. The city where I was staying was a four-hour drive from the airport in Guatemala City. We woke up early enough to get there in time to catch my flight, but they wanted to stop for breakfast. I kept telling them I needed to get to the airport at least an hour before my scheduled flight time, but they wouldn't listen. They thought that the time on the ticket was the time that I had to be at the airport. I knew that we were cutting it really close. As I ran through the airport desperately, I scanned all the lines going to the United States. The last line was empty. Sure enough, that was the one headed for LAX. Boarding had ended. The flight had left me behind.

Before I left home, my mom had told me that if I were in a situation beyond my control, if I were lost or scared or confused, to get an ice cream and sit down on my suitcase. So I did just that. I found a place that sold ice-cream cones, bought one, and then sat on my suitcase. I had about $50 left and no idea what to do. I was alone and totally stuck. I was overwhelmed and felt like I would never make it home. I started to cry. I was really scared; the situation started to sink in. A stewardess came over and asked if I needed help. I explained the situation to her, and she left, telling me to wait right there. She said that everything was going to be okay. Eventually, she came back to me. She was right. Everything would work out. She said that I would make it home, that I could get on the next plane with her. I was frightened to get on the plane because it wasn't going home. It was going to Mexico City. But I had no other idea or plans, so I made up my mind to get on that flight, because Mexico was closer to home than Guatemala City. It was really cool because I got to sit in the front of the airplane with the stewardess who was helping me.

When we got to Mexico City, I got off the plane, and the stewardess told me to wait there for a few hours, and someone would contact me again and help me go home. After a four-hour layover, which felt like forever, someone did come talk to me. Somehow, I had gotten a seat on a plane home. When I boarded that direct flight to LA, I learned something. No matter what happens in life, no matter how alone I feel or how insane the circumstances are, everything will be okay. Sitting in the window seat on my way home, I listened to my Walkman. I played the song "Home Sweet Home" over and over with a feeling of elation inside. *You know I'm a dreamer, but my heart's of gold …*

This was my first real lesson in letting go of fear and trusting God to carry me through even the most hopeless of situations. If I can pinpoint a time in my life when I've learned the most in one day, it was probably the twenty-four-hour period of time between waking up that last morning in Guatemala and walking off the flight in Los Angeles. Life may throw some serious curve balls, but no matter. I was at the young age of (barely) thirteen and able to make it through. Remembering that feeling today, more than twenty years later, it makes me smile. God was right there teaching me things about Himself, about myself, and about life itself that would stay with me forever. I would need to hold onto those lessons in less than one year's time.

Summer 1992

Remembering the summer of 1992 is like remembering an entirely different version of myself. Before then, my posture was straight. I had never tasted alcohol. I didn't understand shame. Sometimes girls tell each other stories about their first time with a boy. Maybe the story isn't always romantic, but usually it is somewhat thought-through. I imagine that the experience is often fumbling and embarrassing—probably not that great but probably not that bad either. I would have liked my first time to have been on purpose, but it wasn't.

My best friend at the time was about a year younger than I was. I'll call her Ella. She was twelve, and I was thirteen. Later that summer, I would turn fourteen. We were planning to go see a movie at the new mall downtown. They had just built the Paseo Nuevo Mall, and the movie theater was supposed to be nice. I can't remember what movie we were going to go see. My mom dropped us off, and we were hanging out in front of the theater. We were early. Right before the movie was going to start, we ran into a few friends of her older brother. I think that is how she knew them. One of the guys was friends with my cousin Aaron, but I didn't know that at the time. I think I found that out later, which made it even worse. They wanted us to hang out with them instead of go to our movie, which felt exciting and sounded fun. *Yay! These older guys want to hang out with us!* It didn't take long for them to convince us to get in the car with them and go out to Isla Vista and hang out at a park. One of them bought beer. I'd never had a beer before, and it sounded really cool to be having one with these guys.

I don't know if I wish I could remember more or less about this. The memories come back in flashes. It has been more than twenty years now, but even back then, I couldn't remember much, not even the next day. The beer was a forty-ounce Mickey's, and I didn't think anything about the fact that it had already been opened when one of the guys handed it to me. I am pretty sure I only drank about half of it before I blacked out. They must have put quite a bit of drugs in it, or maybe not. What do I know? I had no tolerance for anything yet, and I had no idea what I was supposed to be feeling. I don't know what drug it was, but whatever it was made me have holes in my memory and made me sick for three days afterward. Or maybe it was the memories that made me sick. Most likely, it was some of both.

> *Flash:* I'm in a room somewhere, and I don't know how I got here. I'm in a small little garage-like place with two mattresses up on top of an L-shaped platform. There is someone on top of me. I can hear my friend. She is crying; then she is silent. I can't move my arms or legs. They feel like they weigh too much and I can't make them do anything. Even if I try to focus really hard on a part of my body, I can't make it move. I feel like I'm under wet cement or something. I'm naked. It's nighttime, it's very dim, but there is enough light for me to see. The roof is only three or four feet up. We're close to the ceiling. It smells like blood and cinnamon. The guy who is

on top of me is yelling in my face. He keeps telling me to lift my legs up, but I can't do it.

"Lift your legs up! Come on," he says, with a look of disgust on his face. "Don't you know how to do this?"

I think about saying something, but my mouth can't make words. *No*, I think, *I really don't. I don't know what I'm doing. I couldn't lift my legs even if I did know what I'm doing. How long have I been here? Oh my God I am going to be in so much trouble.*

Someone is having sex with Ella too. I hear her make a noise. She sounds as miserable as I am. I feel worried and sad for her. After a while, she becomes quiet and stays that way for a long time.

All around us is plywood, no drywall. I'm on a bare, dirty mattress. This feels really wrong. The place between my vagina and my butt feels torn, burning and stinging. The cinnamon smell is heavy in the air, thick like the blood smell coming from everywhere, and I feel like throwing up. I can't speak or fight against what is happening. I wouldn't know what to say if I could speak. My tongue is fat and limp inside my mouth. My eyes are having a hard time staying on any one thing. I feel humiliated because I have no idea what I'm doing, how I got here, or who these guys really are. This is not how it is supposed to be. I keep thinking about how much trouble I'm going to be in. The guys talk to each other about us.

"This one's tight as a penny," guy one says about me.

"This one's tight as a dime," guy two says about my friend.

Oh my God this is so gross. I wish I could make them stop. I wish I could run away. I wish I could yell something. Why is it hurting so much? How long is this going to last?

As soon as he is done, he starts again. I'm still tearing and burning raw, and then they decide to trade. Now the other guy is on me. *I'm so disgusting. I am such a piece of trash. Ew, I am so gross.* The night turns into forever. At some point, thankfully, I black out again.

Flash: One of them is on my neck and chest, sucking for a really long time. My body feels heavy and swollen. Everything hurts. I just wish I could sleep. I wish I could sleep and never have to wake up. That sickly sweet smell of artificial cinnamon is still in my nose. It's not the real kind of cinnamon. It's the smell of fake cinnamon, like in candles or gum. I still can't move or speak. *I hate myself for letting this happen.* I'm too angry to cry anymore. Once more, everything goes black.

In the morning, I wake up, and I am totally alone. There is blood all over. There are used condoms strewn about. I am surprised by the number of them. I pick one up, and it is covered in bloody slime. I feel disconnected from my body. *Where is everyone?* There are no guys, no friend, no anything but me in this foul little shack. I lean over the side and see that my clothes are on the nasty floor down below. I try to get up and have to stop to clear my head. Finally, I make it down the wooden ladder, although my legs are barely working. Slowly, I get dressed in my jeans and T-shirt. This place is sickening. I am sickening. I feel totally used and beat up. I want to heave. I want to disappear.

I have to get out of here. I have no idea where I am, but I have to get going. I want to be anywhere but here. I can't be here one more second.

I don't know how I got out of there. I don't remember where I went. I do remember getting a clear soda to try to settle my stomach a while later, and I couldn't keep it down. Doubled over, I wretched and wretched and wretched.

After that I stayed away from beer, but I never stayed sober for long. I've asked myself so many times how I became a drug addict. It started way before I met the needle, but was it at thirteen? Maybe so. Maybe I was born this way, and thirteen is when I woke the beast inside. After the rape, I never went back home for long. Covered in hickeys and so much shame, I thought my mother would reject me. I thought that my appearance would upset her. I figured she was really angry at me for not coming home. At the time, I felt everything that had happened was my fault. Worse than anything was the idea that she would want me to talk about it. Truthfully, I don't remember where I went or what I did in those first few days. After a while it became such a big deal that I felt it would be too weird to show up at home, so I stayed away.

The rape changed who I was in every way. I held onto my secret for ten years before I ever admitted to anyone what had actually happened. Later I found out that Ella's family made her go to the police and to the hospital. She did the rape kit and everything, but despite her parents' efforts, the guys were never prosecuted.

As for me, I made my own way, hiding my reality. I learned to live with posttraumatic stress disorder, though at the time I had no idea what I was going through. My mind and everything about my personality changed dramatically, and I was too blind to see why. Suddenly, I hated myself. I had violent and terrifying nightmares that made me wake up screaming or crying. I even had pee accidents as late as sixteen. I've never told anyone about that. Everything felt really difficult. I was angry at myself and the world around me. I relived the rape over and over in my mind. I thought about it a lot and all my intensely negative feelings went inward, aimed at myself. Flashes of the night would pop into my head, and I couldn't get away from my thoughts, no matter how many drugs I tried.

I was a dirty girl. I felt dirty on the inside, so I treated myself badly. I started dressing like a boy, wearing huge baggy pants and oversized T-shirts and sweatshirts. I wore sneakers and never put on makeup or did anything with my hair. I shaved the back part of my head. I smoked cigarettes. I started cutting, piercing, and hurting myself. I burned myself with cigarettes. I made myself bleed and sometimes put my blood in containers. I watched what happened to my old blood, noticing how long it took to coagulate and dry up. I lived in a world all by myself and hated everything about what I had become.

Nobody knew me. Even if they did, they couldn't possibly like me, so I started lying a lot. I lied about everything! I even lied about my birthday. Thinking back, I have no idea why I did that. I made up a lot of things about who I was or what I liked. Finally, a guy I liked a lot caught me in so many lies that he confronted me. I realized how stupid it was and vowed to stop lying. It was much more embarrassing to get caught in lies than it was to just try to be authentic.

One day, at a gas station, I turned around, and my dad was there. He looked as shocked to see me as I was to see him. We hugged awkwardly. I sat quietly in his work truck as he took me back to my mom's trailer. My grandmother was there, and she was so surprised to see me that she slammed her fingers in her car door. It was uncomfortable for everyone to have me around. Nobody talked about why I'd left.

One good thing came out of being there: I was able to be with my great-grandmother when she died. It happened that very day. It meant a lot to me to hold her hand and be with her when she stopped breathing. She had a moment of clarity right before that happened and was able to respond to our conversation and prayers. It was hard to see her body get taken away by the police. They put her on a cloth stretcher with wooden bars on each side and folded them up and carried her away in a bundle. She looked so tiny. I was very moved by it, but it didn't slow me down for long.

I enrolled in Dos Pueblos High School, but I couldn't sit still. I knew one girl, from church when we were younger. She and I hung out, and sometimes she let me stay at her house. Her parents were divorced, and her dad's house was in the neighborhood in which I hung out. It didn't take him long to decide he didn't like me, but she had a pretty big closet in which she let me sleep. When she was at her mom's or when something else was going on, I was on my own. Sometimes I stayed with another friend I met at school. Sometimes I had sex with someone, and he would let me stay the night. I had no self-respect, so I didn't really think it was that big of a deal. One of the men I slept with got me pregnant. Within a month of finding out, I miscarried. He never knew about the baby. More than once, I had no options, so I went to a park where there were enclosed tennis courts. This was a safe place to sleep, because I thought if I pulled my sweatshirt over my knees and got myself into a small-enough ball, nobody would ever notice me. Sometimes I was so hungry I would walk into the grocery store and start eating produce. What could they do? It was already in my stomach. I had no pride left. Sometimes I would hang out in the parking lot of a little place called the Anaconda in Isla Vista and listen to whatever band was playing inside. There was always pot smoking or alcohol drinking going on outside. Smoking pot made me feel more insecure and sometimes paranoid, but I did it anyway. I did anything that people offered, because I wanted to fit in. I wanted to feel liked. No matter what I did, I was never comfortable in my own skin.

After a couple of months, I stopped going to school. It became too difficult to pretend to be normal. I started at an independent study school, but didn't last for more than a month or two. It was a fun school for kids like me. We were all unmotivated to learn and did things to get out of our heads. It was there that I met Anna. She was older than I was and had a car. We drove down to Los Angeles to go to rave parties and did crystal meth together. Back then, it was a nasty pink thing, and just a little line could melt your brain. I'd be up for three days without wanting to eat or drink water. I turned gray and completely disconnected.

Anna had a boyfriend named Rick, whose best friend was named Randy. I met Randy when he was twenty-four and I was fourteen. By then I had stopped going to school altogether, so I had all the time in the world. For the most part, Randy was a good guy. He had a kind heart, adored his mother, and had deep sense of spirituality. Unfortunately he was an addict. We loved each other, but we didn't treat each other very well. It's hard to figure out who was worse. He would get loaded and leave for days at a time, and sometimes he would leave his very young sons with me. When we met, his boys were one and two years old. They were eleven months apart, and I had no idea how to take care of them. I had no idea how to take care of myself. We stayed in various places. Sometimes we slept on a couch or in a garage. We slept in some very dirty and gross spots. After the rape, I truly believed I was a piece of trash. Everything I did in my life was either an attempt to feel less trashy or a validation that I was trash.

I was fourteen when my brother was born. It was wonderful to see my dad so happy. He took me to the hospital to see baby Justin for the first time. I couldn't believe how tiny and cute he was. Weighing in at about four pounds, he was the tiniest little baby I had ever seen.

Eventually, I got stuck on cocaine. Randy sold it to support our habits. There were many nights when we got loaded and got our friends loaded, and it was supposed to be fun, but it would end up stupid. I'd watch as he peeped out of the blinds early into the morning, sure that there were cops outside, always watching. It started to suck. By the time I was sixteen, I was sick and tired of the drugs and waited for him to get sick of them too. I remember the exact moment I was officially over them.

We were staying at a friend's place down on De la Guerra Street, just west of the Paseo Nuevo Mall. Randy scored a big fat sack. Four ounces of coke was definitely enough for a long night and for our friends to come along for the ride too. When you have that much of any drug, you'll find that you have friends. They just come out of the woodwork. It seemed so cool at the time, and I was pumped to do a ridiculous amount of drugs with them. There were also enough drugs for Randy perhaps to make a profit this time. *Yeah, right!* He dumped a pile out on a plate, and like vultures, we swarmed. One by one we walked away, eyes watering, brains burning, a light sweat forming on our furrowed brows, to go smoke a cigarette or to grab something to drink. And so it went, all night long, until the blasted sun rose the next day.

Regret and disgust started to settle in, and I just wanted everyone to shut up. But this wasn't my house, and it wasn't my call. The bottle of tequila I drank made my eyes cross, but didn't make me pass out because I was too high. I had a frigging hangover, and my jaws ached. Lying on the couch, I listened to my boyfriend talking to his guy friends in the kitchen. They had run out. They had been cooking the dope and freebasing for a couple of hours, only pausing to peep through the blinds. *So annoying.* I wanted to hit him. *How can someone so smart turn into such a dummy?* I walked into the kitchen to see what they were doing, and here's where things got really weird. Those numbskulls were actually, in all seriousness, picking their boogers and putting them on the pipe. It caught me so off guard, it wasn't even funny—not yet, anyway.

"You guys are so lame," I said under my breath and walked back into the living room to think things over. I decided to use the bathroom to get some space and think. The sun was shining already, which was such a buzz kill. *What am I doing with this guy? Where can I go and spend a day or two?* All our friends were really his friends, so I didn't feel comfortable going anywhere without him. *Think … Okay, if I take a walk, I can clear my head and then figure it out.* On my way out of the bathroom, I heard the guys talking and laughing. As I got closer, I could hear that they were girl bashing.

"Yeah dude, women are just a waste of cum," chuckled one of Randy's douche-face friends. By the looks of him, with the gummy white foam in the corners of his mouth and a grimy film of sweat covering his face, I doubt this guy could get a hooker to give him a hand job. Those guys were disgusting, and I was out of there.

"I'm out of here!" I shouted from the living room.

"What?" Randy shouted back.

"I'm leaving, I said," I yelled as I stomped into the kitchen. "Gah, you guys are such dicks! I can't stand it anymore, and I don't feel like trying to force my eyes to stay shut while I listen to you!"

"Where are you gonna to go? Pfff. Whatever. K, see you later then," Randy uttered through clenched teeth while I started for the door. Then he called out, "Might want to pull your dress out of the back your underwear, though!"

A roar of laughter followed as I ran my hand down my back toward my butt. Sure enough, my dress was completely tucked into the back of my underwear. *I cannot believe I just did that.* My tough-girl exterior crumbled as I walked away on shaky legs, down the driveway, toward the street, which took me a thousand hours to reach. Don't think that was the last time I ever did drugs. It was just the first time that I ever got sick of them. Looking back, I realize I still had a lot more drugs to do.

It took me a while, but I managed to stabilize myself. I was too young to take the GED, but I took a thing called the proficiency exam, meant for kids under sixteen. I was fifteen when I got my diploma in the mail. I couldn't believe how easy it had been to pass. I did it on an eighth-grade education. Soon after that, I got a job and a place to live. It was great, and I did it all on my own. It was easy for me to get whatever job I wanted. I worked quite a few different jobs here and there—doing everything from answering phone calls to making sandwiches at Subway. I worked in collections doing data entry, and I worked in a call center making outgoing sales calls. There was a period of time where I worked two jobs. I always had at least one full-time job. I took a few classes at the city college. There were times when I struggled to get by financially, but I knew that I couldn't depend on my mom for help. One month, I managed to pay my rent, but had no money left over for food, and I asked her for some money. She said no, so I asked her if she would mind taking me to the grocery store and buying me just a few essentials. Once more, she told me no. I was definitely on my own, and I made it work.

Randy was talented, strange, and beautiful in many ways. He was unlike anyone I had ever met in my life. He was troubled and complicated, but he loved me and he was loyal. One major problem we had was me. My only source of self-esteem came in the form of male attention, and there was always some "friend" of his or boss of mine who wanted to have sex with me. I cheated on him sometimes and felt miserable and full of regret every time I did.

I went back to Asia with my mom the summer I turned eighteen. We stayed with the same family that we had the first time, this time for a little under two months. I taught English to preschoolers for a couple of weeks and freshened up my Chinese. By the time I got back to Santa Barbara, I was ready to get another apartment. I found a place by Cottage Hospital and got a good job with a booming telecommunications company.

After four years with Randy, I was finally eighteen years old. Finally legal. Even though I had been emancipated from my parents for years, I was really happy to be eighteen. It was somewhat anticlimactic, though, as nothing really changed. Randy and I got engaged, and then shortly afterward, our relationship ended. At the time, I thought I deserved someone better, but so did he. I cheated on him with both girls and boys. I let men use me. I still had no self-respect. I had nothing to offer but secrets and misery.

A few years later, I heard that he helped a friend shoot up, accidentally overdosed him, and then left him there, dead. A few years after that, I heard that he was a patient at a methadone clinic, a facility that administers a drug that helps heroin addicts get clean. But everyone knows that the clinic is just another way to get high. Some years later I spoke to him for the last time. A second cousin of mine was doing some work on my mother's house and mentioned that he had Randy's current phone number. He asked if I wanted to call, and I thought it would be interesting to catch up for a minute or two. The conversation was relatively short, but good. I didn't have the heart to tell him the truth about how close our paths had ended up or how far down the rabbit hole I had gone in my own addiction by then.

After Randy and I broke up, I focused on work. Every morning, I either walked or took the bus to my job. I loved it there. Finally, I felt independent and successful. I bought new furniture for my apartment. I always kept it nice and tidy. I felt some self-esteem for the first time since before the rape, and it felt really good.

Around this time, I got a letter with no return address. My mom gave it to me, and I opened it later that night. It was from my biological mother, Mary. After all these years, after all the wondering and wishing, she'd finally gotten in touch with me. It was a dream come true. It took me a couple of days to gather my courage, but finally I got the guts to call her. We talked for a long time. I felt I could open up to her about a lot of things, and I enjoyed hearing everything she had to say. She told me that she had wanted me and that her ex-husband and mother convinced her she was ill-equipped to raise a child. Maybe it was the truth. In any case, it was what I wanted to hear, and it was what I chose to believe. Soon, she flew me out to Spokane, Washington, to meet her and her husband and my two younger sisters. It was a great trip, and I had a lot of fun. Seeing her for the first time was incredible. My heart raced as I walked off the plane and scanned the airport with my eyes. When we saw each other, we walked into each other's arms and laughed. We laughed for a long time, then pulled away to look at each other again, then we laughed some more. Everything she told me made sense. I felt like she loved me and understood me. It felt good to see the similarities in our features. It felt like I was home in a way I never realized I could be until that moment. She asked if I wanted to meet my biological dad, and I told her I did. She said she would try to find him for me.

After I went back home, we kept in contact. Not too long after that, I met my biological dad, Harold. He drove eight hours from Redway, California, with his (soon to be) wife, Ivy, and my two little brothers. They were refreshingly open-hearted, fun, and easy to be around. They wore bright colors and laughed easily. My biological dad put me at ease with his genuinely kind nature and good sense of humor. I loved them immediately. I enjoyed getting to know them and hearing their stories. So many of the questions I had wondered about over the years had finally been answered. Because I had been given away at birth, I had always felt a sense of rejection; now that feeling started to subside. I was no longer alone in the world. The people I met had embraced me as family even though they hardly knew me. It was a good feeling. I felt less misplaced in the world, but there was still a darkness and unsettled feeling inside that I couldn't shake.

Life was ordinary in those days. I worked, read a lot of books, and spent a lot of time alone. I had one-night-stands. Nothing made my heart feel content. I ended up with another miscarriage and a marriage proposal, but it didn't feel right. One day at work, I hand-delivered a message to a guy named Cory. In his office there were pictures of people skydiving all over the place. It was something I had always wanted to do.

"Is that you?" I asked him.

"Yep," he replied, his face lighting up.

"Looks like fun. Do you still go?"

"Just about every weekend," he told me. "I'm part of a sky-surfing team. I fly camera, and this is my friend right here." He pointed to a picture of a guy on a board that looked similar to a snowboard, his arms outstretched to his sides. Beneath him the clear sky went on forever before the ground opened up in sections, the way it does when it's observed from an airplane.

Wow. I was really impressed. *This guy is serious about this! How cool.*

"I wanna go!" I said, feeling a rush of anxiety as the words came out of my mouth. "It's my birthday soon and maybe I'll treat myself. I'm turning nineteen."

"Yeah?" He had a look on his face like he had heard that one before.

"I'm serious!" I told him, trying to convince myself as much as anything. "Maybe I'll ask around and see if anyone else would want to go too. It would be so amazing!"

"Okay," he said, "we can all drive together. Don't get your hopes up too high. People always think it sounds like fun, but they rarely follow through. We might get two or three people to actually go."

"Okay, we'll see" I said, thinking to myself, w*ell over a hundred people work here. I'll bet I can rally at least 10 percent.* Emails were sent, personal invitations accepted, and before long I had nine yeses. *I knew it,* I thought. *It's going to be so much fun. I bet we can even get a group discount.* I called the drop zone, asked about group rates, and made the arrangements.

Then the day came, and guess what happened. One other person aside from Cory and me showed up. His name was Cory too. Wow, what a bunch of scaredy-cats. I should have known he would be right. Oh well, we were going to have a blast. Part of why I wanted to go skydiving was because it had always sounded like fun to me. Another reason was because I felt that I had nothing to lose. I had no real reason to live, and it didn't matter to me if I died.

My first jump was a tandem, and it was the scariest, most incredible, and exciting thing I had ever done. It was almost like an out-of-body experience. I was hooked. The next month, I went back, this time to take the AFF (accelerated free fall) course, level 1.

Part 2

"Live as if you were going to die tomorrow. Learn as if you were to live forever."
—Mahatma Gandhi

September 1997

My AFF instructor was a six-foot, eight-inch guy named Steve. He was tattooed and body pierced and had an energy about him that was undeniably irresistible. After that first jump, we had a drink together, and that was it. I was hooked on him too. I went out every weekend after that. We were like best friends. I believed I could tell him anything. Every night, we talked on the phone for hours. He was easy to love, and I fell hard and fast. We went to Las Vegas and got married in January 1998 after seeing each other for six weekends. The next month, on Valentine's Day, I found out I was pregnant. What a whirlwind!

We decided it would be fun to travel the United States teaching skydiving. While it was a hard decision, I thought it would be the chance of a lifetime. I trusted Steve so I threw caution to the wind and went for it. Even though

I had already traveled a lot, I had never dropped anchor anywhere outside of Santa Barbara. I had a lot of anxiety about leaving. But I felt an even bigger pull to do something big, something most people never get to do.

I spent my entire pregnancy in California. We bought a big trailer and hitched it to the back of a Suburban and got used to traveling while I was expecting. We went up to my dad's in Santa Maria, and we went to Steve's dad's in Thousand Oaks. We spent some nights camped right near the beach, letting the ocean sounds lull us to sleep. We ate good food and spoiled ourselves. We decided to have an "open marriage" with other women right away. I liked the idea because I wasn't able to open up to men on some level and had always felt confused about this. Steve was all about it. If I wasn't into it, he screwed them anyway, as I soon realized.

The first woman we were with together was Jodi, the mother of his oldest daughter, Julia. When I first met her, I was totally intimidated. She was independent and beautiful. She had a way about her that was mature and sexy. She told me lots of interesting stories about Steve and had a contagious laugh that put me at ease. I loved her immediately. Steve told me she might respond if we flirted with her. I let him do the flirting, because I was totally out of my element. He was good at that. I knew right away that I liked her a lot more than he did. She was the first of many women we were with together, but nobody was ever as great in my eyes as she was. She became my friend, and I trusted her. She was fun and didn't want to steal my husband. It would never get as good as her again.

He was really into his tattoo artist, who was also married and not very attractive. She was the first woman he "cheated" on me with; that is, he was with her behind my back. It was so weird and disturbing to see them together that I had to leave. She acted like a teenager experiencing her first puppy love. We were at her house in Ojai, and they were so into each other that it was like I was invisible. It wasn't fun for me, and I had to go. I left them at her house and drove all the way back up to my dad's in Santa Maria. It was already weird, and we hadn't even been married a year. Oh well, open marriage ... what did I expect? Anything outside of the marriage that wasn't agreed upon or was lied about was considered cheating. Thinking back on this, I can see now that it was immature and ridiculous, but it was our arrangement at the time. As anyone could predict, it didn't work out very well. I was huge with child. The tattoo artist was skinny and older, tattooed to the point of being grotesque. She had a green nipple for goodness sake. I did it to make him happy, but I wasn't into her. They weren't done, but I was. After a while, he was over it too, but she wasn't. She even told me that she was "in love" with my husband.

She ended up leaving her husband and pursuing skydiving. Steve never reciprocated any of her feelings. He gave her cheap sex and skydiving lessons. About a year after we left California, we got a phone call that there had been an accident. A plane had stalled at five hundred feet with five people inside. Everyone in the plane except one had died. She was on life-support with a severed brain stem. A couple of days after the accident, she died.

When I went into labor with Rose, we were at my dad's house. It was Elaine's birthday. My sister, Michelle was dancing around and making me laugh really hard, and then I felt my water break. Rose was born the next day. After twenty-two and a half hours of labor, I had my first daughter. The doctor put her on my chest right away. The first thing I did was look at Steve and say, "I love her." He had tears in his eyes too. I looked her over and saw that she was totally perfect. I was a mother. It was what I had always wanted, and now it was real. I was overwhelmed with love and wonder. It felt natural to hold her, kiss her, nurse her, sleep with her on my chest. It was beautiful to watch her grow and change and learn.

Three weeks after Rose was born, we left California. We traveled well together and had fun from the beginning. We took Interstate 10 across the lower part of the States, east through Texas, all the way to Louisiana. We spent Thanksgiving with Steve's mom and then made our way to central Florida. There was a job waiting for us near Orlando, teaching skydiving through the winter. The three of us would live right there on the drop zone, amid the low-hanging trees toward the end of the runway.

When we got close to our new home, I was really nervous, more nervous than excited. Or maybe it was the other way around. We were about a half an hour away from the drop zone when we pulled over to feed and change Rose. She ate and then had one of the hugest and most explosive poos I've ever seen, even after having four more kids. That was the winner of all time. It was everywhere—all over the bedspread, all over the ceiling, and all over me, from head to toe. Steve may have laughed, but I am pretty sure I didn't. Being a mom for the first time wasn't as easy as I had thought it would be. It was more than simply taking care of a little person. It was a serious, full-time deal, and I hadn't learned how to be patient yet. I wasn't even legally allowed to drink. How was I supposed to know how to do it?

It took me about a year to truly fall into my role as Mommy. It wasn't that I taught myself how to be a mom. It was that Rose gently and lovingly taught me how to love. Each of my children have given me very unique and special gifts. Rose helped me see her as more important than myself. She expanded my heart to fit all the joys of motherhood. She guided me step by step into a different way of feeling, not just a role. I began to learn what it truly means to give, to sacrifice, and to love.

Rose was a good baby. She slept eight hours a night when she was six weeks old. At the time, I had no idea how amazing that was. I just accepted it as something most babies do. Now I can see how lucky I was. Rose was also easygoing.

She liked driving, she liked her baby swing, and she liked anyone who held her. She didn't mind being busy and she didn't mind being lazy, staying inside watching movies. She was an agreeable child whose bright blue eyes could light up a room. She was a natural beauty from day one. We had fun together. From the time she was very little, I knew that she had a special bond with her daddy. It was okay, lots of girls are daddy's girls. He had a soft spot for her too. He'd had three other children before her and had no real relationship with any of them. Rose was his chance to do things over, get things right. They were great together. Admittedly, there was a teensy bit of jealousy, but I kept it in check. Every kid has a favorite, and it was okay if Rose chose him. We still had a special bond, regardless.

We stayed in Florida through the winter as planned, skydiving and being reckless. We were reckless with our marriage, our chemical intake, and our lives. We didn't think it was that big of a deal. I had postpartum depression. I didn't know what to do about it. I just kept trying to carry on.

Every girl we slept with liked Steve more than she liked me, and that was depressing. I was just a way for girls to get to him, and I knew it. Eventually, the winter ended and it was time to move on. In Florida, I learned what it felt like to be a mom without any outside help and also about blacking out on rum, the pain of fire ants and ovarian cysts, and how loud hurricanes sound. We had a job waiting for us in New York, so off we went at the end of spring 1999.

We stopped at every drop zone on the way up the East Coast. My favorite place was in Virginia. The drive itself was amazing too. At that time of year, the trees are all changing. Parts of the highway are lined completely on both sides with big beautiful trees, and there is even a center strip with grass, so there is nature and growth everywhere the eye can see. It was beautiful and so unlike anything I'd grown up knowing that I was captivated by it. Every drop zone we stopped at was fun. No matter where you go, skydivers become fast friends. Everyone you meet is someone with a crazy interest in common. You get there, and suddenly you're risking your life with these people. There we were with new airplanes, new landing areas, new names and faces, new drugs, new women. I acted out every fantasy I'd ever had over the years. I came up with new fantasies and acted those out too. My life was outward and wild—so much frivolity, so much meaninglessness.

When we got to New York, it was on! We had some great experiences. A student from the city brought us high quality drugs and gave us tattoos in exchange for skydiving lessons. One student who was a dentist brought out nitrous oxide tanks. By that time, I was good enough at skydiving to make some money at it too. I bought a video camera and a still camera and filmed students doing their first jumps or teams doing their relative work jumps. Every weekend was an adventure. Come Monday, however, my brain was fried.

We had a really good setup on the drop zone. We created a little community with most of the people who worked there. We all parked in a semicircle and hung out in a central area. There was a married couple from the United Kingdom, a couple from South Africa, a couple from Australia, a packer from New Zealand, and Wilson, a cameraman from Canada. We were like a family. On the other side of the community area, there was a tree line, and next to that was a small but constantly running river. We were secluded down there, and we made it a wonderful place to spend time together. We had a hammock, a fire pit encircled by camouflage netting, and Wilson kept us going with really great music. He had a very eclectic taste, but his music always created the perfect mood for whatever trip we were on. We put up Christmas lights shaped like oversized chili peppers in the netting. Pretty soon, someone dubbed it the camo café. Even a loner like me would rather hang out at the camo café than in my own trailer. The place had a buzz about it, a unique energy created by all of us separately, which became an energy in and of itself.

During this time, we were with a girl named Leslie. She was a little older than I was but not as old as Steve. She was a student at Columbia, and she was also the drop zone owner's girlfriend. It sounds really complicated, but somehow it wasn't. In my mind, she liked me more than she liked her boyfriend. Whether or not that was true, I know she liked me more than she liked my husband. She was the only girl who hadn't used me to get to him since Jodi. Truth be told, I liked her more than I liked him too. She made me feel safe. She was beautiful and soft, and being with her was like taking a vacation away from myself.

My postpartum depression progressed to the point that I saw life in the shadows and wanted to step into moving traffic. The drugs didn't help either. I checked myself into my first hospital stay that summer. It was a hospital close to New York City. I learned a lot about the system during that time. I learned that weeks in a hospital feel like months. I learned that if it doesn't help and I want out, all I have to do is answer their questions correctly. I learned which drugs worked for me and which drugs didn't. I learned that the loony bin wasn't the vacation I hoped it would be. I needed to learn how to develop life skills that would work for me so I didn't have to be in a psychiatric unit ever again. I was miserable. I wallowed. I complained. I got Haldol. I drooled on myself. The only person who came to visit me was Shawn, our student- friend who was a lawyer during the week in the city. He was a good man with a magnetic personality and incredible sense of humor.

When I left the hospital, I found out that my husband had been screwing his students in my bed while I had been gone. Heartbroken, but having no other real options, I stayed with him. Again, open marriage ... what did I expect? My respect and trust for him started to fade. I no longer felt loved. It wasn't fun anymore. I got higher and higher, so I didn't have to face my disappointment. There I was, on the opposite side of the continent from family. I felt painfully insecure and stuck. My superman turned out to be human. I thought I had too much invested to leave, so I stayed. My high-speed fantasy life turned flat and dark as the summer came to an end. Pretty soon we had a job waiting for us in Texas.

It was really hard to pack up and leave New York. The hardest part was saying goodbye to Leslie. I never forgot that special summer. I never forgot the friends we made and the times we had. Even though I didn't know then how rare and precious it was to have had friends like them, I still loved and treasured them and the home we made. Wherever I had been, whatever secrets I had or sadness I carried around didn't seem as significant as the loyalty and special moments we created. I got to know them and I got to know myself. It was a great time in my life. Everyone eventually moved away from our little upstate paradise, and years later, the drop zone relocated.

Some time ago, I heard my friend Wilson died. I have pictured him in my mind hundreds of times, remembering the kindness and love that he gave me. He is one of the few men I have ever truly loved and trusted like a brother. He was good to me without wanting anything but friendship in return. He was a good man, and he is missed. I bought his parachute after he died but didn't put many jumps on it. My life in skydiving is over now. I never jumped again after breaking my neck (more on that later). But there are many reasons to remember Wilson. I still listen to that music, and I still can see him in my mind's eye, geared up and getting ready to board the airplane, arms open wide, with a smile on his face.

There we were, leaving New York, heading south for the winter. We were going to Beaumont, Texas, which was only about an hour away from Steve's mom's house in Lake Charles, Louisiana. The winter had its ups and downs. I worked as a waitress in a strip club managed by one of our fellow skydivers. Steve didn't work very much that winter. We jumped for fun on the weekends, but the drop zone wasn't that busy. Slowly, I saved the money I made, and we planned to go back to New York the next summer. Steve kept up his cheating ways. One night while I was at work, he had a girl over, someone I thought was my friend. Turned out she wasn't. As time went on, I got more angry and bitter. My job was a source of negativity as well. It really wears a person down to be constantly objectified. Maybe it's something you get used to, but I just wanted out of there. I looked forward to the end of the winter. Then, in March, Steve stopped taking his medication.

He'd told me from the beginning that he'd been diagnosed bipolar and manic depressive, but I didn't really know what it all meant. Slowly, he changed. He stopped sleeping and started talking about God in very strange ways. Then he began thinking he *was* God. It didn't take long for him to completely snap. It was scary to see him go through it, and I was helpless to make him better. One morning, I woke up, and he was gone. So was my debit card and all the money I had saved at my crap job. By the end of that day, he had spent it all. That night, he called and told me where he was, and I drove to find him. He was in Houston. I drove him back to his mother's house. I knew I had to figure out a way to get him to check himself into a hospital, but he was enjoying his episode, and it was impossible for me to force him. My best idea was to drug him and drag him out to the Suburban and take him to the mental hospital in Lake Charles. When he woke up at the hospital, he was not happy. I told security that they would need to restrain him, because he was extremely agitated, but of course they didn't listen. When he woke up, "agitated" wasn't the word. He yelled at me and told everyone that he didn't know who I was and not to listen to me. Then he took off most of his clothes, grabbed a cross off the wall, and ran out of the hospital in just his shorts. Luckily, one of the officers who ran after him was fast enough to catch him.

It took the professionals a long time to get him to come back down. Rose and I visited him in the hospital every single day. At first he was angry, then his anger subsided, and he got used to being there. It wasn't the first time he had been in a psych ward. Since the onset of puberty, he had been in and out of them every year or two. Here's something funny: his roommate thought he was the devil. *Wow, what were the odds that both God and the devil would end up in the same room in the same mental hospital?*

After three weeks they let him out, and I drove him back to New York. I hoped that the medications he was on would get him back to normal or at least normal-ish. It was a far slower process than I realized. He was still on his high and talking crazy. Driving back up the East Coast, he talked about getting out of the vehicle and walking through the wilderness. He thought that he could gather a following and start a cult. He wanted to keep pulling over to smoke cigarettes every half hour, which was frustrating because I just wanted to get there already. By the time we got there, I was ready for some real alone time. I needed space, and I needed quiet. When I realized that he planned to take students out on tandem jumps in the frame of mind he was in, I decided to leave. I called my mom, and she made reservations to fly Rose and me back to California.

I was done with Steve. I was done with all men. When I came back to California, I was burned out. After a while, I decided to look up Jodi, so that Rose could get to know her sister, Julia. We spent a lot of time together that year. It didn't take me long to fall in love with Jodi. Rose, Julia, Jodi, and I grew really close. I felt that I had a family again, only this time, I could trust my partner not to hurt me. At the time, I was working for my mom's husband, Bruce, a CPA. Whenever I had free time, I drove an hour south to Thousand Oaks to be with Jodi and Julia. Through the grapevine, I heard that Steve had moved on too. He moved on like four times. *Fine*, I thought. *Who cares?*

After the summer of 2000, Steve came to California. He wanted to work it out. Things didn't go very well. I had already moved on in my heart. I couldn't and wouldn't trust him anymore. I told him I was in love with Jodi, which he thought was ridiculous. I also told my mom that I thought I was gay. That went over about as well as saying the F word in your pastor's office. (Yes, unfortunately, I did that once.) My mother's response was, "No, you're not." She and Steve were both mad at me, so they decided to team up and not allow me to see Rose anymore.

During that time, I stole money from my grandmother. I had been handling her rentals and doing her bookkeeping at work, and I took advantage of the situation. What I did was selfish and wrong and I still feel badly about it. I took a few thousand dollars and lost the trust of my family. On my last day of work, Bruce asked if I had taken any money from other clients. Of course I hadn't; that would have crossed the line, I reasoned. What I was unable to see was that any money, even money belonging to my family, was crossing the line. My mom paid for Steve's lawyer. They invited me to meet them at the lawyer's office. The divorce papers stated that I would lose custody of Rose, and my mother and Steve would share custody. There was no way I was signing those papers. I was filled with fear and rage when I left the attorney's office. Worse than that, when I went to go pick up Rose from school, I was unable to do so. They had taken me off the list of people who could pick her up. I was devastated.

My sadness quickly turned to anger, and I decided to confront them. It was useless. As individuals they were difficult to deal with. Trying to fight the two of them together was impossible. *To hell with them*, I thought. *How could my own mother side against me? Even if she didn't love me*, I wondered, *why would she take his side?* I felt more betrayed than I ever had in my life. They wouldn't let me see my little girl unless it was when they said, how they said, and where they said.

It took me a very short period of time to think this over before I realized what I had to do. The only choice I had was to swallow my pride and admit defeat. There was no way I could let my little girl go. I had to beg Steve to take me back. I had to kiss some serious butt. It was disgusting and humiliating to every fiber of my being, but I had to do it in order to get my little girl back in my life. I was a woman scorned, and now I was going to betray my best friend in order to keep my daughter. The seed of bitterness took root. After a blow job, he took me back.

Soon after we got back together, I decided we had to get out of Santa Barbara. We were living in a house that my mother owned, paying more than $2,000 a month in rent. We weren't getting anywhere, and I couldn't let go of the anger inside; if anything it was getting worse and worse. I had to get away. Where could we go? One of the few states we hadn't been to was Utah. Steve had brothers there. It sounded like it was worth a try. We left right after the Twin Towers were attacked in 2001.

When we were first in Utah, we stayed in the basement of one of Steve's brother's. Then we got our own place down the road. We decided to live drug- and alcohol-free for a while. I felt terrible because I'd left California on bad terms. I'd left Jodi and Julia out of fear, and I knew I had hurt them. I had left my mom on bad terms too. I was angry with her for paying for Steve's divorce attorney and for siding with him and letting him stay with her. I was angry that she hadn't loved me enough to take my side or at least not to take any side. Still, she was my mother, and I was unhappy with how things had worked out. Instead of dealing with my problems, I had taken a cowardly way out and run away.

My heart wasn't in my marriage anymore. After some time, I could see that Steve still wanted to be with other women. I wanted to cheat too. I felt no loyalty toward him. My heart wasn't in it, and I couldn't force myself to be his friend anymore. We stayed together for years like that, and then one day, I left. Becoming interested in someone new was the final push I needed. This time, I wrote the divorce papers.

Part 3

"Out beyond ideas of wrongdoing and rightdoing
There is a field. I'll meet you there.
When the soul lies down in that grass,
The world is too full to talk about."

—Rumi

Winter 2003

When I left, I asked Rose, who was six at the time, with whom she wanted to live. I knew her answer before she told me, but I needed to know for sure. We did weekends here and there. I had my own apartment in downtown Salt Lake City, but I rarely stayed there. I spent most of my time at my "boyfriend's" house. Those were confusing times. I wanted to start something new with Walter. I spent time with him. Then I'd feel guilty and go back home and spend time with Steve. It was incredibly difficult and unhealthy, but I went back and forth for a period of time. As much as I wanted to let go, I felt guilty and torn. Eventually, I was able to let go of Steve and move on.

Remember the *boy*friend I mentioned at the beginning? Let's talk about Walter for a bit. Walter was my boss, I'm pretty sure I mentioned that already. He was a tough guy to get close to. Falling for him was a slow process. I worked for him for about a year before I ever even thought about him that way. The first time I realized I was interested in him was when we were e-mailing back and forth while he was on a buying trip overseas. Walter was smart and intelligent, interesting and complex. Once I saw past his stoic business side and through to his heart, I wanted to see more. I realized that he had a lot of sensitivity and beauty. He was a reader. I love people who are readers. He also loved music and art and traveling. There was a lot to Walter, and I thought I was just the woman to get to the center of him. In my mind, nobody had ever given him enough of a chance. He had a lot of love to give, if only someone could love him and open his heart. It was my mission to be the perfect girl for him. I wanted to please him and gain his approval. At the time, the age difference didn't seem like that big of a deal. It made me feel protected and safe. It made me feel like he was so settled down in life he wouldn't cheat on me. I wanted someone whose wild years were behind him.

My divorce had been final for about a month when he tried to strangle me the first time. We were in Atlanta on business, and we got into a big fight. Honestly, I can't remember whose fault it was. I'm sure every fight I've ever had was at least partially my fault; surely, this time was no different. I don't remember what it was even about—maybe jealousy or something. Whatever it was, it was stupid. I should have known that he wasn't my Prince Charming on the flight to Atlanta; he sat in first class with his friends and left me alone in economy. It was the first of many instances when he made me feel like a second-class citizen. When I asked him why he left me back there, when his seats had been upgraded to first, he said it was because the food was just so much better in first class. *Well, sure. When you put in that way, it makes sense. Who wants to be stuck in economy with crap food?*

The trip went from bad to worse. I was limping around on a sore leg from a skiing accident, and the usual three feet he walked ahead of me became more like five to ten. The one person who always seemed able to keep up with him was Poppy, a friend of his I couldn't stand. She was a complete snob. I always thought she either wanted to be with him or believed I wasn't good enough to be with him. She was always snubbing me or correcting me about things like how I dressed or shaped my eyebrows. I tolerated her for Walter. Watching the two of them hang out in first class made me dislike her even more. After a night that went on too long, during which I dealt with her mean, snarky remarks, I finally spoke up. I made an idiot of myself and yelled in her pruny, disapproving face. She yelled back, threatening me, getting her gross, old lady spittle on my glasses. I was kicked out of that restaurant. Walter and I went back to the room. Then it got scary. His hands were around my neck in an instant. Instead of walking away from the fight, I fought back at him. It got out of control. The police came and took me to get my own hotel room someplace else. That night should have been the last fight we ever had. I *should* have gone back to Salt Lake and stayed alone for a while. Back then, I rarely did what I should have done. When I went back to Utah, I was back with him in a week.

Don't get me wrong. I'm not saying he is a bad guy. We just weren't good together. We didn't understand each other. Looking back, I think he did love me. He was mature, loyal, and generous, and he tried to make it work. I know I loved him. I loved and trusted him very much. But I had so many issues in my heart, I wasn't any good for him. I was unappreciative and immature. I wasn't ready to commit so soon after my marriage. My heart was broken, because as time went by, Steve stopped letting me see Rose. Presumably, he was mad at me for not coming around to see him anymore.

Finally, we get to where I started this story. Clearly, I wasn't okay inside. I was trying to get beyond the past, but I never dealt with it or even talked about it. Nobody in my life—except my mother—knew about the stuff that went on when I was a kid. Few people knew about the rape. I tried to live my life as though those things never happened. I was a total faker. While I was trying to get by in life, those things from my past were boiling right under the surface. I was screaming inside, and nobody knew it. Surely Walter knew I was a mess, but he never really understood why. Bet he never would have gotten involved with me if he'd realized I had so many daddy issues.

In the beginning of my relationship with Walter, I finally called my mom after three years of not talking to her. I was ready to let go of our past and, slowly, build a better relationship. I missed her. Sure, she wasn't perfect, but neither was I, and I needed my mom. One day I called my biological mother to catch up. We had been talking fairly regularly back then. This time, I can't remember her exact words, but she said something like "I'm really busy right now, why don't you call me when you have less drama in your life." *So, like never. Okay, fine.* I'd started off that relationship with huge feelings of rejection, and it felt really terrible to be rejected again. I felt like such an idiot for believing that she loved me. I made up my mind to never contact her again.

At the hospital, after we found out that we were expecting, things changed for the better for a while. I believed the only reason I lived was to be Payton's mom. I was in love with her from the moment I knew she was inside me. I thought she was my little guardian angel, and I wanted to do everything I could to take care of myself and grow a healthy and happy child. While I was pregnant, my mother called and said she wanted to make a trip out to visit me. She told me the date that she would come to Utah, and I told her I was looking forward to it. I was apprehensive but excited. I wanted very much to let go of the past and move forward.

When she came, I was about seven months pregnant. The first day she was there, she showed me a wedding invitation.

"Open it," she said. So I did. Inside the invitation were two names; one was a woman I did not know, and the other was Steve.

"Wow, he's getting married already?" I asked. "When?"

"Keep reading," she said. The wedding had been two days earlier.

"Why do you have this invitation?" I wanted to know. I had a feeling, but I wanted to hear her say it.

"That was the reason that Bruce and I came up here, so we could go to his wedding." I couldn't believe my ears. Within minutes, I started having contractions. It was like someone had punched me right in the chest. I couldn't catch my breath.

"Are you okay?" she asked, a look of concern on her face.

"No, I'm not." I wanted to tell her that my reaction wasn't because he got married, but because she had betrayed me again, right when we were trying to rebuild our trust. I knew if I tried to explain, she wouldn't understand, so I just kept my mouth shut. Inside, I felt fresh rage at her. She'd acted like she wanted to come visit me, but the trip had nothing to do with me. It was all about her relationship with Steve.

What is wrong with me that my moms don't love me? Nothing changed. They were the ones who should be getting married. My mom and Steve. That would be perfect. Why is he so important to her? He doesn't even say nice things about her. He is just involving her to be mean to me.

I was fuming, but still I said nothing. Now I knew why he wouldn't answer my phone calls or allow me to have any contact with Rose. My mother's visit was characterized by forced niceness and many platitudes. I wasn't able to forgive or forget. I did manage to ask her one important question that had been bothering me again.

"Why didn't you leave Dad when I told you that he was touching me?"

She was quiet for a bit before responding. "Well, I thought he stopped," she said.

"He didn't, Mom. I had a bladder infection for years and years. You had to know something was wrong. I mean, that's just not normal!"

"I thought you were giving it to yourself," she explained. "I thought maybe you were touching yourself, and maybe your fingers were dirty."

It was what I wanted, I guess. It was an answer. At least it was something. At least she remembered the conversation. After all those years, I had started to wonder if it had all really happened the way I remembered. It became a secret that was ignored and forgotten, but not by me. It made me feel crazy to carry it around when everyone else acted like it never happened.

Walter and I had good times, but often the good times were overshadowed by my depression, my secrets, his controlling nature, and his bad temper. We also drank a lot. He took me on a buying trip when I was pregnant. We went to India, and it was amazing. The following section is from a handwritten journal that I wrote while we were there.

March and April 2004

Yesterday we flew from Salt Lake City to Cincinnati, then to Paris, finally landing in Delhi, India. This morning, we're flying to Lahore, Pakistan. We will be on the Afghan border by tonight. The hotel we stayed in last night is called the Taj Palace. It is the biggest hotel I have ever been in. The room was gorgeous, and the bed was perfect. It was made up in all white with a down comforter and four down pillows. It felt very luxurious, and after such a long and exhausting trip, I slept really well. Walter has the whole trip planned out, and I am just along for the ride. He does this trip twice a year and has done so for around twenty years, give or take.

The sun is setting behind me. We've just landed in a small prop plane that flew from Lahore to Islamabad. Here, we will drive to the border. I can hear hundreds of birds flying toward the west, where the last bit of sun is outlining silvery clouds. There are men everywhere. By that, I mean that there is an obvious absence of women. Many of the men are in blue uniforms with guns, who either look at me with curiosity or mistrust. The few women I have seen are in long garments covering them from head to toe. Usually, the top piece is black, which covers the entire head, with an opening for the eyes. The material flows down mid-leg, where I can see a lighter colored garment on the legs going down to the ankles. This outfit is called a burqa. They wear sandals on their feet. A few have adorned their toenails with polish, but most women are as unidentifiable as the next. They look out from the small hole for sight with silent, observant eyes. There are no other white girls around. I wonder what these women think about me. Maybe they think I'm a heathen, void of morality. Walter says they probably wish they could have the freedom that I do. He tells me that they are not allowed to speak unless spoken to.

When we got to our hotel, all I wanted to do was take a shower. Meanwhile, he wasn't happy with the room because of the sound of traffic outside. So he moved rooms while I was showering. In a country full of women who wear burqas, I had to walk through a huge hotel crowded with people in nothing but a towel! I was so embarrassed. It is little things like this that are always making me feel like he doesn't really care about my feelings. I called him a princess for being so picky about the room. That didn't go over very well.

We took the car to a bus station, then took a bus back to Peshawar. The bus was really chilly, but it was great because we had a front seat with an excellent view. I slept most of the way. The baby growing inside me is taking a lot of my energy. I don't mind. I think about her every minute, and I can't believe she is already a world traveler! Right now, I'm at the Khyber Bazaar. It isn't an outside bazaar like I was imagining it would be. We are in a tiny little room, maybe twelve by twelve feet, in a tall building filled with rooms identical to this one. All the men (including Walter) are a bunch of hard-nosed business men. They are negotiating, and it's like pulling teeth. Nobody wants to budge! I've never felt so many eyes on me in my life. I'm supposed to try to avoid eye contact, but it's really hard! I mean, where else should I look? At the ears? The neck? The feet?

Now Walter is asking the men if they want to eat lunch. They are tossing around ideas. Walter suggests chicken. Somebody else says "mincemeat," whatever that is. Before coming here, I asked my doctor about being inoculated. She told me I couldn't have the typical shots people get before traveling to third-world countries because of the baby. She told me to avoid meat, dairy, uncooked fruits or vegetables, and obviously water, unless it had been boiled first. I don't want to have to eat any meat, but if I do, I will just employ the old tricks I learned from traveling with my mom. Be polite, and pretend to eat while discreetly disposing of it in any way possible. Smile and give lots of compliments.

The man we are buying rugs from is beautiful. He is dressed in all white. Even his beard is white. He has a large build and kind eyes. His ears are big and floppy and hang down. He drives a hard bargain just like Walter and the other men, but he does it with a smile on his face. Walter likes to use phrases like "old customer" and "that's a tourist price" a lot. It's funny and endearing. He periodically glances in my direction to check on me. I feel like cracking up, but I know better. This is how he makes his living, and this is how people do business here. Walter knows how to get what he wants. At the moment, I'm sitting on a stack of rugs in a corner of the room by an open window. A warm and fragrant breeze flows in. I can hear the sounds of the street below. Horses and motorcycles are taking people where they want to go. It looks like Walter and Mr. Floppy Ears have settled on a price.

I survived lunch. The thing I liked most is called naan. It's a flat bread that is baked in a special oven, and it is DE-LISH-US! Right now, we are across the street, and Walter is haggling with another set of tough guys. He tells me not to laugh or try to make him smile, because he can't "lose his momentum with these guys." He tells me that they "want to eat him for lunch!" When they are right in the middle of their business, Walter suddenly says the funniest thing I have ever heard him say. He raises his hand and extends his index finger and pointedly says, "I will not be a chicken kabob!" He is totally serious too. I have to stare down at my hands so that nobody can see me smiling and on the verge of laughter. These guys must think we are totally nuts, but who cares.

Today we are at a factory owned by an Afghan man with whom Walter has done business for a long time. This place does everything from shearing and dying the wool to weaving the rugs. It's a huge compound. At lunchtime, the men roll out a big runner and eat quietly. After they are done, they roll out long flat rugs and begin their prayers. An older man sings verses from the Koran while the others wash their hands and feet. Then each of them begin their individual worship. Gradually, they all line up and begin bowing at the waist, standing, kneeling, standing again, then repeating the process. I watch as all of the men do their ritual silently and in unison. There are even some children participating. The children here aren't like I was when I went to church as a kid, always giggling or talking to somebody. These kids are serious and reverent. After the man in front is finished singing, he joins the rest of the men. The only sounds to be heard are that of the men's robes rustling with their practiced movements and the birds chirping in the trees.

We were invited into the home of one of the men Walter buys from last night. It was a really amazing and eye-opening evening for me. They treated us so well. I worried that after 9/11 we would be treated poorly. Not so. The people here have treated us very graciously. The family consists of three brothers, their wives, eleven children, and the men's mother, the matriarch of the family. I sat in a room with eight women as they got ready to eat dinner. The female camaraderie here is totally different than anything I've ever witnessed at home. There is no sense of resentment or competition. They seem to truly enjoy each other. I'm guessing the reason that they have such a close relationship with one another is because they aren't friends with their men. Their role as wife is one of servitude and submission. Their friendship comes from each other. They have such a remarkable kinship and companionship together. It is a wonderful gift to experience other cultures. We take so many things for granted at home. It's also surprising to learn about the things that we miss out on in our society. I'm learning a lot from these beautiful people.

Today, we took a car from Lahore to Wahga. From there, we crossed the border back into India on foot. After being thoroughly scrutinized in customs, we walked to a place where we could get a taxi. We took the taxi to the train station in Amritsar to catch the Shitabe Express. The drive was hilarious. These people honk their horns so much that nobody would believe it back home. There is always some camel or motorcycle or pedestrian in the road, and the cars constantly honk at everyone they are passing. Nobody gets offended or angry about it. The train is wonderfully air-conditioned. In six hours we will be back in Delhi.

Last night we were back at the gorgeous and comfortable Taj Palace in Delhi. I love that place. Today we woke up and had breakfast with one of Walter's business partners, Raj. Raj is a nice fellow, whom I had the pleasure of meeting once before, when he visited Walter in Utah. He has great energy and smiles a lot. He is an easy guy to like. Gregarious is the word that comes to mind to describe him. Raj will accompany us until we leave India and head to Kathmandu. After eating, we drove through Rajasthan. One of my new favorite things about Raj is that he is Hindu, which means he is a vegetarian. We stopped at the best little place for lunch. It was this little side-of-the-road joint that I would never think would be safe or good. It was by far the best eating I've had since being away from home. Now we are in Jaipur at Raj's palatial home, where we will stay for three days. It's incredibly beautiful here. Outside, just down the street, there are homeless people living in the dirt on the side of the road. There are hordes of children that approach oncoming vehicles begging for money. Some children are in critically bad shape. One little boy looked about eight. He had leprosy, and he was missing an arm. He came up to our car and started thumping his cloth-wrapped stump on the window. He had a sadness in his eyes that caught me so off-guard that I was brought to tears. As a mother, I couldn't help but want to do something for him.

"Don't look at him," Walter said to me. "This is his job. Just ignore him."

On we drove. Not even a quarter-mile away, we are in a mansion with beautiful decorations, expensive tapestries, and servants. I can't get the sight of him out of my mind. After our stay here, we will be in Agra for a day, and then we will go to Calcutta for two days. We will take two overnight sleeper trains and one plane. I'm pretty drained, and I know it isn't the jet lag anymore. It's my little tiny baby growing inside me. I feel so lucky that I get to have another baby. I'm so in love already! I miss Rose more than ever, and thinking about the new baby inside eases that ache just a little bit.

Tonight we went to a little pizza place overlooking the Ganges River in Varanasi. The pizza was unexpectedly good. The ice cream we had after dinner was even better. Following dessert, we drove down to a different part of town. We stopped at a place that looked somewhat ordinary with tall buildings all around. The street was filled with people, cows, and stray dogs. We got out of the car and started walking down a narrow street that went in between two looming buildings. The road was so narrow that if I had lain down across it, I could have reached out and touched both sides. Motorcycles, bikers, pedestrians, and cows moved along with us down the street until we were deep in the five-thousand-year-old city. It felt like a maze to me, and I doubted that I could have ever found my way out without help. In some spots the street became so dark that I couldn't see what was in front of me. On either side of us there weren't any individual houses. It was a continuous long brick wall connecting buildings together. The doors were painted dark red, and the windows were dimly lit. There were also little shops along the way selling things like sodas, cigarettes, and sometimes big black balls of hash. The thick night air smelled like incense, trash, blood, and burning wood. We went deeper into the ancient city.

After walking some more, the street opened up, and we could hear a man singing. As we got closer, we saw there was a crowded outdoor café where people were dancing to the music. There were arches built into the walls containing big piles of firewood all around. Now we could see all the way down to the river. There were people sleeping on big cement staircases that led down to the dark brown water of the Ganges. The entire place had an almost tangible vibration. There were crowds of people watching some fires that had been built down by the water line. There were about six or seven fires that were giant and roaring. The energy was palpable, and I was totally enthralled. A group of people appeared, walking down one of the narrow streets toward the river. They were carrying a wooden cot on their shoulders. On the cot was a human body wrapped in white cloth with a golden blanket draped over the top. They made their way down to the river and bathed the body. Then they brought the body up to one of the fires. It was then that I realized what I was seeing. We were at an outside crematory.

We walked closer to get a better view. We were on a huge concrete slab near the outdoor café. We had a perfect view of the river and the fire where the body had just been placed. The fire shifted and began to lick at the body. Slowly, the body began to catch fire. At first, I was so overwhelmed, I thought I might cry, but no tears came. The scene was too intense for tears. Nobody else was crying either. Everyone was happy and celebrating life. I watched the fire so intensely that I couldn't have turned away even if I tried. It was as if there were magnets in my eyes, and I couldn't pull them away. I was hypnotized. It was amazing to see death dealt with in this fascinating way while carrying a brand new spark of life inside me. People talked, mangy dogs scratched themselves, firelight glowed, revealing trash heaps along the bank. Nothing was sacred. Everything was sacred.

The heat from the fire was warming my face, and the smoke drifted toward us. The ashes found their way to our clothes, our hair, and inside our noses. I wonder how much of this person I brought back on myself or even in my lungs. I breathed the air in thoughtfully to properly analyze the smell. I wanted to remember it, so that I could write it down and never forget. It smelled bitter and heavy like burnt coffee, burnt hay, and burnt plastic. All mixed in were the more familiar scents of wood and incense burning. The smell was so distinct that I would recognize it instantly even after fifty years passing.

As the fire eventually consumed the body, it burned off the cloth wrapped around it, revealing an ankle here, some fingers there. It felt very intimate for me to watch that happen. I was spellbound. I have no idea how long we stood there, watching as the body turned to ash. I looked at Walter with a smile on my face, but hadn't the words to tell him how much I loved it. He had taken time out of his business trip to show me something incredible. It had been one of the most amazing nights of my life. "I knew you would like it," he said. Awestruck, I simply nodded in agreement.

This morning he did it again. We went back to the river. He hired a man to row us in a little boat that looked kind of like a kayak. We went out on the calm and dark water to watch the sunrise. What an incredible trip. It is something I will never, ever forget.

I haven't written in a few days. After Varanasi, we went to Calcutta where we spent two days. I got really, really sick there. I ordered a noodle dish that came with little slivers of vegetables in it. I didn't think anything of it at the time. Apparently, they weren't cooked well enough. I am struggling. My insides feel like they are twisted up in knots. I'm constantly cramping and feel like I have to go to the restroom. When I try, nothing comes out but bloody mucous. It is intensely painful and disgusting. I was so careful too! I can't believe this happened. What really worries me is whether the baby is okay. As soon as I can, I want to see a doctor. I think I'll have to wait until we get to France, because I don't think going to see a doctor here would make much sense.

I feel like I've been away from Rose forever. As beautiful and special as this trip is, I can't pull my mind away from her. I wish Steve weren't punishing me anymore. I wish he could just let me be a mom to her. Why can't he see that he is punishing her too? What kind of father wants to rob his own child of having a mother? It is cruel and heartbreaking. I don't know what to do anymore. I try to think positive, but it's impossible to always see the bright side when I know my little girl is missing me and probably thinking I stopped caring about her. I want to see her smile. I have her pictures and I always look at them, but it isn't the same. I want to put my arms around her. I want to watch her play and hear her laugh. I'm tired of crying about this and knowing that Steve gets to tuck her in every night while I cry myself to sleep, missing my beautiful girl. I am grateful that I have another baby on the way, but Rose is my first daughter. No one will ever take her place. Having another baby doesn't make Rose any less important. I am in Kathmandu, Nepal, in one of the most beautiful cities I've ever seen. But I don't need the Himalayas. I don't need Paris. What I need is my little girl.

I'm in Paris now. The flight over was so awful. When we were getting ready to take off, I had to use the bathroom, bad. I tried to hold it but I simply couldn't. My body was revolting against me. Doubled over, I started to cry. Finally, when I realized I was about to go in my pants, I pushed past the flight attendant and told her that I HAD TO GO. She would have to let me. I was going to poo in my pants, and then what? Oh, it was so embarrassing and awful. I bet Walter wished he could have upgraded to first class on that flight. He must have been even more embarrassed than I was. Oh well. I really do try to do the best I can. It's never good enough.

It's April now, and I decided to try Steve on the phone. I accidentally called him at three in the morning, but he told me to call back at eight and that he would let me talk to Rose. It was so great to hear her little voice! She is so cute. She was talking about her yoyo. I love her so much.

It's been over a week and I'm still sick. I feel like I need to buy tampons to put in my butt. I'm leaking blood, and it is so gross. I can't stop this thing. I finally did see a doctor here in Paris. I was so worried. He said that everything was okay. The coolest thing was that I got to get my first ultrasound pictures of the baby! It made me cry happy tears.

Right now I'm sitting in a French café all by myself. I ditched Walter this morning because he was being a jerk. We were fighting about something really dumb. Most of our fights are about dumb things. Stuff like him getting upset if I sleep in another room when he snores. Stuff that shouldn't be an issue. This time it was because I wanted to buy something nice to wear to the opera tonight. He has a friend named Sylvia here. She is very sophisticated and classy. She is a really amazing lady who lives in Salt Lake City part-time and also has an apartment here in Paris. That is actually where we are staying while we're here. One thing about Sylvia is she is always dressed like a million dollars. She oozes good taste and class. The word that comes to mind when I think of her is aristocrat. One of my favorite things about Sylvia is that she knows how to treat people. She is funny and thoughtful, and I have never felt the least bit "second class" in her presence. I really like her. When she asked us to go with her to a Parisian opera house, I was thrilled! The only problem was that I didn't pack anything nice to wear. All I have with me is jeans, T-shirts, and some traditional Indian clothes that I bought in India. There is no way I'm wearing jeans to a Parisian opera house! I told Walter I needed to go buy a nice sweater at least.

"I can't wear jeans to an opera house, Walter," I said.

"Well you can go buy a sweater, but then we won't be able to go to the museum," he replied with irritation in his voice. It turned into a big argument. Why does everything have to be such a big deal? Why can't he allow me to make any decisions? It's his way or no way. In the end, he said that he would just go to the museum alone, so I left by myself.

I've been out on my own in the city for hours. What a cool place. The people here don't seem to like Americans much, but that's okay. I actually had somebody ask me if I voted for President Bush before selling me a poster. "No," I told him truthfully. "I didn't."

I don't know how I'm going to continue to have a relationship with someone who can be so one-sided. I know I'm not the best girlfriend in the world, but I still have feelings. We'll just have to get through the trip and deal with the relationship issues when we get back home. For now I'll just eat my sandwich, drink my soda, and enjoy myself on this beautiful day in this perfect spot in Paris, France. It's every girl's dream, and here I am.

Back home, we continued to fight. I'm guessing Walter felt resentful that I wasn't more appreciative of him and all he'd done for me. I couldn't settle down if I didn't feel loved. He couldn't really love me and at the same time constantly act like my feelings don't matter. I didn't like the insinuation that I was less important than he was. Just because I had experienced poverty didn't mean that I was stupid or inferior.

Some people thought I was just with him because of his money. It had nothing to do with that. Walter knew I wasn't the kind of person who cared about money. He knew that when I left Steve I didn't ask for our house or any of the furniture in it. I took nothing but my books and clothes.

Hopefully, Walter knew that the feelings I had for him had nothing to do with his money. What I felt for him was deep and meaningful. Unfortunately, we couldn't seem to make our good times last.

Our fights were two-sided. We were both stubborn and strong-willed and didn't want to let anything slide. I held onto a lot of resentments and didn't like being bossed around. From the outside, it looked like he took very good care of me. I wanted to settle down and drop anchor with him, but couldn't get past my inferiority complex. Maybe it was my own problem with insecurity, and I was to blame. I don't know anymore. I do know that I tried. When I was about eight months pregnant, we had a big fight, and I ended up getting a black eye. I can't remember what the fight was about, but it was at my favorite place in the world at the time—his cabin. The next day I drove to the house and wanted to take all my things and leave. He said he didn't trust me, so he called the police to "supervise." That was a stupid move, because of course the police noticed the bruises on my face. We both were arrested for domestic violence that day. Of course, when you have money, you don't spend much time in jail. He bailed out, but I had to wait to get out on my own recognizance.

Things went on like that for a while. Our fighting became a way of life, and he always got the last word. He would give me the silent treatment for days at a time. I've never been around anyone who can literally clam up for two or three days at a time and not say a single word. I always felt like I was walking on egg shells. Those were hard times, and I felt very alone.

The day Payton was born was wonderful. My mom was visiting. It was Election Day, 2004. I cast my ballot while I was in labor and made my way back home to our heavenly bathtub. I spent an hour or so in labor in the tub and then told Walter it was time to go. Off we drove in his SUV, to the University of Utah hospital. Payton was the only child I've had without any pain medication or epidural. Walter wanted it that way, so I agreed to a natural childbirth. That's how our whole relationship was. In retrospect, I can't believe I agreed to that. I don't recommend it. It didn't really matter though, because as any mother knows, as soon as they give you your baby, the pain goes away and all that matters is the new little life in your arms. So it was for me that day. As soon as the doctor handed her to me, nothing else existed. It was all about her. She was beautiful, and I loved her immediately. I had already loved her when she was growing inside me, but that love was amplified a million times over when I held her the first time. She was my life. She was perfect. It was a priceless moment, and I still have the pictures from that day. The only thing that belonged to both Walter and me that I kept after our breakup was the photo album from the day she was born. It is one of the few possessions that I have been able to hold onto since then.

Life was good for us for a while. Falling back into the mommy role was wonderful and easy. I became content inside. Things made sense for me again. I loved watching Payton grow each day. I loved to read *Goodnight Moon* to her every night. She slept with us until one day Walter decided that it was time for her to sleep in her own room. I wasn't ready for her to be away from me, but there was no talking him out of something once his mind was made up. More than once, I remember crawling into the crib with her if she woke up in the night, just to get some baby cuddles. The only memories I have of my girl are from when she was a baby. My favorite times were when she would wake up right before dawn. I would go get her out of her room as soon as I heard her and bring her into my bed to snuggle. Because it was morning, I could keep her in the room. I would hold her as close to my body as I could, so that I could feel her breathing, and nurse her while the sun rose. As I lie there, smelling her soft sweet hair, I would drift in and out of sleep, and listen to the wetlands outside the house wake up for the day. I could hear the birds start to chirp and the horse start to make his happy morning noises. It was a special time of my life, maybe one of the happiest times I can remember being alive.

November 2005

My step-mother, Elaine died. She was only forty-two. She had been sick for just a few days with pneumonia, which is what technically killed her. The doctors blamed it on the alcoholism. But we, her children, know what really took her down. It was my dad. It took a while for the news to sink in. Memories came flooding into my mind of phone conversations I'd had with her over the years.

"Your dad's evil," she would cry. "I don't know what to do. I want to leave him, but I can't."

A few times she confided that she was so tired of feeling bad all the time, she wished she were dead.

"I'm just done trying," she whispered in a hoarse voice, full of fear and exhausted tears. "I just wanna die."

At the time, my heart broke to hear her desperation, but by the time their fights and dysfunction had progressed to this point, I had moved out of the state. Maybe it had progressed to that point before then, but he hadn't broken her spirit. A deep depression set in, with the added darkness of a life utterly controlled and consumed by alcoholism.

There had been times when she tried to quit. She would go for three days, a week, once even three weeks when she was in medical detox. But she couldn't ever stay away from it, not when she had to leave the recovery program and go home to an unsupportive husband who not only triggered her drinking but refused to quit himself. She would walk into a house with an already-drunk husband and a bottle of their favorite poison. For a period of time, he kept "his" liquor out in the garage in a locked cupboard and kept her completely penniless in an attempt to control her drinking, without taking responsibility for his own. Like any addict, she always managed to figure out a way to get what she needed. His self-serving manipulation and blame-shirking also forced her into hiding. It created more fights, and caused her alcoholism to evolve into a whole new kind of monster. Frustrated and isolated, she began to drink from the time her eyes opened in the morning to the end of the day.

Their fights, already verbally and emotionally abusive, became violent. She always had been a fairly petite woman, but the alcohol strung her out and sucked her body dry of all the nutrients she could keep down. When my dad got mad, he had no problem picking her up and throwing her around. Her body bruised easily, and the fights occurred more and more often, until she felt isolated not only from her husband, but also from her entire family. This eventually included my sister, Michelle, who ended up going to live with her dad. Then Elaine's mother died, and Elaine's will to continue trying died with her. When I heard that Elaine died, I imagined that she'd finally gotten her wish. My grief rounded off at the edges as it combined with relief for the end of her pain.

The trip home for her funeral was miserable. My neck was ruined, healing from a nasty car crash that had broken it in three spots in July. I was given lots of very strong drugs and healing slowly. The doctors switched me from OxyContin to Percocet, just around the time I found myself lugging bags through the airport with Payton, who was about a year old. We flew from Salt Lake International to LAX. To save money, Walter booked us on the LA flight, and then made arrangements for a shuttle to drive us the rest of the way to Santa Barbara. From there, we were picked up by my mom who drove us the remaining hour to Santa Maria. The trip would have been grueling even if my neck felt normal.

Somebody, I don't remember who, asked me to read Psalm 23 at the funeral. It was something I didn't look forward to doing, but I knew I could manage it. As soon as I got there, I was approached by the funeral home director.

"Excuse me," he said. "May I have a word with you in private?"

"Sure," I say, wondering what to expect.

"You are the daughter, right?" he asked. I nodded in response. "I'm not sure how to put this." His posture was awkward and his expression was pained. "Uh, we've had an extremely difficult time trying to prepare your mother's body for an open casket. You see, the bacteria in her body from the pneumonia continues to multiply, and the body is still weeping. We have drained the body of the blood, but the body is swollen, and the embalming process has not had the effect that we would have liked. The body has been placed inside of a large plastic bag to keep the fluids contained, but nothing can be done about that swelling in the facial area."

Sick. "Have you talked to my dad about this?" I asked.

With a look of sincere agony on his face, he furrowed his brow and continued. "That's why I'm talking to you. Your father is extremely emotional and will not listen to any of our recommendations. We strongly advise against having an open casket. Your father seems unable to listen or understand."

Of course not. "Do you want me to talk to him then? What are your suggestions?"

"Please do. The staff and the management here are asking that the service continue as planned, but with the casket lid closed. We have done our best, but the way she looks may be very upsetting to your family and friends." There was pleading in his eyes, and since he was in the business of seeing dead bodies all the time, the situation must have been pretty serious for him to approach me like that.

Gross. "Okay, I'll do my best," I say, forcing a smile. "I'm pretty sure I can talk him into that." I walked away with a sinking feeling. My dad was easy to find, which was good because I didn't want to waste any time.

"Hey, Dad," I said, trying to think of the best way to word things. The best way, I guessed, was to be honest, harsh as it may have sounded.

"Listen, they can't do anything with Elaine's body. She's seeping out all over the place, and she is so swollen that her face doesn't look right. It's so bad, the guy who is in charge of this place is pretty much begging for us to do this thing with a closed casket. That's okay with you right?"

I knew I was talking too fast, and my smile was too big, but I was doing my best to handle this all without freaking out. Sure that he was going to agree with me, I slowly turned my head, looking for the manager so I could be done with this subject, and get on with other conversations I didn't want to have with other people I didn't want to talk to.

"Absolutely not," my father barked. I looked back at him, my smile still plastered on my face, because I was sure that he was joking. But the look on his face told me he wasn't, not even the slightest bit. I exhaled loudly and waited for an explanation.

"I want to be able to say goodbye to my beautiful girl, and I want the top open. They already talked to me about how she looks, and I saw her. She's my baby, and she looks beautiful."

I want to believe him, but I don't. She's leaking dead person fluids and is wrapped in a garbage bag for heaven's sakes. "So what, then? Michelle and Justin have to see her like that? Don't you care what they think?"

"Michelle and Justin love their mother and need to see her to say goodbye to her. She doesn't look bad. The lid stays up."

Wow. "Okay then, I'll go tell him to go ahead and leave it open," I said, trying to keep my voice even.

Inside, people were taking their seats, and I made my way through the crowd. Several people stopped me to give hugs. After a lot of milling around, I made my way to the front and waited for things to start. The coffin was carried in and set on a platform in the front of the room, surrounded by flowers. A podium was set off to the side. My dad sat next to me, and on his other side was my aunt Sarah, his youngest sister. My mother sat on my other side and helped me with Payton. I didn't go up to the coffin immediately. I decided to wait out of respect, since the only reason I'd be going up there would be to gawk at an expected mess. I preferred to wait and go up after the service when everyone else did. The coffin was raised and far enough away from the rest of the room that even the people standing couldn't get a peek inside at her. Yet. I felt as though I knew a dirty secret. Staring at the coffin, I tuned out whatever the priest was saying. *At any minute*, I thought, *we'll watch, horrified, as liquid starts dripping onto the red carpet beneath the casket*. This, of course, did not happen, but what did was every bit as disturbing.

Soon it was my turn to get up and read. I started with a Bible verse and finished with a short letter that I had prepared the night before. It went by fairly quickly, and I was back in my seat. I was proud that I didn't cry in front of all those people. The last person up was my dad, whose voice was clear at first, then choked, and by the end nobody was able to make out a word he was saying. At the same time, a cry that turned from weeping to wailing came from outside the room by the entrance of the building. I could not see whom it was coming from but could hear that it was getting louder and louder. The minutes crawled by.

Finally, the priest stepped up to take center stage back from my dad. He told us it was time to say our goodbyes. *God help us.* I was not in a hurry, so I sat quietly until the rush of people slowed down. There were three steps to climb before I reached her coffin. Then there were a few more feet to walk over to the platform and the coffin, where at long last I took a look inside. *Oh. My. God.* No warning from the funeral director could have prepared me. Elaine was always conscious of her looks and kept her figure no matter what. She would have been more horrified than any of us. Her face was so swollen that her features no longer resembled her; the stitches to keep her mouth shut weren't even concealed. Her eyes were swollen and so were her cheeks. The pallor of her skin was greenish gray underneath a thick coating of makeup. For some reason I can't figure out, instead of a dress, she was wearing Eeyore (from Winnie the Pooh) pajamas. They were so thin it was obvious she was in a garbage bag, which had holes for her bloated and deformed-looking hands, which had been positioned around a bouquet of red long-stemmed roses. As everyone stared, I could see them all trying as hard as I was not to look aghast at the body lying before them. That wasn't Elaine.

My dad stepped out of the line going toward the podium to watch the people go by, staring at his dead wife. I wondered if he ever thought that this day would come during his lifetime. I'm guessing he didn't, since she was fourteen years his junior. I wondered if he knew how fragile she was every time he lifted her up and threw her or hit her, if he ever guessed that her little body would give up from the inside out. This was the product of all the hundreds of bruises he gave her. What I saw when I looked at her is that he finally got his wish, and so did she. I felt as though the wind had been knocked clear out of me. My only relief was that my brother and sister didn't end up seeing their mother that way.

After everyone finished the viewing, my dad remained in his spot, staring at the body that had been his wife. Suddenly, he made his way toward her and did something nobody expected. He put his arms around her and started sobbing, so violently that everyone in the room was shocked and silenced.

"My baby," he sobbed. "My beautiful baby!" This went for what felt like forever, until his sister finally came and helped me pull him off of her. "No! I won't leave her here! I can't leave her alone!"

He yelled, choking as we tried to convince him to sit down. He was way stronger than both of us, so we all made even more of a scene than he did on his own. What else was I supposed to do? As we urged him to stop, he struggled against us and moaned and sobbed some more. Then he grabbed at the bouquet of roses that were in her puffy hands.

"I want one of these roses to keep," he cried. Unfortunately, the stems still had the thorns attached, and one of the thorns got caught and tore a hole through the pajamas and the plastic bag containing her body. Finally, we freed the rose and got him away from her. Hastily, I made my way out of the doors and away from the open-mouthed stares. On my way out, I realized the crying was coming from my sister, Michelle. She was really going through it, but I bet no one would remember her for that. It wouldn't be what anyone remembered from that day. Luckily for her, my dad stole the show. The rest of the day was a blur. I struggled again to remember what the hell I was thinking when I decided I didn't need the heavy drugs anymore.

The rest of the trip wasn't as bad as the funeral. Eventually, I got back home. Walter and I immediately began fighting. Christmas sucked. The last fight that we had was the worst ever. I hit my head so hard, I had to go to the hospital. I was completely knocked out. Walter said I fell. I don't know because I can't remember, of course. Whatever the details were, we had a fight, and the head injury was so bad the next morning I couldn't even sign my name, my ears were bleeding, my hands were shaking, and I couldn't think straight. Walter had been too busy to celebrate Christmas with me. I had spent a lot of time picking out really great presents for him and Payton, and he hadn't made the time to open them with me. It was Christmas Eve 1985 all over again.

My therapist came to the hospital that morning and told me that if I didn't leave Walter, the fights would to continue to escalate. "You have to take your daughter and leave him before he kills you," she said.

Hastily, I planned my way out. Payton was fourteen months old, and I needed to make a fresh start for both of us. Walter was going to go back to Atlanta for his annual tradeshow, and I figured that was a good time to leave. I told him I wanted to go back home for a while to regroup, and he bought my plane ticket with his airline miles. My mom came up and helped me pack. I even consulted with a lawyer before I left town, asking if I were doing anything illegal by leaving the state of Utah. My lawyer assured me that everything would be fine, since I could prove that Walter bought the ticket for me. Before Walter came home, I was gone. I took most of my things with me when I left. The most important thing to me was that I had Payton. No matter what, I knew everything would be okay as long as we were together.

Being back in California was an adjustment, but as long as I had Payton, I knew I could make it work. I had to build a life for us, something safe. I started working for Bruce again. After a week went by, I started to feel guilty about leaving Walter the way I had, without talking to him about things. I made the stupid decision to get in touch with him and tell him that I was sorry for leaving the way that I had. I apologized for my bad manners, but I told him I wasn't ever going back to Utah. I explained that I hoped he could someday forgive me, but that I just couldn't be with him anymore. Very soon after I sent that e-mail, I was served with papers. Then he showed up in California to take my little girl. In three days, there would be an ex-parte hearing. He accused me of kidnapping my own daughter; I was on the wrong end of a restraining order. That was the beginning of a very dark and lonely time for me.

I remember very well the day he took her from me. That morning, I woke up slowly, and nursed my darling girl. I enjoyed having her next to me as I always had. I knew that later on that day, he would be coming for her. Every fiber of my being wanted to take her and run, to do the awful thing he had accused me of. I knew it would be idiotic and wrong, so I did what I had to do. I got her ready to go. I dressed her in dark pink corduroy pants and a white long-sleeve shirt with snaps on the bottom. Over the top of her shirt was a light pink, dark pink, white, and gray sweater. She looked perfect, just like she always did. After her breakfast, she fell asleep in my arms, and I didn't want to put her down. I carried her all through her nap. Auntie Carol came over to take me away so that I wouldn't make a scene or have to watch him physically take her. Before we left, I decided to wake her and hear her voice one more time.

"I love you, Payton," I told her.

"Love you, love you, love you," she replied in her sweet little baby voice. She always said that back then. I can picture her face and hear her saying this to me as if it were yesterday. It still makes me cry after all these years.

Three days later, I showed up at my court date, and it was an absolute disaster. My mom went with me. I was surprised to see Steve there. Stupidly, I thought he was there to support me. He wasn't. Somehow, through bribery or just pure maliciousness, Walter had gotten Steve to side with him. Steve and his smug little new girlfriend were there; so were Steve's dad and Walter and his big, expensive entourage of legal and moral support. Steve handed me a letter he had been carrying around with him. It was a sworn statement about how *crazy* I was and what a terrible wife and mother I was. It was really harsh. It was everything stupid or ugly I had ever said or done, along with some major exaggerations and outright lies. I was horrified when I read it.

It was almost impossible to convince my mother of the reality that was happening.

"Mom, Steve isn't here for *us*. He is here to support the opposition. He is on Walter's side!"

"You must be mistaken. He wouldn't do that. Right?"

I handed her the letter. It took her a minute or two to scan the first page, and then she sat there, dumbstruck and wide-eyed, wanting to disbelieve, but forced to understand.

"I don't want to read anymore," she finally said, handing me the pages back.

"Okay, well, stop trying to talk to him or smile at him anymore. He seriously hates me," I whispered angrily.

When we all were settled in our seats, it was humiliating. Walter's side of the courtroom was full, and ours had four people in it. My mom and me, my ridiculous attorney, and my therapist (the one who had told me to leave Walter before he killed me). Anxiety rose in my guts and I felt the weight of the world on my shoulders.

When my attorney began his defense, he mispronounced my name, and at that moment I knew for sure that my ship was sunk. There were so many lies, so many ugly things thrown at me to make me look bad. If I was so bad, why would Walter have left me alone with our daughter when he went on his buying trips for weeks and weeks? It was insane. I knew I was a good mother, and so did Walter. Walter's problem was that he couldn't stand losing. Actually, I take that back. *My* problem was that Walter couldn't stand to lose. He had all the money in the world, enough to pay attorney's fees and court costs until the end of time. Everything I had went to pay my lawyer and I had nothing left. He would never let me win. He would never let her go. He even made it look like I wasn't nursing her anymore. It was terrible! I stood up and told the judge in desperation that I certainly was still nursing! What an easy lie to uncover! I was still lactating. But, of course, how would anybody ever know that?

The sting of betrayal from that day still makes my heart pump fast. There is no real need to go any further into this. Suffice it to say, Walter won, just like he always did. What he couldn't see was that in winning, everyone else lost, especially Payton. How sad that a little girl would end up growing up without a mother. Because eventually custody wouldn't be enough for Walter. In time, he would push to have my parental rights taken away from me. Could I have fought harder? Absolutely. This is one of the few "I wish I could do that over" moments I have in life. I wish I could prove to her that she was worth the fight. I wish I could go back to that courtroom and pull myself together and do everything differently. I wish I could show Payton that she is and has always been so loved. There has never been a day that I have not thought about her and wished that I could talk to her. Oh, how I've longed to hold her in my arms. At this point, it isn't about what Walter did. It isn't even about what I did wrong. All I care about is that my little girl knows she is loved. Unfortunately, I doubt that she ever will believe that. When Walter got his legal team together and formulated a plan to win, he hurt his little girl more than he will ever know. No child should ever grow up questioning whether she was ever loved or special enough to have a mommy in her life.

I had one more visit with Payton at Walter's brother and sister-in-law's house. The visit was heartbreaking. She had lost her smile in three days' time. I read somewhere that a child's connection to her mother is so strong before she is two years old, if that bond is broken suddenly, the way ours had been, her very innermost being might be fractured. I could see that had happened to her. Try as I did to get her to smile, I could not. My heart broke for my precious little girl. I nursed her one last time. I bathed her one last time. I held her one last time. It was the hardest day I had ever lived in my life to that point.

Later on, I read in some court documents that Walter had claimed that I was on drugs that day and that he had turned me away, not letting me have my visit. No, I hadn't been on drugs that day, and yes, I did have my last visit at Walter's brother's house. There was no end to the lies he told to make me look like a bad mother. I have never claimed to be perfect. I have made many mistakes in life. But as far as Payton was concerned, I hadn't done things wrong. But soon, my ability to do the right thing would run out. Soon, I would give up and make Walter look right about every lie he ever said about me.

Part 4

"I would rather work with God in the dark than to go alone in the light."

—Mary Gardiner Brainard

January 2006

When I left Utah, I didn't call my mom. I stayed at my sister's friend Amber's house. A guy named Chuck also lived there. Chuck was bad news from the beginning. I knew it, and I didn't care. A week after coming home from Utah, I killed myself. I died that day. I cut myself and took a bottle of pills when I was alone at Amber's house. For some reason Michelle showed up. This is all a blur, of course, but I'll tell you the parts I remember. She took me to her boyfriend's house. I knew he was into heroin, so I told her that I wanted to get loaded.

"I thought you didn't shoot up," she told me, with sadness and shock in her eyes.

I had never shot up any drug in my life. I just wanted to act like I did it all the time, so he would give me enough to finish the job. I was desperate and couldn't face the world for one more miserable second. My life was over already; I just needed to make sure that this day was my last. It was a terrible thing to do to my sister. Hopefully, someday she can forgive me.

"Sorry, Michelle, I've been doing it for a while," I told her as convincingly as I could.

"When did you start?" she asked with sadness.

The last thing I remember saying was "I'll tell you tomorrow." I had no intention of being alive the next day. That was it. Lights out. I floated out on a wonderful cloud of fog and bliss.

Until …

I was in a very small white room, with only a small bed with a very thin foam mattress on top. The walls were all white, and the door looked heavy. It was shut and had a very small window near the top. I knew where I was before any staff showed up. It was the hardest time I'd ever done in a psychiatric hospital in my life. The minutes went by like days. I didn't have the energy to deal with anybody. I didn't even bother lying to the staff. I didn't care whether I got out. My feelings during that time were wrong and deadly. My self-worth was gone. I had no purpose. The loneliness inside was over-powering. I learned what it meant to be in despair.

I don't remember how many weeks I was there. It wasn't quite a month before they let me out. Amber picked me up and took me back to her place. From there on out, things got worse. Instead of trying to kill myself again, I learned how to put a needle in my arm.

I'd like to recount some details here, but my memory escapes me. I can't think of many. I remember Chuck's mess in Amber's kitchen—an enormous pile of clothes, trash, tools, and shoes that took over the entire table and everywhere underneath it. It was disgusting. I didn't really even like him. I just got stuck one day and couldn't figure out how to get out. He had a daughter a little older than Rose, and I started watching her while Chuck worked. He rented a house for us.

It was bad, as bad as any relationship I've ever heard of. I was a wreck back then. I was high all day. I was holed up in a filthy room in a filthy house that I constantly tried to keep clean. Mostly, I stayed in my bedroom. My depression was so extreme that I was unable to return a phone call or even check my voicemail messages for a year and a half. It was the darkest time of my life.

I realize now that if I hadn't gone through this unbearable darkness, I would not have the relationship I have with God today. If I had to do it all over again, I guess I would—if only it would get me to this point. It is hard for me to recall how I became unstuck after being stuck for so long, or even to describe what was going on in my mind during that time, but I'll try.

When I was a kid, I saw that my dad and Elaine's relationship was bad, and I couldn't understand how anyone would ever stay in a relationship that miserable. By the time my brother, Justin, was born, I was already out of the house, and doing my own thing. One year I went there to spend the night before Easter. My dad was so out of control with his anger and name calling, he pulled out all of Elaine's dresser drawers and dumped them into the mucky fish pond outside. He raged and told her how bad her pussy stank and called her a slut and a cunt. Elaine, of course, was also drunk and fought back as best as she could. Finally, I took my little brother and sister, and we went shopping for candy. It was the only thing I could do—get the kids away from their parents. Sadly, it was just a regular, everyday type of thing for them. We were all scared and crying by the time we got out to my car, and I thought, *Why do they stay together?* But they did stay together. They stayed together until Elaine's alcohol-saturated body couldn't recover from pneumonia. That fight was just one of hundreds that my brother and sister had to live through. Every time I visited them, there was a scene like that one. It was never normal. It was always something.

When I'd call my dad and Elaine from New York or Florida or Utah or wherever I was living, Elaine would cry on the phone, telling me, "Your dad's a monster." I would think, *I know.* I couldn't understand why they didn't just get a divorce. It didn't make sense at the time, because I had never been in her shoes. Shortly after Elaine died, I had the opportunity (if you want to call it that) to find out exactly what she was going through and why she wouldn't or couldn't leave my dad.

February 2006

After I died, I woke up with big, fat staples running like railroad tracks up my arms. They were not very pretty. I was supposed to be gone. I was on stolen time, a dead girl walking. Who cared if I shot up? Who cared if I killed myself a little bit every godforsaken day? I was dead already.

This sounds pretty crazy, but I truly believe drugs saved my life. I got so high and stayed that way for so long, I forgot to try to kill myself. Living in a tweeker house is disgusting. There's always someone around who smells weird. There is always someone there you don't know. My living room constantly smelled like old cheese and dirty socks. At first, it was depressing. But I got high every day, and spent a lot of time alone or with Chuck's daughter. It was a trade-off. He got me high every day, and I stayed home and took care of his child. I spent most of the time at first trying to keep the house clean. Eventually, the house was in such a state, I couldn't clean it. The carpets turned gray. Then the kitchen became impossibly trashed. Finally, the living room was so full of litter, clothes, and pieced-apart junk that I gave up on the entire lower half of the house and stayed upstairs in my room all day, every day. My relationship wasn't too bad during this time, because I never went anywhere. Our fights were mostly verbal and never so bad that I felt I had to leave. I just got high enough to forget about it. When I say I never went anywhere, I really mean that—not to visit a single person, not to go to the grocery store, not for one reason at all, ever. Then one day, I got to know Tara.

I had met Tara earlier, because she is Amber's mom and Michelle had been living with Amber for a couple of years. But Tara didn't like me, because she thought I was a crazy person. Not even drug addicts understand the suicide thing unless they go through it themselves. One day, for whatever reason, Tara came over to my house. She brought her little travel dope kit. We got high together and realized we enjoyed each other's company.

"Why don't you ever leave here?" she asked.

"I can't" was all I could say.

"Let's go shopping sometime," she said.

I told her I'd think about it. I have no idea how much time it took, but eventually she did get me out of the house. It was hard, but I finally went out. And we went shopping. We totally went shopping. Like, a lot. She told me that I dressed like an old lady and taught me what kinds of clothes are worth wearing. We had no money, so we stole everything. I became really good at it. It's embarrassing to think about what my life was back then. I became a big shoplifter. I stole anything and everything. Then other people—tweekers— stole all my stuff from me. I have nothing left from that part of my life, although I stole entire wardrobes, thousands and thousands of dollars' worth of ridiculously expensive clothes. It was all to look pretty and smart on the outside, because I was empty and ugly on the inside. But I was staying so high and busy, there was no time to kill myself. So that was good.

I slept maybe once every five days for a couple of hours. Tara taught me that I had to try to sleep every day, even if for a short while. And I had to at least eat a little bit, just to ground myself. And I should never pick my face. Get really high once in the morning and move on. I learned how to function, and I wanted to hang out with her rather than be stuck at home with Chuck. I went out, and I stayed out.

That's when the real fights started. The more he complained that I wasn't ever home, the more I wanted to stay away. The more I stayed away, the worse our fights got. I'd come home for a little while to appease him, and we'd fight. He'd yell or cry or throw something and I'd fight back. Our fights got really bad. Sometimes I crawled out of the second-story bathroom and hide, like a ninja in the night. I got him off me that way a couple of times. I'd lie down so flat, he'd think I had jumped off or something and would leave or go tweak out on something else. He was a tow-truck driver during that time, and he worked all night. He slept very little even when he was not working. His mental state was never quite right. He was always revved up or coming down or paranoid or angry. A lot of the time, he was angry.

In his defense, he did hold it together the best way he had learned how, and he tried to take care of me. But I didn't want to be stuck in a room to rot anymore. I needed to be **SHOPPING**! When I was shopping, I wasn't thinking, I was focused on getting away with something. When I was shopping, I was made up, with my shopping attitude on, and people were nice to me, the fools. I felt very good about how easily I got away with everything. I hated coming back home to my dumpy, dirty house with all the gross tweekers and their tweeker smells and tweeker junk. I thought I was better than they were, and I couldn't stand the fact that we even had the drug in common. I liked Tara, and I liked that she made the drug look more fun and less trashy than Chuck or his dirty friends did.

One time I came home, and Chuck was in such a foul mood I knew I'd better just turn right back around and leave, but I didn't. I probably wanted to get high or something, I'm not sure. Forgive me if I am vague, but my mind has done its self-protection thing and blocked out many of the details of this time of my life. He was at the computer, yelling at me about being gone so much. I was standing next to him, and he put a cigarette out in my ear. I ran away, threw a box of nail polish at him, and started yelling. Then we hit each other once or twice, and he punched me in my stomach, just the way a man would hit another man. I had never had the wind get knocked out of me like that before. I couldn't breathe air into my body. I lay down on the messed-up bed, trying to make air go into my lungs. All I could think was that once I could move, I would kill him. But I was beaten, and I knew it. He was stronger and meaner than I was, and there was no way I would ever win a fight with him. Still, the fight didn't stop there. I picked up a plate off the floor and hit him over the head. He then jumped on me, grabbed one of the porcelain shards, and tried to jab it into my neck. Luckily, I was able to get my arm under it, and he plunged the pointy part into my blocking arm instead. There was blood pouring out of my face and arm, but I was still so angry I didn't want to give up. Afraid to get caught with a drug charge, I didn't call the cops. I just left the house and went back to Tara's. Later that night, I went to the hospital under a fake name to get stitches, because the inside of my arm started to poke out of the hole, and I couldn't push it back in. *So gross.*

I thought about Elaine and how she couldn't or wouldn't leave my dad. I realized I was just like her, even worse probably. Soon after that fight, I became pregnant. Unable to stop using, I planned to have an abortion, but we ended up getting in such a bad fight, he threw me on the bathroom floor. It was just like that: he picked me up and slammed me down so hard that I couldn't move. When I was finally able to get up off the floor, blood started running down my legs. Around this time I stopped fighting back anymore, and I started to give up in a whole new kind of way.

One day I laid in bed, locked in my room. I looked around, staring at the shadows on the wall, on the floor, and around the bookcase that held the television. The muck smell had started to infiltrate my room, and the warm air was thick with the stench of stale cigarette smoke, full ashtrays, and dirty laundry. Stuck in my own negative thoughts about wanting to leave, and wanting to get high and feeling miserably guilty about what I had become, I stared at the shadows. I stared *into* the shadows. I wished I had died or that I could will myself to die. It was as if everything good inside me was fading, and the fight that I had inside my heart to try to overcome was cracking into pieces. My resolve seemed to be melting; I could actually feel myself breaking down. At that moment, in my mind, I gave up completely to the darkness and the ugliness all around me. Whatever I had done to live *above* it, instead of *in* it, faded away. I was becoming part of the devil that I shot into my veins; I had finally become one of the zombies who walked in and out of my house every day. Whether or not I dressed like them or picked my face or went to prison, I was exactly the same as they were. I was death. I don't know how long I stayed that way, lying there, welcoming the darkness, but it became part of my very being. I sensed, with my heart, mind, and soul, those shadows shifting, coming toward me and merging with my very essence. I had lost the will to be anything better or do anything else; I had nowhere to run, so I let the darkness invade me. I felt both terrified and exhilarated. I felt an actual shift occur psychically and sensed that the worst was still to come. I was right.

The physical abuse became a daily issue. My fear made me unable to fight back, and my level of addiction got worse. I loved to get high. I couldn't take care of his daughter anymore, and I didn't even try. Again, I stayed in the room all the time. I got back in touch with my mom and tried to get clean, but I couldn't make it to five days without getting loaded. I made it to four days quite a few times at her house, but I could not get to day five. My emotions, anger and guilt had me in a cycle of horror. As much as I tried to reason with myself or intellectualize my problem, there was nothing I could do to free myself from my shackles. I was a slave to the needle. When I couldn't stay clean one more minute, I would call Chuck, who would pick me up at my poor mother's house and take me back to our disgusting shit hole, where I immediately put the needle in my arm. The instant rush I received helped me block out the disappointment and heartbreak I caused my mother, the guilt I felt about being a terrible mother to my kids, and the sting of failure I felt about whom I had become. I felt disgust when I found condom wrappers around the room I'd called home only days before. I had no self-respect. I had no will. I had nothing left inside. All I wished for was my life to end. One day, Jodi came to my house and couldn't believe how I was living.

"Help me get out of here," I pleaded. But before she took me with her, I shot up one last time in front of her. It's always *one last time*. I was pathetic. I was a size two. I was gray and my body stank because Chuck had given me some kind of bacterial infection. I was sickening, and I knew it. I lasted maybe two days at her house. Again, I hurt her. I ran away from her like a fool. I even stole Julia's phone before I left, because Jodi had tried to protect me from myself by keeping my phone. I left her house feeling like the biggest loser that ever lived. But I needed to get high! I simply could not stand my feelings or myself without the drugs.

Very soon after I returned to Chuck, I cut all my hair down to just an inch or two off my scalp. My hair had been all the way down the middle of my back, and now it was gone too. When I looked in the mirror, I didn't even recognize myself anymore. I was down to 115 pounds. My arms were scarred, and though my track mark was always in the same spot, it was an angry bruise all the time. My skin had taken on the pallor of a Hollywood alien, grayish-green. I looked ill. My pupils were always intensely dilated, and I had a dull spaced-out look on my face.

Underneath it all, my soul screamed out in absolute desperation. My expression was lifeless, but my heart cried out every minute of my sleepless days and nights. I never slept, I never ate, and every second of my life, my mind experienced the epitome of hell.

One day, I got hungry and went to the kitchen to eat something. It had been maybe four days since I had put anything other than tap water in my stomach. There was cereal in the cupboard and milk in the fridge. I made myself a bowl of Frosted Flakes. After taking the bowl upstairs, I realized the milk had soured so much it was chunky. It was totally rancid, but I was starving, and there was nothing else in the house to eat. I ate it anyway. There are no words to describe the darkness that enveloped me during this time. Every breath was filled with self-loathing. Accidental glances in the mirror caused waves of disgust within me. I looked away from the ugly girl in the mirror as quickly as I could. *Whose eyes are those?*

I turned my back on God. I thought He was to blame. Somehow it was God's fault all this had happened. After all, I was innocent and didn't deserve what Walter had done to me. In my mind, the fact that I gave up and chose to do drugs instead of fight Walter wasn't the point. It should have never happened, and God had let me down. I couldn't own the fact that I had let myself down. I felt I was wronged, and I couldn't let it go. I knew God could have made things different if He wanted to, and I was mad that He didn't fight my fight for me. I wanted Him to fix things, and He wasn't doing it for me. I was angry! I didn't stop believing in Him. I just stopped liking Him. In my prayers, I even told God I hated Him. I yelled out loud to Him, cursed Him, said I was through with Him. I closed my heart. Inside me, the darkness grew. My heart was broken, my inner light turned off. I had shut down so spiritually and emotionally, I was no longer a human being. I was as sick as any girl could get. But though I closed my heart to God, He never closed His heart to me. Patiently, He heard my prayers, and with love, He waited for me to come around.

Things got worse before they got better. But eventually the end of this period came, although the fights never got resolved. They just merged, one into the next. Either I ran away, or he went to work. I got so beaten up I didn't even want to get out of bed. One fight was particularly bad, and I called Tara. As always, she came to get me. She had been evicted and was living with her daughter; she said I could come hang out. While I was there, Chuck called my phone and left me a message. One of his ways to get to me was to say mean words. I've never met another person who could say such mean things. It's a bad habit I picked up from him.

The message was: "Pick up the phone. You need to call me back. All you want to do is spend time with Tara! Why can't you just come home? You need to come outside! I've been parked out here all night, and I'm not leaving. Can you understand that? I hope you have no place to go. I hope Amber kicks you out, and you end up homeless and you get raped again! If I hear about that happening, I'm going to laugh about it! You're a piece of shit, and I hope you suffer. I hope you end up getting hurt and having nothing. You deserve to have nothing, you stupid bitch. You probably don't even care what I'm going through. Look what you're putting me through, being parked out here for hours when I should be working, you fucking whore!"

His messages went on and on and usually ran into each other. The voicemail would cut him off, and he'd call right back. Over and over and over. Call after call, voicemail after voicemail, and text after text—usually all from right outside the door, right across the street, right down the road. I've never seen anyone get something in his mind and obsess like that. The drugs made him stay up forever, and he'd spend the whole time stalking me and freaking out when I stayed away. What a scary time. For whatever reason, the message about him laughing if he heard I got raped again was a breaking point. He had said a million mean things, but that one really hit me in a sore place. You tell your secrets, and some people will hold those secrets against you, learn how to turn them around and hurt you with them.

I'd had enough. I called Delta and bought tickets with my air miles. I needed to get out of Santa Barbara.

Unfortunately, I had nowhere to go but back to Utah. Steve had his own house. Since I'd asked for nothing in the divorce, the least he could do is let me go there and come down. Get away from that maniac and get my head back on straight.

Delta said I had enough miles to get me to Utah, so I booked the earliest flight I could. Amber said I could stay with her until I left Santa Barbara. I don't remember how long I had to wait. It was probably a week or two. I passed the time getting loaded and shopping, running unnecessary errands with Tara, going to the laundromat, taking midnight walks to the rose garden at the hotel down the street. It was all fun again, because I thought it would be the last time I'd hang out with these people, and they thought it would be the last time they'd have to deal with me. I planned to come down, so that once I got to Utah I could be normal around Rose. Thing was, I couldn't live with someone who got high every day and stay clean. It was totally impossible.

May 2007

I got high right up until the day I flew out of the Santa Barbara airport. The details of that trip are foggy. I just remember getting there and coming down hard. It was as hard as coming down in jail, but worse in a way because I had to act like I was okay in front of Rose. I didn't want her or Steve to know what I was going through, but I could hardly hide it. My emotions were all over the place. I was edgy, I was grouchy, I was tired, I was mad, I was overwhelmed, and worst of all I still wanted to get high. Steve was mad at me for not coming down before getting there, and he wanted me to take a drug test to prove I wasn't still getting high. I told him it would take five days for the drugs to get out of my system, and then I would take a drug test. I even flushed a little baggie I found with dope inside it down the toilet. That was how serious I was about wanting to make it work. But as the days went by, I didn't feel better. I grew frustrated with Steve, because he wanted me to be back together with him, and I didn't feel comfortable sleeping with him. I guess it was a misunderstanding. Maybe I had flirted with him when we talked before I flew out. Whether I did or didn't, he'd obviously gotten the wrong idea, and he was mad at me and hurt that I wanted to stay in a spare room. My feelings all came back at me full force. Everything I had gotten high to forget was right there. It hadn't gone anywhere. It was like a giant tidal wave of emotion waiting to crush me. I kept thinking about that day in the courtroom, the betrayal I'd felt, how he looked sitting next to Walter. I hadn't been able to forgive him for that. We fought about that, and we fought about how visibly different I looked. I was disturbingly thin, and my hair was still extremely short from my meltdown. I was wearing it in a boy kind of style, dyed dark red. I thought it looked cute at the time, but it probably didn't. I was moody and not functioning normally and I'm sure I made them both feel really sad. I was nothing like the *me* they remembered.

After a few big arguments, I decided to stay at a hotel. I called my mom and asked if she would pick up the bill for me, because I had no choice. Of course, there was no way I could call Walter, and I had no friends in all of Utah who weren't his friends too. I was way too embarrassed to put myself out there like that, so I waited and decided on the sixth day to take the drug test to prove I hadn't been using while I was there. The drug test came out positive. That's how saturated my body had been. I looked like such a liar. I even told Tara this story, and she didn't believe that part about flushing the dope down the toilet. But it is the truth.

After I tested dirty, everyone was sick of me. I really should have cleaned up before going out there and making such a mess of things. I wished I had, but the truth is, I wasn't strong enough to do it. I hadn't the resolve or the ability. Making matters worse, I was somehow unable to come down like a normal person. *How do "normal people" come down, anyway?* It was way too hard. It hurt way too much.

89

There I was in Utah, and I had blown my opportunity to get my life back. Chuck started texting again. He said how sorry he was and how he wanted me back. It was just what I needed. I was out of time at my hotel, and I had no options left for my chance at a life again. He bought me a Greyhound Bus ticket back to Santa Barbara, and I took it. *Seriously. I KNOW. So dumb.*

Before I returned to California, I had a wonderful experience with a couple who showed me real human kindness. I was walking down the street with my suitcases. I had everything I owned in them. It wasn't much, but it was certainly enough to weigh me down. I had to get from Draper, Utah, all the way to downtown Salt Lake City, about a half-hour drive, maybe a bit more. I planned to take a city bus, but I didn't know which one. The bus would not leave until the next day, but the hotel had kicked me out. My plan was to make it to the bus station and wait there. All I had to do was figure out how to get to downtown Salt Lake. I walked down the street, lugging my suitcases and feeling totally overwhelmed. I was lost, and I didn't know what to do.

Suddenly, a nice couple in a car pulled over. "Do you need a ride?" a sweet-looking lady called out to me.

"Yes," I said. They had no idea how much help I needed, and I had no idea how much help they were prepared to give me. They were an older couple. They invited me to their home and made me stir fry. They let me sleep at their house, and they drove me all the way to the Greyhound Bus station the next day. They even let me have $40 to get me going, so I wouldn't have to be hungry on my trip. It was one of the nicest things that any stranger has ever done for me, and I still think about them today. I hope they realize how much that meant to me and know that, even today, their kindness puts a smile on my face. There should be more people like them in this world.

The bus pulled into downtown Santa Barbara late at night. Chuck picked me up in the tow truck. He took me back to the house, which he had let get filthy beyond all reason or explanation. It stunk, and I didn't want to put my clothes away. It was so gross that I didn't want to take my shoes off. It was piled up with trash. There was a funk in the house that smelled rotten. He'd had women there. Everything was covered in grime and old clothes and car parts and mechanical pieces of things. Everything felt dark. The air was thick. I needed to get high. He made me wait until the next morning, probably as a way to punish me for leaving him. When I did finally get high, it was like getting into a comfortable bed and pulling the sheets up to my neck. It felt good and it felt safe. I did a big enough shot to zap my brains hard, so I would stop thinking or feeling. My eyeballs danced in their sockets. I couldn't focus. I couldn't do anything but lie down and stare at the ceiling, seeing nothing.

It only took about two weeks for us to have a major fight. It wasn't the biggest fight we ever had, but it was in public. Chuck called me up one morning when he was out working, saying he needed help because he couldn't hit his vein. I drove out to a grocery-store parking lot at Turnpike Road, and got into his tow truck to help him hit it. I hadn't gotten high that day, but he said he was in a hurry and it was all he had. He said he'd bring me some at the house later. I filled up the syringe and helped him get high. I pulled back on the plunger, registered it, and watched the blood come back into the needle, signaling that I was in the vein. Then I pushed the drugs into him and heard the exhale of breath he always made when I hit him. He was happy. He wanted to get going. He wanted to know when we could talk. I was pissed off, because I wanted to get high too, but I knew I wouldn't be able to, so I was in a bad mood. I took the piece of cotton that I'd used to get him high and put it in a little container of beads that I had. I thought I could use it to get a little bit high later on. Soon after that, our conversation got off track and turned ugly, so I went back to the van and left.

He had wanted to leave, but as soon as *I* wanted to leave it triggered something in him. Whenever I wanted to leave, he tried to control me and make me stay, so we got in that familiar tug of war. I decided to drive away. For whatever reason he followed me in his tow truck. I drove faster. He kept up behind me. The chase was on. I got on the 101 Freeway going south, and still he followed me. I got on the 154 going toward Santa Maria, and he kept following me. I didn't really have a plan, but I thought that if I kept driving, eventually he would give up. The thing about Chuck was, he didn't give up. He actually gunned it and hit the back of my vehicle so hard, he lifted the minivan up off the ground. Somehow I controlled the wheel well enough to make sure I didn't get thrown off the road. Part of me was scared to death; the other part watched the whole thing unravel, disbelieving and kind of excited that I was able to drive like a stunt car driver in a movie. It was scary but also thrilling that I was somehow living through it!

Of course before long, someone else on the road called 9-1-1 to report a tow-truck driver ramming a minivan down the freeway, and we were pulled over. The police found the piece of cotton, which I hadn't even used to get high. I ended up going to jail for possession of methamphetamine. Given all the times I'd had drugs on me, I had to get charged for drugs that weren't even mine. Oh well, I was skin and bone and had drugs in my system, so I got put in jail. That was July 11, 2007. When they took me to jail, they asked where I'd gotten the drugs and who I knew. I wouldn't tell them anything. So they put me in a cell with no bed, no blankets, no toilet or toilet paper, and they left me in there for two days without food or water. I had to pee in a river like thing that was cut out of the floor and had water flowing in it. I didn't know that police could be so mean or cruel. That was my first experience with how awful police can be when you don't do what they want you to do. Starving, freezing, exhausted, and drained, I was moved to the main part of the jail. They asked me routine questions, one of which was when my last period was. It took me a little while to answer it, but it was then that I realized I was a couple of weeks late. Testing confirmed that I was pregnant.

One of Chuck's other girlfriends bailed him out of jail so he was out way before I was. Eventually, I got out too, and we went back to where we started. Around this time, we were evicted from our house. The landlord was a decent guy who had given us a lot of chances, but we got too far behind, and we were kicked out. We left that house a terrible mess, with the carpets sticky, stinking, and soiled, dirty needles and trash everywhere, and stuff we had no room for discarded and left behind. I still feel shame thinking about the shape it was in when we left. Not only did we owe thousands in back rent, but we had totally ruined the house, which belonged to the landlord's parents. I'm really embarrassed to this day, and hope to figure out a way to someday make it right.

Things get spotty for me about this time too, because I don't remember the actual sequence of events. As with the rape, I remember certain moments that stick out. I had another fight with Chuck and ended up back at Amber's house with Tara. I started bleeding and had the cramps and pain of another miscarriage. Everything felt stupid and circular, like an endless cycle from which I couldn't escape. Each day seemed more empty and depressing than the last. Amber and her boyfriend got sick of me. I went back and forth a lot with Chuck. I hated him, I needed him. I wanted him to die, I forgave him.

I got really mad at Tara, because I had gotten the settlement (finally) from the 2005 car accident in which I'd broken my neck. The insurance company bought Walter a brand new car. (Walter always wins!) Tara had convinced me that it was a good idea to keep the money behind a photo in picture frame at Amber's house, and, like a fool, I trusted her. The money slowly disappeared. She even bailed someone out of jail with part of it. That someone, of course, never paid me back. The last straw was when she asked if she could buy a big screen television, because someone she knew had stolen one exactly like it, and we were going to do some kind of return swap on it. It was all worked out, and I was to get my money back, for sure, right away. She ended up keeping the TV, and that was the last of the money I'd broken my neck for. I was broke. She wasn't sorry, and I couldn't stand how cold she was toward me all of a sudden. Best friends? Yeah, right. Maybe she felt I owed her the money for all the times she had gotten me high. Whatever the case, in the end, I felt used, and it broke my heart.

Chuck and I both had a court date for the drug charges. He had been caught with some needles in the tow truck, and I think he had a paraphernalia charge. I showed up alone, and he showed up with yet another one of his girlfriends. She was young and better looking than the one who bailed him out of jail, but she was a picker, and her face was pretty much one big scab. After they left, I attacked him right in front of the court house. This, of course, facilitated yet another reconciliation. My self-esteem and self-respect were completely out the window. Just when I thought I hated myself as much as anyone could ever hate herself, there I was hating myself even more.

Chuck had pitched a tent at Cachuma Lake, and suddenly that looked like the only place to be. I was as miserable and broken as I had ever been. There was no love in my heart, and there were no ideas in my mind. My body was malnourished and weak and that foul bacterial infection was back. He was dirty and didn't have any concept of personal hygiene. We stank. I'm not really sure if he knew it or not, but I did. I looked at him sometimes and felt such disgust I couldn't even speak to him. He was filthy in every way a man can be filthy. He didn't even bother to brush his teeth anymore. I never got that bad. I still had enough inside me to brush my teeth every day. When I had quarters, I would put them in the public showers at the lake campground and rinse myself off. Life was unbearably painful. I hated everything about myself and the people I'd considered friends. I had no money left. I slept about eighteen hours a day. Chuck spent most of his time doing who-knows-what in Santa Barbara, and I stayed in the tent. Sometimes he brought me a needle with a little bit of drugs in it, but most of the time he didn't.

Something I couldn't quite put my finger on had changed inside me, and my mind wasn't the same anymore. I wasn't living my life. Instead, I was slowly physically dying. The darkness and mold that had crept under my skin and into my body a little over a year prior finally took a complete hold of me. It had won. It had rotted me from the inside out, and I was a stinking corpse. I was either blank with utter and absolute depression, or I felt an animal rage that came out in bursting tantrums. I was a mad woman on the edge.

August 23, 2011

It was my birthday morning, only about six weeks after I was put in jail. Chuck and I had another massive fight. I ended up very badly bruised. It was so bad, I went to my mother's house. Her friend Howard was there giving her physical therapy, and she let him work on me too. He was nice to me. His niceness broke my heart, because it felt so foreign. I had become an alien and found it incredibly difficult to trust anyone, especially a man. My mom helped me through the night. I knew it was time to quit for good, and I told her I wanted to do whatever it would take to make that happen. She knew she had to get me away from Chuck to really help me, and she knew of a rehabilitation program in the desert.

The next day, my mom and Bruce drove me to a drug rehab in Perris Valley, California, called U-Turn for Christ. They helped me check into the place, and I committed to live there for six months. This place was strict and, as far as I was concerned, not as great as it claimed to be. In all fairness, it is an excellent organization, and an astounding percentage of the graduates stay clean. I just wasn't ready to commit at that level, not yet anyway.

You know how it is … if you want to find a problem with something, it's easy enough to do. Here was my problem: the rehab had a quiet time after six o'clock in the evening. "Word fast" is what they called it. By quiet time, I mean absolute silence—no talking, no whispering, and no laughing. I tried to live by the rules at first, though my efforts were half-hearted. Waking up early felt really hard. When a person comes down, sleep is like a force of nature beyond all control. I'd fall asleep sitting up with my mouth open quite a bit and got in trouble for it. The thing that I got in the most trouble for, though, was my inability to respect word fast. When silent time was over the next morning, I would have to be silent again all day, wearing a bright orange vest so everybody would know not to talk to me. For a while I did okay, but then I would think something was funny and laugh about it. I developed a crush on one of the girls and we became close friends. She made me laugh the most. In my mind, if I were able to laugh in a crap-hole place like that—stuck in a terrible, hot little room with a bunch of bunk beds at night, getting way too little sleep, and then working all day—then it was a miracle from God. Who was I to stifle the joy that God had put in my heart? I even told the people in charge my ideas about this, but it got me nothing but more silent treatment and homework.

I had to read and copy all of Psalm 119. That's 176 verses. Eventually, I was allowed to take off my orange vest and, soon after that, go to work during the day with the other girls on the outside. Sometimes we worked at a thrift store, and sometimes we cleaned the rooms of the hotel at Marietta Bible College. Cleaning rooms was my favorite, because we were paired off, and I felt a little less policed by the staff. The college also had a nice, big cafeteria, with a delicious salad bar, where we got to eat all we wanted. By this time I was getting pretty hungry again and putting on a little weight.

I don't know how long I stayed at U-Turn, but I didn't last the whole six months. I made it hard on myself. Mainly, I was stubborn about the laughing issue and got into loads of trouble. Unfortunately, I got other girls into trouble too, when they communicated or laughed with me. Finally, I was told that I had to dig a hole for punishment. Digging a hole doesn't sound that bad, right? Wrong! I'll tell you why. The hole was to be out in the middle of the hard desert earth, and because we worked all day, I had to dig at night after the other girls went to sleep. I was to go out into the night for two hours at a time, for as long as it would take to dig a hole measuring five feet long, five feet wide, and five feet deep. It took me more than a week to dig that monstrous hole. After a couple of nights, I got used to the routine. One of the staff went out there with me to make sure I wasn't slacking on the job. She would read scriptures to me, which was fine. The nights were warm and clear, and the stars were as bright as I've ever seen them in my life. When I stopped feeling sorry for myself, I was able to appreciate the beauty of life. Slowly but surely, I felt the light coming back into my heart and soul.

When I finally finished digging, I felt a sense of accomplishment. It was the first really hard thing that I had set out to do and actually completed. I was proud of myself, which was a foreign feeling. I jumped down into my grave-like hole and acted like I was digging out the corners, but what I actually did was lie down. Lying in there, I felt the tickle of a bug or spider go across my arm or leg, but I was used to the creepy-crawlers already, and they didn't bother me anymore. As I lay there, staring up at the sky, I asked God if He would come back into my life. I said I was no longer angry at Him, and asked, with a hopeful heart, if He would please live in my heart once more. As I smelled the warm earth and watched the clouds float past the moon, I realized that He had never left me. Silly me, He had been right there waiting for me the whole time.

With a quiet smile, I got myself out of that hole and asked the girl to measure it, so I could be done with that job once and for all. She measured the corners. She smiled at me and then sat back down.

"Good. Now go ahead and fill it back up," she said.

The feeling inside me was so peaceful I didn't even get mad. I just got back to work. It only took three days to fill it back in. You would think that experience would have shut me up, but of course, it didn't.

However long my stay had been at this point, I realized I hadn't started my period again. I told the staff and asked for a pregnancy test. The test was positive. From the very first moment I knew about the baby, I was elated.

The next time I got in trouble for laughing, they wanted me to go back out and dig another hole. This time, they gave me a slotted serving spoon and covered the holes with tape. After working hard all day, I went out into the night with my watcher, who read to me from her Bible. I began to dig. This time, though, I was a lot less serious about it. I knew I'd never get anywhere with the spoon, so I didn't care about the progress I made. Instead, I sang praise songs to the night sky and the dirt, using my tape-covered spoon as a microphone. My levity was not received well. Within a day or two, I was shown the door. I don't know if they forced me to leave, or if I chose to walk out, but either way, I was out on my own. Lost and alone in the desert, I called none other than stupid, frigging Chuck. In my mind, I thought he had a right to know I was pregnant and that this time I would have the baby. He told me he would be out the next day to pick me up. I slept outside under the stars. I was cold, discouraged, mad at myself, and also hopeful that what I was doing made some sense in the world. Chuck said he wanted to get clean too and that he would be there for me and for our baby.

The first night back showed me that he was lying, *again*, and that nothing had changed. On the second night back in the tent by the lake, I had a dream in which a beautiful bright little baby, wearing nothing but a diaper, ran up to me. I thought it was Payton, so I asked, "Do you know who I am?" I thought that by this time, she wouldn't recognize me anymore. She looked at me in the eyes, and very seriously said, "My daddy's going to try to kill you," and then she ran away. When I woke up, I knew the dream was important. Thinking it was Payton, I thought, *Why would Walter want to kill me at this point? He's already won.* I couldn't understand what the dream meant, but I knew it was significant. Within hours, I was having the worst fight I would ever have with Chuck.

I can't remember what started the fight, but it was most likely the fact that I was mad at him because he was still loaded. I wanted to leave. I wanted him to take me to my mom's. I had screwed up by calling him, but I hadn't gotten loaded. I hoped that maybe she would let me stay there. I got in the van and wouldn't get out. Eventually, he relented and drove me down San Marcos Pass. It was the most terrifying drive of my life. He drove like a bat of out hell the whole way, more than ninety miles an hour on a fifty-five mile per hour stretch of a two-lane highway, curving down the foothills toward Santa Barbara. The whole time, he was raging and hitting me, telling me he wanted to drive right off the cliffs, killing both me and the baby growing inside me. Once when he slowed down, I opened the door and made a move to jump out. At this point, he swerved into the guardrail and hit it hard enough to slam my door shut. I was lucky I didn't lose my leg. By the time we got to the bottom and off the fastest part of the drive, I took the first opportunity to jump out. I tucked in my arms and legs to protect the life inside me, taking the brunt of the injuries on my elbows and knees. The car behind us called 9-1-1, and Chuck left me there, bleeding and terrified. Since I wasn't high, and I didn't want to get high, I knew I could stay away from him.

An ambulance took me to the hospital, and I spent some time alone. They gave me an ultrasound and told me that the baby was fine. A lady from a domestic-violence (DV) shelter came to the hospital and talked to me. There was a shelter in town, she told me, and I was welcome to stay there. I did so for a couple of months. The staff treated me really well. The women there were just like me, wounded but strong. They were incredibly open-hearted and kind. I loved them like sisters. The hardest thing about being there was that the jail was so close by. Many nights, I woke up in a cold sweat, thinking Chuck was right below my window, waiting in the dark. The location was confidential, but surely he knew someone who knew where I was. My fears were irrational, but real to me nonetheless.

While I was in the DV shelter, all the women got together and threw me a baby shower. They hardly had the money to do anything for themselves, but they chose to do that for me. They were all as down in their lives as I was. It was one of the most touching and thoughtful things anyone had ever done for me. They made it really great. There were balloons and games, food and cake. They even broke the confidential location rule and allowed my mother to come. She and I had begun to build a relationship again. She loved seeing me cleaned up. She told me she still believed in me.

During my time there, a doctor confirmed that I was having a little girl. The dream I'd had was actually the baby warning me about her father, Chuck. I had already seen her and felt an intensely strong connection with her. I was totally in love. I was excited to be able to name her all by myself. Eventually, the shelter put me up in an apartment. When I was on my own, I started to feel guilty about Chuck being in jail. Like a complete idiot, I helped the defense get him a lesser sentence. I even visited him in jail a couple of times. *There really is no end to the stupidity.*

It had been a while since I'd talked to my dad. One night I called him; he sounded really sad. He was all alone by that point. Child Welfare Services had taken Justin away. Apparently, when my dad was under the influence, he had gotten violent with my brother. My dad's drinking had gotten really bad. He had gotten hurt somehow and wasn't working anymore so he was able to start drinking first thing in the morning. My dad sounded so sweet on the phone, so lonely, so broken-hearted. I could relate to him. He asked me why I was living in Santa Barbara by myself when I could be living in Santa Maria with him. *Good question*, I thought. To stay in my apartment, I had to get a job, which wasn't easy to do, since I was so close to having a baby. Going to Santa Maria sounded like it made sense. I felt a pull inside telling me to go, so I moved in with my dad.

$\mathcal{P}art$ 5

"Come to Me, all you who are weary and heavy leaden and I will give you rest."

—Matthew 11:28

Winter 2007

My sister drove me to Santa Maria right before Christmas 2007. My dad let me have Michelle's old bedroom. Elaine used to sleep there when their fights got really out of control. It felt awkward at first, because my dad and I hadn't spent much time together in a while. Soon though, we developed a pretty good relationship again. It was fun for the most part, though his alcoholism had really progressed. Since he didn't have a job to sober up for, he spent all day, every day, drunk. He was on an array of different medications, which lessened his ability to function normally. He took Ambien for sleep and was always trying something new for his depression. He also took various drugs to manage his psychotic episodes. The doctors were always changing his medications, and he would get too drunk to remember if he had actually taken his pills that day. He either took too many or none at all.

Unfortunately, psych meds don't work that way. He was a mess, but he was my dad and I was grateful to be there. It made things a little easier for me.

My dad was constantly fooling around, always up to some silly thing or another. My thing was keeping the house tidy and making us dinner. One night, after the dinner things had been put away, he got up. He had a T-shirt on but had forgotten his pants, so I went to grab him some shorts. I went into the kitchen to help him because he was really unsteady on his feet. He decided he was hungry, so he started to make a sandwich. The first thing that tipped me off that he was blasted was when he asked where Elaine was. Who wants to be the one to say, "She's dead, Dad." Not me.

"Uh, I don't know right now, Dad," I managed to say. I watched him as he fiddled around with ingredients. He pulled bacon out of the fridge, then he put butter on some white bread. I didn't know how to stop him when he started to eat it without cooking anything. *Ew, seriously? A raw bacon and butter sandwich? Don't argue. Just make sure he gets to bed without falling down.*

Another night, he came out on another mission to get snacks. As usual, he could barely hold himself up. *Too much Ambien again,* I figured. He opened the fridge and pulled out a bowl of mashed potatoes I had cooked for dinner and started eating them cold. Suddenly, he started to choke. Stunned to silence, I watched and tried to figure out what to do. I had never given anyone the Heimlich maneuver. Also, I was almost nine months pregnant at the time, and my belly was so huge, I wasn't sure I could get my arms around him. But I had to try something. His whole head had turned a deep, disturbing purple. It was awful, like a big eggplant. I had to take action. I grabbed him around his waist from behind, sucked in my giant stomach, and heaved! I heaved two times, three times; finally, he coughed it up. Then he started to throw up all over the counter top and floor. His basset hound came in and ate his puke. I tried to shoo her away while I caught my breath, but it was useless.

"Oh my God, Dad! I just saved your life. You were completely purple! Go to bed right now." I was upset and fed up with his shenanigans.

"Oh sweetie," he said. "Stop it. I'm okay."

"No, Dad. You are not okay. Bed! Now!" I led him to his room and made him lie down. That was that.

Many times I'd find the milk in the cabinet where the dishes go, or the freezer left open, or my dad roaming the halls talking nonsense to no one. Sometimes it was funny. Mostly it wasn't.

Right before I had the baby, I went to Aunt Carol's house. When I left, I had a bad feeling. I just knew my dad was going to overmedicate himself and drink too much. He did. He had gone outside looking for Elaine, wearing his favorite outfit: a T-shirt and no pants. He was also wearing Elaine's slippers. He ended up at the side of the house, stuck in the wooden fence overnight and all the next day. After the sun went down, Tugs, the dog from next door, alerted our neighbor Laura that something was wrong. Laura found my dad mostly naked, completely cut up, and face down in the dirt. He was in bad shape. My dad asked her not to call 9-1-1, but she did anyway. She had to. By the time he got to the hospital, his body temperature was way down, and he had blistered burns on his butt cheeks from being exposed to the sun all day long.

When I got back to Santa Maria, I went to see him in the hospital.

"Have you had the baby yet?" he asked when he saw me. Still very pregnant, I stood there and assured him that I had not.

"I love you," he told me. It was the first time he'd said that in a long while. I had gotten used to feeling like he didn't really love me. Since we'd been living together, all he did was talk about Justin. There were pictures of Justin and Michelle all over the walls and not a single one of me. I had never felt it growing up, but now I felt very *adopted*. I knew he didn't mean it. He was going through his own guilt about letting his son down. But I was there for him. I took care of him every day. I made sure he was fed, cleaned up, in bed, off the floor, or whatever the immediate need was.

My dad ended up getting violated for that little stunt. He was on probation and trying to get Justin out of foster care. He just couldn't handle staying sober. The system was easy on him though and gave him a lot of chances. By the time Sunshine was born, he was in detox. Michelle moved up and stayed with me at my dad's.

The day that I went into labor, I was about three weeks overdue. She was already a mommy's girl. Michelle had driven me to Target, and I was eating one of those yummy little individual pizzas when I first felt the kind of pain in my tummy that I knew meant business. The doctor's office had called earlier that day to make an appointment for induction. Now it looked like that wouldn't be necessary. We walked around Target, and the pain got pretty intense so we decided to go home and get ready to drive to Santa Barbara.

When we were at the hospital, I started to feel the old irrational fears. I worried that somehow Chuck would find out that I was there. I made sure that no men were allowed in the room. Again, I knew that the fears were probably not founded in reality, but I couldn't shake the fact that I was afraid. I just wanted to feel safe. The next morning, I had my little girl in my arms. The nurses asked if they could take her and give me a break.

"No," I told them. "I don't want a break. I want to keep her with me." When I looked at her, I was surprised by the feeling that I already knew her. She looked exactly as she had in my dream. She was perfect. As I held her, I thought, *She has nobody else in this world but me*. I knew nothing could or would ever come between us. Nobody would ever be able to take her away from me.

My dad was unable to stay sober, and because he was on probation, he kept getting in trouble. It was truly amazing the number of chances he got before he finally went to jail. Finally, after he was caught enough times under the influence, he decided to max out, which means he took the jail time and did not have to be on probation anymore. He knew he wouldn't ever be able to pass the constant alcohol tests. He was in jail for about a hundred days.

One day Chuck called my dad's house, and I answered. He assured me that he was in a program and just wanted to meet his little girl. For whatever stupid reason, I decided to allow him to see her. *Idiot move.* That lasted only weeks before it went bad. But first, we got high together. *Yes, really stupid.* We went by Tara's house and though I didn't get high the first time I saw her, I did the second time. Chuck had befriended my cousin Aaron in jail, and they came to my dad's house a couple of times together.

The last time he came up, he came up alone. We weren't getting along. He wasn't even nice to Sunshine. He called her spoiled and sat on the couch, waiting for me to make him food. I was so through with him at that point I couldn't even stand to be around him. I had no feelings for him anymore. His sense of entitlement and his lack of caring about my daughter made me sick. I couldn't wait for him to leave. He eventually admitted to me that when he got out of jail, he immediately went to the house of another girlfriend to smoke crack with her (not the icky one who bailed him out of jail, but the one with the scabs). I lost the tiny bit of respect I had for him and any hope that he might be a positive influence on Sunshine.

He forced himself on me and I vowed never to open my door to him again. It wasn't a rape in the other way I experienced rape. It wasn't violent, but it wasn't consensual. I told him I didn't want to, and he didn't care. He didn't listen to me. He got what he wanted, but I promised myself I would never see him again. He didn't like it when I ran away from him, but running away when you live in a different city is a lot easier. He started to blow up my phone and email inbox. One day he called me from Aunt Carol's house. He was hanging out with Aaron. He sounded drunk or loaded or something. He was rude and making threats. He said that he would come up to my house, slit my throat, and take my daughter.

When I told my dad, he said that if I didn't call the cops, he would. So I did, and Chuck called the house while they were there. He made threats to the female officer who picked up the phone. She later testified on my behalf in court, where Chuck sat, smugly, and made kissy faces at me in front of everyone. It was unbelievable! One thing that really hurt my feelings was that my cousin was there that day—but to support Chuck. He asked me ahead of time if I would be hurt if he did that.

"Do whatever you think is right," I told him. I was really devastated, but I loved my cousin anyway. After that day in court, Chuck was sent to prison. It finally was the end. I have not had any contact with him since that day. *It sure took long enough.*

Once Chuck was out of the picture, my life was peaceful for about five minutes. I had a crush on a strong, sexy, mysterious guy named Jevon who lived across the street. It was exactly what I needed to move on emotionally, but it was wrong. I had to keep it to myself, because Jevon was my friend, Patty's boyfriend. He was supposed to be totally off-limits. They had been together for fourteen years. They both said they were unhappy, but it was none of my business. They had a child together, a boy named Talon, whom I had grown to love. I broke the girlfriend code, and I hurt a child I cared about. It is, by far, the worst thing I've ever done on purpose.

By Thanksgiving, we had been together a little over a month, and he told her. It was awful. Patty confronted me, and I told her I felt terrible. Jevon moved out of their house and into his workplace, a temporary solution to a problem that had gotten way out of hand at home. I felt like a disaster. I'd moved into a new neighborhood and ruined a family. I was like a bomb that flattened everything around me. Jevon told me that he'd stopped seeing Patty, but he told her he'd stopped seeing me. Nothing had changed except that I didn't feel so guilty about seeing him anymore. One night he went to his house and stayed there. I went out front all through the night, checking on his truck, which never left. I realized he'd been lying to both of us. He tried to convince me that he was there to spend time with his son. I was sure that he didn't sleep in his son's room. But what right did I have to be jealous anyway?

I got loaded the day after that. (This is why they tell you to lose all your drug-dealer's numbers. It's too easy to get high when you have a bad day.) Pretty soon, I didn't care whether or not he was across the street. I decided (not for the first time) to let Jevon go. He needed to be with his family, and they needed to be with him. I got down on my knees and apologized to his son for hurting him. What I had done was worse than wrong, and I wanted him to know that I was truly sorry.

Our separation lasted about a week or two. We went back and forth like that for a while. It got really weird. Patty knew what was going on, and so did I. Then Jevon quit his job, and he had to move back home. I was too emotionally invested in Jevon to stop caring, but I tried. I even told him that I had a drug problem and that I had started using again. He told me he thought that was disgusting. He acted like he was mad at me for using drugs, which was surprising since I knew he drank and smoked pot every day. *What a hypocrite,* I thought angrily.

I broke up with Jevon at least ten times, maybe twenty. We never lasted more than two weeks apart. I couldn't get him out of my mind. It was ridiculous. He told me he was sleeping on his couch. He told me again that they had never been happy. He told me he had cheated on her many times over the years, but that he had never fallen in love with a woman until he met me. He told me that the reason they never got married was because he had never really loved her. It all sounded great to me, but the fact was, he was across the street, and he was playing us both. Back and forth we went. Back and forth.

Around this time, my dad had another surgery on his shoulder. He always asked me to let him take Sunshine on walks or drives alone. I never let him take her anywhere without me. Heck, I wouldn't even let him give *me* a ride, so of course I wouldn't let him take her anywhere. The best bad thing that could have happened was a car accident. I'm sure I don't have to say what the worst scenario would have been. All he wanted to do was be around Sunshine, to give her candy and popsicles, let her do whatever she wanted, to be sickly sweet to Sunshine but hardly tolerate me. Maybe I was overly sensitive. It seemed like he was never nice to me anymore. I wasn't nice to him either. I didn't want to condone his drinking or let him hold Sunshine. His drinking and falling down, which had become everyday things, were no longer funny. I was a nervous wreck. Adding to my anxiety, I thought I had to be on top of Sunshine's every move. She was just starting to crawl. It is hard to never take your eyes off of a little person. I lived in constant fear that he would do the same things to her that he had done to me. Even if I were right there watching him, he did weird things. He was never steady on his feet, and I thought he might fall on or drop her. It was irritating and frightening. One night, I heard him masturbating loudly in the next room; his door was open. Things got so strange, I couldn't handle it anymore. My mind was a mess. I needed an escape. I started to get high again on a regular basis.

One day, my dad got mad when I said, once again, he could not take Sunshine. I always told him no, and this time was no different, except he got really angry. He kept insisting. Jevon happened to be there that day. I was in a foul mood. Leaving Jevon in the hallway but still within earshot, I stomped around the corner.

"Dad!" I yelled. "I am sick and tired of you asking me if you can take Sunshine all the time! Just stop asking me already!"

"Why?" he asked loudly. "What is your problem?"

I felt gutsy. The drugs probably gave me the courage to say it. "Dad, just stop it okay?! I remember everything you did! I remember you coming in the bathroom when I was in the tub, and everything you did to me! You're fucking sick! I think about it all the time! How could you do that to me?! You act so innocent, like nothing is wrong, but it is wrong, Dad! I'm tired of acting like there's nothing wrong! That's why you can't take Sunshine anywhere, okay, so just stop asking! Don't ever ask me if you can take her anywhere, EVER AGAIN!"

And that was it. I was as surprised that I'd said it as he was, particularly after twenty-five years of silence. But nothing surprised me more than his response.

First, there was nothing, and then: "Oh come on, it didn't go on that long."

I couldn't believe it. One time would have been "too long." There he was, justifying and making it seem like I was overreacting. As I looked at him there in his room, I wanted to throttle him, to put my hands around his neck and not let go until he stopped breathing.

I had to leave. If I didn't get out of there at that moment, I would have done something I would have regretted. I had nowhere else to go but across the street. Yes, weird turned into twisted. As anyone can imagine, this was a really bad idea. My stress level was through the roof. I had to come down immediately, and everything was awful. I heard them loudly having sex in their bedroom that night. Everything sucked. I wanted to kill myself again. I filled a needle with Raid one day, but chickened out right before I put it in my vein. Sunshine was the only reason I didn't do it. Eventually I went home, but things were never the same.

I brought it up one more time. I wanted to know why he had done the things he had done. I confronted him alone. We were in the kitchen.

"Listen, Dad, I hate to bring this up again, but I need to know why you did those things when I was a kid." He just stared at me silently, his eyes open really wide.

"I just need to know if someone hurt you. I want to understand why you did it. If you tell me, I can try to understand you, and then I can let it go. I promise that I will never bring it up again."

Still, there was nothing. He just sat there, staring at me. It was looking as though I'd never get an answer.

"Please?" I asked one more time, but he still said nothing. Not a single word.

"Okay," I resigned, walking away. "I'll never bring it up again." And I never did.

Later that year, I got a DUI. The legal limit is a .08, and I was a .09. The cop had me call someone to pick up Sunshine. I called Jevon about ten times and finally had to call Tara. I spent the night in jail and the next day, Tara brought her to me. Now I had no license. But I hadn't learned my lesson. *Of course, I hadn't learned my lesson the first time.* I borrowed my dad's Expedition and took off one night, angry at Jevon, and got pulled over again for driving like a maniac. When the officer asked me my name, I told him I was Elaine. It was the only thing I could think of. I thought that if I told him who I was, he would realize I had no license and would impound my dad's vehicle and maybe put me in jail. I thought he would take Sunshine, and I worried that she would end up in the system. So I lied. I had Elaine's birthday memorized, of course. It was a stupid lie. The cop who pulled me over was one of the few nice cops I've ever met. He let me go, but not before telling me that it was really strange, because the DMV had Elaine listed as deceased. Better check that out.

"Go straight home," he told me. "Stop driving crazy." It was a kindness from a stranger, and I appreciated it.

Somehow, however, the cop found out that I wasn't who I said I was. The next day, he came to my dad's house and arrested me at the front door. Luckily, Jevon was home, and he took Sunshine for me. It was awful. My life was spinning out of control, yet again. With or without drugs, I was a mess. I could blame everyone in the world, but the truth was, I needed to get a handle on my own life. I needed to stop acting like an idiot. I needed to become someone on whom my little girls could depend. I was tired of myself and all my antics.

Sometime later, I was walking Sunshine to the CVS down the street. I was buzzed and needed to get out of the house. I'd quit drugs again, and drinking helped take the edge off. Jevon and I were off again, and he was out shopping with Patty. I was burned out on my life. Everything felt pointless. I needed to move out of my dad's house and make a new life with Sunshine. For some reason, the clerk at CVS thought I stole something. When they confronted me outside the store, I opened my purse and showed them everything I had. I was in a huff. I wanted to make a scene because I hadn't stolen anything, and I was offended. I yelled at the clerk and the manager, and they decided to call the cops on me anyway.

"Fine! Call the cops!" I yelled. "I didn't do anything wrong!" I was very angry. When the cops got there, they threatened to call Child Welfare Services, because they smelled alcohol on my breath.

"Fine," I said again. "Go ahead, I didn't do anything wrong!"

Idiot girl. What kind of a person tells the cops to go ahead and call Child Welfare Services? I think I am the only person who has ever been put in a treatment program for drunk stroller-walking with her baby. So stupid. They wouldn't even let me take her home with me. Jevon had to come and get her. Again. I was losing it. Walking home alone, I cried so hard that I peed my pants.

Jevon and Patty had Sunshine for a few days; then she went to my mom's for a week. It was a very long and stressful week. Jevon disappeared for a couple of days. Adding to the difficulty, my dad left to go stay at my mom's while Sunshine was there. I begged her to not let him be alone with her. Later, she admitted that she had allowed him to take Sunshine on walks and watch her alone. I couldn't believe she actually left the two of them alone together. When I asked her why she would allow that, she said she had to because she was too busy. I couldn't believe my ears. Some things never change. I was sure my dad would do the same things again if given the opportunity. Too selfish or blind, my mother was potentially letting it happen all over again, in the exact same house! I was infuriated and determined to get Sunshine out of there.

Finally, I had a meeting at the Child Welfare Services office. They let me have Sunshine back, but I had to be in a program called Project PREMIE for six months. Good, I could handle that. Every day, I rode my bike to the program. I was tested for drugs and alcohol and participated in group sessions five times a week. I took Sunshine with me. There was a childcare program on-site. I liked the program manager, Heather, right away. She was a little intimidating at first, but was honest and a good ear when I needed to talk. I looked up to her. She had once been stuck on the needle too, but had been clean for almost twenty years. She showed me that I could be something someday. She gave me hope that I wouldn't ever have to be dependent on drugs again.

At the end of six months, my case was closed. It was a hard road, but I'd done it. I felt good about myself. Jevon and I were together again, and finally I could see that he'd stopped going back and forth between Patty and me. He lived up north with a friend from work, and I saw him often. We went on that way for a few months, and then his roommate asked him to move out. Reluctantly, Jevon moved in with me and my dad. He got a new job, working for a local electrician. Things in our lives were changing for the better. Around March or April of 2010, I found out that I was pregnant again.

June 2010

It's summer, and instead of my mom flying Rose out this year, I flew her out here myself. She arrived this afternoon. I found myself speechless tonight, unable to express anything but silent prayers of gratitude. I have been weeping with joy at the sound of her laughter. I had forgotten how deep the emptiness had become inside me. There was a hollow ache that I'd gotten used to feeling. I almost lost touch with the pain that has resided so long in my soul. Nothing comes close to the desolation of a mother who has been separated from her child.

I realize now that fault, situation, and circumstance don't matter anymore. Blame is as useless as a bad habit; excuses and guilt are pointless. What matters now is that at the end of this day, and at the beginning of this summer, my firstborn daughter is here with me. There is nothing to feel but pure enjoyment in this moment. There is an ease in my chest, and a lightness in each step I take. Was I fooling myself every day I said I was happy? I don't know if that's true or if I've just reached an ability in life to find contentment no matter what. That said, nothing comes close to the profound wholeness of having my children near me, and that includes the newest love I feel growing inside me.

My mind constantly wonders how it might feel to be with my Payton. I imagine how it might be some day when I am able to hold her and look into her eyes as I am doing with Rose tonight. But the luxury of daydreaming about her is dangerous, and

I cannot allow myself to dream too long, because it accomplishes nothing more than making me feel pain and regret. I think about her and dream about her all the time. She is the one failure I've yet to make right. So I tuck her memory back into the deepest, darkest pocket of my heart. I know that in loving her, it is not necessary to mourn her or make myself miserable on this night. As my mother would say, "Baby steps." And today giant steps have been made. I'll allow myself happiness in this moment.

My dad's dad is dying. The family has offered to fly my dad out to Oregon so he can say good bye, but for some reason, he won't go. There is nothing tying him here. They are offering to pay for the trip and figure out all the transportation to and from the airports. I can't figure out why he doesn't want to go. It's really sad and confusing. Part of me wonders if it has anything to do with the bad thing. I promised him I wouldn't bring it up, so I won't. Thinking about it makes me realize how lucky I am to have this time with my dad before he dies.

At first I thought I could save my dad somehow, but that's not happening. Hepatitis C is a disease that can be lived with for many years. A person has to make healthy choices and actively survive with the virus. A big thing one has to do to live with Hep C is quit drinking alcohol. That is something he can't do. He did the Interferon treatments years ago. He went into remission for a period of time, but now he isn't doing very well. He doesn't have a lot of years left, I fear. I can either use this opportunity to spend time with him or throw it away. Just yesterday I realized that when my dad does die, I will mourn him. I want to fix him. I want to make him feel happy. Trying to take care of him accomplishes nothing. I feel I am not helping him at all.

Sometimes being sober feels great; other days it totally sucks, and I feel frustrated beyond rational thought. The biggest frustration is fighting myself. What I want to do and I what I don't want to do are the same thing. Why do I have an innate thirst for self-destruction? Today I'll force myself to be good to me, because the life inside me needs me to be. It won't save me forever, but it works for now, and that's all that counts.

One of Rose's favorite things to do is to play in the water, whether she is swimming, playing on a Slip 'N Slide, or just running through a sprinkler. It makes me happy to see her running around having fun. She tends to want to stay in her bathing suit for a while afterwards, and today I told her that she can't do that here. She was confused and asked me why, but I didn't have the heart to tell her. "It's just not appropriate" was all I could manage. It sucks that it should have to be an issue at all, but I know I did the right thing by bringing it to her attention. Living here feels hard at times. The other day, my dad went to his bedroom window totally naked. We were all in the backyard watching him stand there in front of his window. When these things happen, there are no words to make it right. Just guide the kids away from the part of the yard with a clear view into his bedroom. Apologize, and try to move on.

Today Rose told me that the worst thing about going to my mother's house is that she makes her go to church. When she made this comment, I knew it might also be her way of asking me how I feel about God, so I chose my words carefully. I told her that I think church is a good foundation, but that religion and spirituality are different and separate concepts. I want her to know that my connection with God these days is a huge part of my life. The only reason why I am capable of the unconditional love I have for her and her sisters is because of God. I explained that I think people without spirituality can experience joy in their lives, as I experienced joy in my life before. But it's comparable to looking at a photograph of a sunset as opposed to experiencing a sunset in real life. Hopefully I didn't do a bad job of trying to describe something so profound. It's nearly impossible to find the right words. She was sitting in the backseat of my car at the time, so I was unable to see if at any point she rolled her eyes. It was our first conversation about God. I am hoping it won't be our last.

Earlier today, I was thinking that my eyeliner doesn't work anymore. When I apply it to my top lid, it will not make a straight line. Instead, it misses spots creating little hyphen marks, and right when I was ready to toss it in the trash can, I realized it's not the makeup, but the application surface. I have wrinkles. Ugh. I've always told myself I would age gracefully and have rejected the idea of plastic surgery. I feel sorry for older women who feel the need to have artificially colored hair to cover the grays that, to me, look sophisticated and wise. Now, I stare at my reflection, mouth gaping, realizing that my own grays have begun to make me look old, not sophisticated. My wrinkles are hampering my attempts to look pretty. Have I grown vain at the age of thirty-one? Have I always been so confident about my appearance that I haven't even been able to be honest with myself? The real story is that I have always hoped that by the time I started to visibly age, I'd have done something with my life. It has always been one drama after the next, me … in some stage of coping, managing, manipulating, escaping, or recovering from life's inevitable ups and downs. Now that I have finally learned how to live and let live without taking everything so personally, I'm getting old. This is an easy lesson for some people I suppose, but I learn my lessons hard, and it usually takes me a long time. *What now?* I ask my weary reflection. My eyes look back at me, and I see tears. These aren't tears of vanity. I'm smudging my already shoddy makeup job even more. It's more that I know I'm ready for the next stage of my life, whatever that may be. My life is wide open, and I'm ready for whatever comes, knowing that I'm finally strong enough to trust myself to keep on going. So I pull the edge of my eye tight with one finger, and grin at my silly self while applying an almost straight line with the other hand. I'm going to be just fine.

Days after that last entry, I remembered that I'd hated being a kid. Did I want to turn back the hands of time to look *younger*? Heck, no! Finally, I was starting to know who I was. Finally, I understood my own sexuality and had no hang-ups about what it meant. I was able to be loyal and monogamous and to be happy about that! I felt comfortable in my own skin. I was okay, liking whatever weird things I liked. I accepted myself for not liking the things I didn't like. I was willing to take my wrinkles and grays if they came with peace of mind and a budding sense of self-love.

One morning, before the sun rose, I woke up sweaty and upset. The details of my dream swam around in my head, some of them coming to the surface, others sinking down into my murky subconscious. I used anger to steel myself against crying. With a grumble, I waddled into the bathroom to go potty *again*. Getting back into bed, I noticed that Jevon had rolled over, giving me lots of room to crawl back into bed and into his arms. My anger dissolved, and as I snuggled in next to his warm body, my tears started to flow. *This is exactly what I need,* I thought as I wept silently, making an attempt to control my breathing. His hand slid up my pregnant body to rest on my rib cage, which shuddered with each breath. Still, he said nothing. Surely he knew of whom I was dreaming when I'd wake up and cry. He's never known me another way.

"I was dreaming of Payton," I said softly just to reassure him.

Again, he was quiet, and in that moment, I felt loved. We both knew nothing either one of us could have said would have made it any better. I rarely allow myself to speak her name, though I'm always thinking about her. Nothing I can say will ever change the reality with which I live. I want her. I miss her. I need her. Eventually my breathing returned to normal as I allowed my gratitude to grow larger than my sorrow.

"I love you," I whispered, without knowing for sure whether he was awake to hear me.

August 2010

On her last night in California, Rose finally asked me about God. Some of her questions were easier to answer than others. "Mommy," she said, "do you think God is a boy or a girl?"

"Neither," I answer. "I say He, but in my heart, I believe that God is a combination of both and is also a combination of all the other energies in this world. It says in the Bible that God is everywhere at the same time. So I think that God is the force that brings life to you and me, the animals, and the plants. We are all part of God and God exists in every life on earth."

"Oh, so then you think animals go to heaven?" she asked shyly.

"Well, sweetie, I have lots and lots of ideas, but nothing is for sure. I've given it plenty of thought and had a lot of my own experiences, but that doesn't mean I'm right. It's just what I think."

She said nothing, so I continued. "My idea is that God is like a giant magnet, and when anything is done with the body, its energy is drawn back to the original source, taking with it whatever it learned in that lifetime. So, since animals are living beings, yes, I believe they do go to heaven." I thought I might have lost her, but I also knew she was smart. She was pretty advanced for her age. Her little wheels were always turning.

"Where's heaven?" she asked. It would be so much easier to give her short answers without thinking, but I was in a talkative mood, and I'd been waiting for her to ask me about these things for a long time.

"Okay, love," I said. "I'm not really sure. I believe our journey to heaven or hell starts here on earth. I think we begin our path to heaven or hell long before we die. Here's an example. At my dad's house, on a beautiful sunny day, we're making food for a barbeque, the weather is perfect. You, Talon, and Sunshine are all playing on the Slip 'N Slide in the backyard. I am watching you guys, hanging out with Jevon, and feeling very happily pregnant. In my mind, in this moment, I am in heaven. I am at peace knowing that my life has brought me to this place, on this day. On the other hand, your grandfather is in his room, completely wasted and in a miserable hell. He hates his life, hates his decisions, has immeasurable guilt and regret, and has become completely immobilized by them. Follow me?"

"Mm hmm," she said. "So you think we don't go anywhere?"

"Yeah, I think we do, but it starts a long time before we die. It starts in our minds. And if we have died spiritually in life, then maybe we make more bad choices after our bodies die."

"Do you think we can live more than one life?"

"I do," I said after a moment's hesitation. "I think it's a possibility because God's love for us is so limitless that He gives us lots and lots of choices. I've always known about God, but was never really close to God. Here's something that may surprise you. Even though I always believed in God, there was a time when I felt separated from Him. I even told Him that I hated Him." I heard her inhale sharply.

"I know, right? Pretty bad," I said. "Well, after I was done blaming God for where I was in my life, I took responsibility for my own bad choices. Then I spoke to God again, hoping He was still there for me. Not only was He still there, He was actually a part of me. The aloneness and separation I felt was my own personal hell. I had put myself through it, but it was only an illusion. That is when I found out who God is to me. I opened my heart, I opened my ears, and I waited on Him. God showed up in dreams and became so fully present in my life that I gained an entirely new understanding of Him. God is not some judgmental guy sitting on a cloud. What I found was radically different from my childhood understanding. God is absolute and unconditional love. It's hard to describe, but all I can say is that God is perfect love. Anything that does not line up with love is not what God is. I don't know how I know it's true. I just do.

"Someday, you'll feel alone or separated. Try to remember that it is all in your mind. Everyone experiences this at some point. You will either ask for God to show up, or you will turn your back on Him. If you knock, God will always answer, no matter how many mistakes you have made in your life. This is when you will find out for sure who God is to you. God shows you little by little who He is. It all depends on what we are ready to understand at the time. That's all I have to say about that. The rest you'll just have to find out for yourself, 'kay?"

"Okay, Mom," she said. She had one more question. Giggling, she asked, "If God was a man, do you think He'd wear glasses?"

I knew she was playing with me, and I loved how she lightened the mood. "No, love, I think God would be able to afford laser surgery." Then we both laughed and decided to go to sleep.

The next day, I took her to the airport. I watched her as she turned back to smile at me twice while she walked up the steps to the waiting jet. After she was beyond my sight, I sat down alone at the gate, missing her already. I had a good cry before I went outside to find my mother and Sunshine.

Things finally got to the point that we needed to move out. We're at our third hotel in a month. It's the most affordable in town. Needless to say, it's cheap for a reason, but we have no choice. I guess I'll start with the accidents.

My dad had a new prescription, Seroquel, I think. He took it sporadically and sometimes took way too many with lots of alcohol. He had three accidents in three consecutive days. Usually I tried to pretend like I was minding my own business, but I was always aware of his comings and goings. When he walked inside with a tail light in his hands, I raised my eyebrows. I snuck outside to total up the damages: missing tail light, dented bumper, bent license plate, area around the light smashed in and scratched up. I would have walked to the store for him. I decided to ask him what happened. I walked into the house; he was still standing in the same spot where I left him in the kitchen, still holding his tail light.

"Hey Dad," I asked. "What happened to the Ex?"

Turning most of the way toward me, he looked me straight in the eyes and muttered, "I hit a pole."

"What pole?" I asked, even though I know there's no pole at the corner liquor store.

"Well, see I don't really know, 'cause while I was in the store, some guy hit me," he stammered, the light glimmering in his unfocused and yellowed eyes.

"Hmm," I said, grabbing Sunshine and making my way to the back door.

"Laura!" I yelled, scanning the yard for our neighbor. Most days, I could find her in her backyard, which butts up to ours, separated by a fence with an access door in the middle. Hearing a muffled response inside her house, I slid open her backdoor and was immediately and excitedly greeted by her dog, Tugs, a black terrier mix who was always happy to see me. He gave us a friendly couple of barks and jumped up on my legs, wagging his entire lower half. Laura greeted me with a hug.

"Hey, I think my dad hit somebody's car at the Short Stop," I blurted out. She was used to that kind of thing. She had been my dad's neighbor for almost twenty years. She was like family. Sunshine even called her auntie.

"What? Why do you think that?" she asked.

"Because he's wasted and came inside holding his stupid tail light, looking baffled. When I asked him about it, he lied. I checked out the truck, and it's obvious he's been in an accident. I'm not sure if he had a hit-and-run or what."

"Well, I need to take Tugs for a walk anyway. Let me get the leash on him, and we'll walk over there."

It was the response I'd hoped for, and with Sunshine right behind me, we all headed for the corner store. After stopping to let Tugs do his business in his usual spot, we went to the store. One of the owners, Dan, was behind the counter. Two people were in line, waiting to be rung up. While Laura went to grab her usual three tall boys, I blurted, "Has anyone had an accident here?" There were blank stares from everyone.

"See, I think my dad was just in here and hit someone or something, and I'm trying to make sure everyone is okay."

"Oh that," Dan replied. "Yeah, he was in here, and he was so plastered I refused to serve him again. After he left, he backed into a parked truck whose driver was making a delivery."

My eyes grew wide. I couldn't help but feel embarrassed.

"I'm done with him," Dan continued. "I know you guys live right around the corner and that he's been a customer for a long time, but this is it. Lately, I've had to refuse him service so often that it's more of a liability than what it's worth. I told him to stop coming in all together, but I doubt he'll remember later. I'd appreciate it if you'd remind him he can no longer come in here for any reason."

"Sure, Dan," I said. "I'm so sorry. I knew this was probably coming and tried to avoid it by offering to walk here for him, but he doesn't listen. When he walked in just now with car parts in his hand, I asked questions, and he lied to me. I just wanted to come and make sure that he didn't just drive away, that everyone was okay, and that he gave out his insurance information to whoever he hit."

"He did. I saw them outside. He was parked right there in front, and I saw the whole thing go down. He was lucky the guy didn't call the cops. I saw him give out his information. It was the last straw for me though. Sorry. I hope you understand. Every time he comes, he swerves in here and can sometimes barely stand up straight. I just can't stand being put on the spot like that all the time in front of my other customers."

"It's okay," I said, lamely. Laura paid for her beers. Sunshine threw a bag of gummy bears up on the counter, for which I dug out some change. We made our way for the door.

"I really am sorry about my dad. I don't know what to do for him anymore. I'll tell him he can't come in again. Have a good one." We round the corner to free Tugs from the pole he was tied to.

As we walked home, Laura listened to me rag about how stubborn, incompetent, and difficult my dad was. By the time we got back, I'd lost my patience. At home, I demanded the car keys from my dad. I spotted them on the counter and just took them.

"You're done," I told him and walked away without listening to what he had to say. Sunshine and I went straight to our room, where we spent the rest of the day watching cartoons with the door locked, ignoring the pounding and loud threats coming from outside the door.

When Jevon got home from work, we evaluated the damage done to the Expedition. There was also a giant scrape across the bottom passenger side, indicating another accident. Rolling my eyes, I decided to say nothing, as usual, just to avoid a confrontation. It was his car after all, and there was nothing else I could do.

The next morning, before I could give him the keys back, he had already called AAA and had new keys made. I knew this because of the receipt on the counter for $180. He had already been to the liquor store. Frustrated and lacking the ability to reason with him, I grabbed snacks for Sunshine and myself and walked back to my room, where I planned to spend as much of the day as possible. An hour later, I heard him in the driveway, attempting to start the Expedition over and over. In an attempt to ignore it, I rolled over and put the pillow over my head. But after he'd tried about fifteen times, I got up, and slowly walked out to where he was in the driveway. "What are you doing?" I asked.

"The key won't come out. It's stuck, and I'm trying to get it out," he mumbled.

After he moved away from the driver's side door, I slipped into the seat and turned the key just a bit more. It went into the off position. It was as easy as that. I was able to pull it out. My dad had an array of tools laid out on the passenger seat. Apparently, he had been preparing to remove the entire ignition just to get the key out. *What a spaz.*

"Here," I said, holding the key out for him. It's mean to give someone a hard time for being like this, so I just walked away.

The day went by slowly; Sunshine and I hung out in our room, listening to him struggle with the car now and then to go to the liquor store. When Jevon got home from work, I was really happy to see him. With him there, I feel like Sunshine and I could leave the room. My dad rarely started fights when other people were around. I didn't complain too much; I just filled Jevon in on the basics and started dinner. Later on that evening, my dad decided to go to the liquor store again. After watching him stumble and nearly fall on

125

the front patio, Jevon offered to go for him, but of course he was too proud for that. Off he went.

We watched him leave and wondered what to do. He was in really bad shape. As he backed out, he went too fast and backed right into Patty's driveway and into her truck. *This is so ridiculous.* Then he went forward and acted like nothing happened, continuing on his way to the store. This put us in an awful situation. Either Patty would call the cops or we'd have to. It wasn't what I wanted to do, but I called while Jevon surveyed the damage. My dad could not keep doing this. I could not keep living like this. His moods were too unpredictable. He was dangerous. I should have been enjoying my pregnancy, but instead I was babysitting my dad, and he didn't even like me anymore. Within a day or two, we moved out. I would have thought he'd be happy to see me go, but it was a big fight. He probably just didn't want me to take Sunshine away from him.

After we'd been gone for about four days, he finally called me. I didn't pick up the phone so it went to voicemail. Later that night, after Jevon got home, I checked the message.

"Hi." He sounded wasted. "I just want to tell you that I hope you give birth to a dead baby." *Ouch, jerk.* I played it on speaker for Jevon, then saved the message. I wanted to keep it in case I ever felt sorry for him and to remind me why we couldn't live there anymore.

While I was reading in bed, Sunshine sat next to me, watching her favorite TV show, *Dora the Explorer*. She came close to me to give me a kiss, and I opened my arms to her like I always do. For the first time, she took her soft, little, two-year-old finger and traced the shiny white lines that run vertically along the underside of my arms.

"What's that?" she asked.

"Scars," I replied.

"Scarves?" she asked.

"Scars," I said once more, knowing it would be the end of her interest in this subject. For now.

"Scarves!" she happily repeated and then gave me a kiss before turning her eyes back to her show.

Part 6

"See, I am doing a new thing! Now it springs up; do you not perceive it? I am making a way in the wilderness and streams in the wasteland."

—Isaiah 43:19

September 2010

We found a house and promptly worked to make it a home. It was our first real home together. For some reason, I had overwhelming anxiety the day that we moved in, but every day afterward was better. My anxiety disappeared, and in its place was something new: contentment. Life was good.

Today is our fifth day in our new house, and I ran into my dad. I was out on my bike, coming home from the dollar store, and he was leaving Gateway Liquor, the second-closest one to his house. He pulled over, and we talked for a few minutes. He was trying to look tough, standing there with his shoulders back, but he was visibly wavering on his feet. I got Sunshine out of the bike trailer so that he could say hi. He started crying right away.

"Wow" was all I could muster when I got over the shock of seeing him. Looking at Sunshine, I said, "Sunshine, who's that?" I was trying to add a smile to my voice. I love how having a child around can be a distraction from any negative situation.

As they said their hellos, I struggled to decide if I should offer to go over to his house and bring Sunshine, so he could see her for a bit. It's so difficult to know how to handle him. One thing I know for sure is that he is sad and lonely, and I should probably try to resolve things. I don't have to move back in, but things could be better between us.

"I might be going back to jail," he said, breaking my train of thought.

"Why's that?" I asked.

"I broke my probation."

"I thought you didn't have a probation officer. Aren't you just on informal probation?"

"I was," he admitted. "But I went over to my drunk-driving class, and the lady at the window smelled alcohol on my breath, and she ratted me out. Then I got a probation officer." He was obviously ashamed. I felt for him, but what does he expect to happen if he shows up drunk to a drunk-driving class?

"That sucks." I said, and I meant it. I wished him no ill will. "You know if you have to go to jail, I'll come by to take care of the dog and water the lawn or whatever you want me to do. I just moved into a place not that far from here, and it would be pretty easy for me to stop by everyday to do whatever needs to be done."

All he gave me in response was a slight nod of his downward turned head. "You can have my car if I go," he offered.

"I still have no license, but don't worry, I'll take care of your stuff if you go away again."

"Justin got busted for smoking pot," he said with a slight smile.

"I know. He texted me. I can't believe he would do that in public. He's old enough to know better," I said, realizing what hypocrites we both sounded like. Then without thinking, I said, "Hey, we'll come by some time before you have to go to jail. When is your next court date?"

"September 13."

"Okay then, we'll come by so we can talk about that and you can see Sunshine for a little bit," I said, inwardly cringing at how stupid I was all the time. I wondered what Jevon would think.

"Okay," he said.

"Well, we have to get going. I need to get Sunshine home and start on dinner," I said, picking her up and putting her back in the bike trailer. "Come on, sweetie, let's go," I continued, while she starts to cry.

"I love you," he said, to Sunshine, of course.

"I lo ... I lo ..." *Wow, have I just developed a stutter? What is wrong with me?* "Okay, love you too, Grampy," I finally blurted, caught off-guard by my sudden inability to say the words. "See you soon, then."

"Bye, Sunshine. Okay, see you soon," he said, looking at me instead.

Uncomfortably and awkwardly, I tried to get on my bike. I am seven and a half months pregnant, and I was towing a trailer behind me. I tried to seem confident even though I know I looked ridiculous. I rode as quickly as I could without looking rude or spraining my vagina muscles. *I just had to go and get a potato masher tonight, didn't I? Couldn't just let Jevon do it, even though he offered ...* Riding home, I went over every word we said and beat myself up about everything, including my bad timing.

That old saying "you get what you ask for" was true in my experience, especially regarding my prayers. For a while, I'd been praying to get to know this child before she was born. I knew she was a girl before the ultrasound, and I had lots of different dreams about her essence and her appearance. She came to me and gave me a few deeply loving messages. It became clear that she loved me as much as I loved her. I learned things from her, and I hadn't even held her in my arms yet. I couldn't wait for that day.

Some of my dreams weren't as happy as other dreams. In the past, a really intense relapse dream may have triggered the real thing. One week, I had at least three nights of relapse dreams. The dreams got progressively worse and kept coming back over and over throughout the whole night. When I woke up, I thought, *Okay good, I'm glad that's over,* and then the dreams would happen again. Some were exhausting as well as disturbing:

> I'm using in a bathroom, but I drop the needle in the toilet, then fish it out to put it in my arm. Or I'm using a needle that is too dull and won't pierce through the scar tissue on my vein, so I have to use a lead pencil to make a hole there first. Or I have a needle full and ready to use, but someone is always lurking nearby, hampering my ability to inject it without being noticed.

That is how I used in real life toward the end—always a secret, always alone. Nobody knew how big a deal it was to me, and that was how I protected myself from judgment. I judged myself harshly enough. I hated myself when I was on drugs. I hated who I was, I hated what I did, and I hated my thoughts. I hated the death in my eyes. I couldn't even stand to look at my reflection. It's amazing how dreaming about a substance that creates such self-loathing could make me want to experience it all over again in my waking life. That is one thing I can't figure out about myself. But despite my long night of dreaming about getting loaded, hiding, and running away, I did not get high. I had a beautiful little girl to take care of and a belly growing with another gorgeous love inside. It felt good to make the choice to stay clean. I wanted so much to build a life worth living, something of which I could be proud.

One Saturday, while we were running errands, I threw out a suggestion: "Hey, how 'bout we go by my dad's?" Without missing a beat, Jevon nodded his head in agreement.

"Okay," he said but without judgment or making a face, which made me feel better.

"Let's stop by and pick up lunch on our way over," I said. "We can take him something since I'm sure he'll need to eat." And we did. The afternoon went smoothly. We spent most of our time outside, enjoying the day, watching Sunshine run around. After three hours, we decided we'd spent the appropriate amount of time with him and headed home.

The next weekend, he showed up at our house. After catching up for a while, he asked how we managed without a TV. Then we talked about how much his cable service cost. The conversation was nice, and we kept it light. I filled him in about our morning; the most exciting thing was that Sunshine went poo in the toilet for the first time ever. Hearing me tell the story made Sunshine smile and gave us all a good reason to be happy in the moment. My dad sat down to read books with Sunshine for a few minutes; then he decided to get going. When we walked him outside, he said "I love you" to both of us, which really surprised me. I hadn't heard him say that since he was in the hospital, and even then, I said it first. Well, wonders never cease.

Another day we spent some time with my mom and grandma. They came to our place for a visit. Right before they left, my mom dropped a bomb.

"We went down to San Diego and saw Payton," she said.

Good thing I'm not drinking, I thought as I held my composure. Sitting next to me, she told me how Walter had treated them. Usually I would have cared more about that, but at that moment all I want to know about was Payton.

"How was Payton? What is she like?"

"She asked me if I am her mom's mom, and I told her yes." Then she switched gears back to her interactions with Walter.

"Did she say or do anything cute that you can remember?" I pressed.

"I don't know," she said. "We only had about an hour together, and I didn't even get any pictures for you. Sorry," she said, trying to keep a lightness in her voice, but I could tell it was forced.

My grandmother came out on the back porch to hang out with us. "Hey, the last time I was at my gyno, she remarked on what great shape my boobs are in. She actually took pictures of them to put in a catalog." She beamed with pride.

Perfect timing, Grams. This was turning into a real bummer. Later, this would be the highlight of the visit in my mind, and I would happily remember her smiling face.

"She asked my permission, and I was more than happy to let her take my pictures, but they didn't show my face. Only my boobs!"

"Wow, Grandma, that's great. What a wonderful complement. I'm jealous," I told her.

"Yeah well, I was flattered. Hey, wanna see 'em?" she asked. I was not sure if she was serious, but I nodded my head, and there on my back porch, in front of my mother and me, she lifted her shirt and bra.

"See? Now how about that?" *How about that, indeed.*

"Thanks, Grandma. I hope I look that great when I'm your age, although I haven't taken care of myself as well as you have."

"I breastfed both my kids," she continued, smiling shyly.

"Mom, we really need to have a private talk now," my mother said to her mom.

"Okay, well, I just want to tell you, dear, I love you very much," my grandmother said to me, looking lovingly in my eyes. "No matter what has ever happened, I just want you to know that I never gave up on you and always have loved you from the moment you came into our lives."

My grandmother always made me feel special. Some of my fondest childhood memories include her. I often spent the night with her during my parents' divorce, and she let me stay up late, watching *Golden Girls* reruns, and rubbed my back until I fell asleep or tenderly touched the insides of my arms until the fear and anxiety melted away. I always knew I was safe with her. She gave me unconditional love, attentive ears, and homemade desserts.

"I'll go wait in the car then," she said as she straightened her shirt and turned away from us.

Whatever my mother said after that didn't stick. My mind was full. I heard all the information that I could and the rest would have to wait until the next time we talked. Sitting by my mother in the sun, I realized that, for once, I was not angry at her. Usually, whenever she saw my kids, and I couldn't be there, I felt bitter and jealous. Sometimes Rose visited her in the summer and she never told me until Rose had already left. It hurt me a lot. Looking back, I know it was because I was high and living with stupid Chuck. Of course she couldn't let me see Rose. My mom should have been able to see my kids, even if I was not allowed to. My situation was not her fault. Besides, I should have felt glad that my kids could have her in their lives. The more people who love them, the better. It was time for me to put any negative feelings I had about my mom to rest. We were building a relationship as adults. Nobody is perfect, but my mom was trying to be the best mom and grandma that she could be. She may not have told me beforehand what she wanted to do, but was that so malicious? All in all, our relationship was taking a step in the right direction.

Later that night, I was at the laundromat, and my mother called to check on me. She realized what a huge deal it was to tell me about Payton, then leave right away. I told her I appreciated her concern, but that I wasn't as upset as I would have been in the past.

"I just want to make sure you're okay," she kept saying, which warmed my heart. It meant a lot that she cared how I felt, even if it were after the fact.

"Mom, you should know that I was never really that mad at *you* so much as I was mad at *myself*. I was on drugs and in a bad place. I was unable to look at myself honestly. I needed someone to be mad at other than myself, and you were the one that got the brunt of it. I want to apologize for doing that to you."

"Okay," she said, hesitantly. "Thank you for saying that."

"I mean it. I made really bad choices after Walter took Payton. If I hadn't made those bad choices, he wouldn't have been able to keep her away from me. I gave up the fight, and that's nobody's fault but my own. It was really horrifying to look at myself in the mirror and to know that I failed the person I loved so much. She and I needed each other, and when I felt I had lost, I rolled over and decided to die. I needed to be stronger. I blew it, and that was hard for me to handle. I couldn't stand myself, and my anger was misdirected. Now that I've cleaned up and can be honest, I can work on forgiving myself. I'm not angry at anyone else. I'm not even angry with Walter. He has after all, been there for her all these years. I know in my heart that he loves her. Even though he hurt me very badly, he still does take good care of our daughter."

"I've never heard you talk like that," my mom said slowly. "You have matured a lot."

Ah, sweet nothings from the mother. I love those.

"It makes me happy to hear you say that," she said. "You know, she isn't gone forever. Just because it looks like she's out of your life, don't give up just yet. Walter sounds like he's more receptive to allowing you to be part of her life. Don't give up hope."

I couldn't stand to hear that, because although I am an optimist, I did have my parental rights taken away. I rolled my eyes. This wasn't the first time I'd heard that pep talk. I appreciated the sentiment, but I knew I'd probably lost Payton forever.

"Okay, Mom, I'd better go. I'm at the laundromat. Got to get these clothes done. Love you," I said, and I meant it.

"I'll talk to you soon then. Love you too," she said and then hung up.

Normally, that conversation would have been a huge trigger. I'd have made calls, pulled together funds, texted, ranted, and made all the necessary stops to get needles, dope, and enough time alone to kill my brain cells as well as my self-esteem. Not that day. But I can't say the thought didn't cross my mind. It was not a real itch though. It was vague, just a passing thought, that it was something I would have done before. I just wanted to check out mentally. I would have loved to drink right then. As though he were reading my thoughts, Jevon showed up with a black plastic bag containing my favorite kind of adult beverage. It sounded so good it was sinful.

"Here, you probably need some of this," he said, handing it to me. It took every ounce of strength I could muster to turn it down.

"I do need it. That's why I'm not going to have any. I know that even if I taste it, it will not be enough. I'll be off and running tonight, with this little baby inside me along for the ride. It just wouldn't be fair, and I can't do that to this little baby. I'm just not willing to do that, hard as it is to say no."

It was so hard that after a silent evening of washing, drying, and folding, I wept silently in the dark truck on our drive home. My emotions and hormones were all going, and as much as I wanted to say I was fine, I was not. I was weak, and the awareness of my weakness, the craving for some numbness, crushed me. Thinking about it brought hot, angry tears to my eyes. But I remained stone-cold sober. I'm happy I made the right choice. I heard somewhere that it's never too late to turn it around. I believe that, and I held onto it that night.

After leaving the toxic environment and constant stress of living with my dad, my impulses to do stupid and self-destructive things went way down. That doesn't mean that the thoughts never crossed my mind, they just popped up less often. I thought about what a great life I was living. It was wonderfully normal.

I was eight months pregnant, and we were eating a healthy dinner in our new home. I was trying to teach Sunshine how to use a fork.

"Hold it down a bit lower," I said, showing her with my own fork. As she struggled to stab at a piece of her chicken, I added, "Well, you have to aim."

Jevon laughed, and so did I, but a flash entered my mind: a memory of me holding a needle in just the right spot above my arm, aiming at the vein. Aim and stab. It was not a feeling of guilty pleasure or a feeling of desire. All I felt was disgust at myself because I had not gotten far enough away from it yet. *Why am I still so susceptible to these thoughts? How can I have done that to myself so many times, hurt myself, over and over?* I pushed the thought out of my mind before Jevon stopped chuckling. Then I looked at my salad, grateful for the beautiful and ordinary gift it is to have an appetite and to be eating with my little family.

So much in my past had the power to unravel me if I gave it enough thought. I didn't live in denial. I was very aware of who I was and where I came from. I just didn't give myself any excuse to dwell. On Payton's birthday, I allowed myself a good cleansing and thorough cry. Nothing had the power to break my heart the way that did. Everything else had been compartmentalized and talked out at the rape crisis center or in other therapy. I had so many issues, and I didn't feel the need to evaluate and rehash them anymore. What was done was done. But where was the story of survival? I didn't feel like I was surviving. I was still trudging through my life. I still sucked my thumb when I felt really bad. I still had nightmares all the time. I still felt the past, and had the need to numb myself so I didn't have to feel like *me. Perhaps*, I thought, *in time I'll exhaust myself and finally put it all to bed*. I knew eventually it had to stop haunting me. I was terrified of what could happen if I didn't learn how to deal with my past. I knew if I had the courage to live through it the first time, I had to have the strength to survive and move past those things, once and for all.

October 2010

My due date was exactly two weeks away. The last month always drags on so slowly. Overall, I was still feeling great. I'd figured out how to afford Christmas presents that year. Lying in bed one morning, it came to me: sell my skydiving gear—parachute, helmet, altimeter, and all. After I figured out the logistics, my mind came to a sudden halt: *Sell all my skydiving gear?* Suddenly, I realized what a huge step that was. Since the car accident, when I'd broken my neck, I hadn't seriously considered jumping again, but still, this was pretty major. The interesting thing is, despite my realization that I thought I *should* be freaked out about doing this—*it's my skydiving gear!*—the reality is that I wasn't. I wanted to buy nice things for my family. I knew exactly what I wanted to buy for Jevon, and the kids are what Christmas is all about. It was settled. After a few more moments, I concluded that I was happy and that I'd never been so in love before. I'd known it for some time, but this was another reminder of that truth. I realized that I was finally growing up. That was a good thing; I had to catch up with those wrinkles.

Dad came over looking pretty bad. It must be the time of month when his prescription got refilled. He seemed slower than usual and looked like he'd been beaten up. After shuffling inside, he eventually sat down and said that he had fallen down the night before. I noticed a Band-Aid on his arm and a cut on his lip. His color was purplish, but then again, his color is never good. On that day, however, the purple was more obvious than the yellow, which was usually more dominant due to his failing liver.

"I tried to ride your bike in the backyard last night," he told me.

"That's great," I said, smiling at him. It was good for him to do some moderate exercise.

"I kept falling down," he explained, his voice cracking with emotion. About a year earlier we had taken Sunshine out for a bike ride around the neighborhood and had to cut it short because my dad kept falling in the street, just barely missing the traffic. I was so scared, I wanted to ride home, get the car, and come back and get him, rather than watch him fall again. It was a terrible wake up call for me, but not for him. I had almost forgotten how incapable he'd become at doing even the simplest of things in life.

"Are you okay?" I asked.

"The last time I fell," he said, "I went down right on my shoulder and couldn't hardly move. I had to roll around on the ground for a while before I could get myself back up."

"You'd better stay off the bike," I said. "I bet your shoulder makes it too hard to steer that thing." It was the only thing I could think of to make him feel better. I knew it wasn't the shoulder that made him fall, but I didn't want to hurt his pride by making judgments.

"You'd better take it easy. Don't try to get back on it for a while." I could not look him in the eye. He nodded his agreement. I was happy when Sunshine started walking toward the door, saying she wanted to go outside.

"Go peddle bike backside, Mama?" she said as she ran to the backdoor.

My dad tried to get up from his sitting position on the floor. We still hadn't been able to afford furniture, so his only choice was to sit on the floor. His struggle was obvious and, knowing his pride would be bruised if I tried to help him, I patiently waited for him to do his thing. It was not the first time I'd stood next to him while he tried to get up off the ground. It never got any easier for either of us. After another few seconds, he fell down from his knees. Not wanting to grab any of his scabs, I offered my hand.

"Here, put your weight on me," I said. "I'm strong enough to support you, but I don't want to pull your arm and hurt your shoulder any more than it already hurts." Together, we managed to get him up.

"Pathetic, isn't it?" he said sadly, not with self-pity but embarrassment.

"No, I'm just sad that you're hurt," I replied.

After we went outside to watch Sunshine run around, I thought about what he'd said. *Pathetic. What a harsh word.* A brief, heavy sadness filled my chest. I envisioned him rolling around on the concrete trying to get up, all alone, and it broke my heart.

One of the few photos I have of my dad and me when I was growing up is at a school, on an expanse of black pavement. He was standing tall, and I was on my bike, just learning to ride the dang thing. My mother has told me I had a lousy time learning to ride a bike with the training wheels off. My dad never gave up on me, though, and that photo was the first one I put up in my room at his house when I lived there. I found it, took it out of the album, and taped it up to the mirror in my room so I could remember over and over again the good times we'd had. No human being is ever entirely good or entirely bad. While I had some memories

I wished weren't there, they should not overshadow the fact that there were some very good ones too. I wanted to hold onto those.

But all I saw of the strong and determined man in that photo was a shell, an unrecognizable empty person who had suffered the consequences of too many bad choices and too little impulse control. He came into my home, bruised and bleary-eyed, admitting he couldn't remember how to ride a bike. It left me speechless and so very, very sad.

Dad was headed to jail again for violating his probation. He was getting too old for this crap. He was too old for it last time he went to jail. I couldn't imagine spending my sixtieth birthday in jail, but he did. This time his attorney told him to expect a sentence of thirty to sixty days. He'd just stopped by to drop off his car and house keys. Of course, according to his version of things, everyone else was to blame. His lack of responsibility for his own actions made it impossible for him to do anything else in life. Unless he took ownership, how would he ever make the necessary changes? He'd just keep thinking that things keep happening *to him*. I hoped he'd have enough time to sober up and enjoy his life a little bit, even if it was behind bars, but I knew different. He was not ready, and he never would be. I just had to learn to accept him and his choices. Love means accepting people exactly the way they are. There was nothing anyone in his family could do for him anymore. He lived a very sad and lonely life. I do wish he didn't hurt the way he did.

Chuck was arrested at the rescue mission where he'd been staying. Of all people, it was my mom who called to tell me. Someone who worked for her was staying at the same shelter and overheard him talking about me. It's pretty creepy to think about him hanging out at the homeless shelter, talking to random people about me. Anyway, it turned out he'd absconded a few months earlier and, after he'd been at the shelter for three weeks, his parole officer finally caught up with him. That was my mom's story. Of course, I called Santa Barbara County Jail to see for myself. They confirmed that he was in custody but couldn't give me a release date, because that was up to his parole officer and the judge. What they did know was that he is going back to the prison at Wasco. It was a good morning.

The previous weekend, Jevon had been in Las Vegas at a business convention. Spending two nights alone was scary for me. I'd never been a scared person. I always felt able to handle myself. Bad things may have happened, but I was a survivor. Chuck changed all that, and spending those two nights alone had me restless and edgy. I was very pregnant then and would have been totally defenseless.

Sunshine asked me all the time about monsters, and it was my job to reassure her. I told her I would punch them in the butt and kick them in the face. Inside, I knew I couldn't defend myself against Chuck. Being out of my dad's house was good because he could have easily found me there. I kept my name off all the utility bills, because those can be tracked online to find a person's address. I also had a post office box and didn't receive mail at my new address. Even my cell phone was in Jevon's name. But there were ways, and this was a relatively small town. In my heart, I knew that as long as he wasn't behind bars, there was one monster I couldn't protect my little girl from.

November 2010

My water broke on a Friday morning. Our daughter Halo was born just after the clock passed midnight on Saturday, November 13. At times, Jevon and I felt like we were the only ones in the room, but we weren't. We chose to share the experience with a few loved ones. Grandma Mae was there during the delivery, something she had always wanted to see. It made me feel good to include her in her great-granddaughter's birth. She came with her daughter-in-law, Susan. Auntie Carol was also there, despite the fact that the last time she was in that hospital was when her son, Aaron died. She showed up in tears, but she still showed up. Bless her heart. Looking in her eyes, I remembered the pain she had been forced to deal with, less than a year earlier, a pain no mother should ever have to experience: the death of a child.

$\mathscr{Part}$ 7

"So with you: Now is your time of grief, but I will see you again and you will rejoice, and no one will take away your joy."

—John 16:22

December 2010

Halo died thirty-nine short days later.

Monday turned into Tuesday, and she was inconsolable. I'd been sleepless every night since she was born. It was around one in the morning, and she was crying that painful little cry of hers. I finally gave into my own exhaustion. I put her in her car seat, and in the living room, and shut the door; then I went around the corner into our room and shut that door as well. After a half an hour of crying or so, I heard her go quiet. Feeling guilty, I went into the living room to gather her up and bring her back into our bed, where she had always slept, right next to me. I picked her up, walked back into our room, and felt her head drop back on her limp little neck. Immediately, I knew there was something wrong. Her body was still warm but completely limp in my hands.

"Halo!" I shouted, waking Jevon. Quickly I turned on our bedroom light and dropped to my knees, laying her tiny body on the floor in front of me.

"Call 9-1-1!" I yelled, while Jevon, stunned, stared at his daughter's lifeless form. "She's not breathing!" I spit. "Call 9-1-1!"

Grabbing the phone, I dialed it myself and shouted into the receiver. "My baby is not breathing!" Then I handed the phone to Jevon and listened as he continued the conversation. As adrenaline rushed through my veins, I realized it was up to me to try and save her life. Tilting her head backward just a bit, I plugged her nose with my fingertips and breathed into her open mouth. *Oh my God. This isn't happening.* My breath went into her chest, but nothing changed. All that happened was that her chest rose up from the air I forced into her. *How many times am I supposed to push down on her?* I couldn't remember what to do, so I just started pushing, but not too hard, because I didn't want to hurt her. The air trapped inside her escaped as I pushed down the first time. I pushed a few more times and then breathed into her again. *This has gotta work, right? I mean, she just stopped breathing. She must still be alive. Why isn't she breathing?* I breathed again, I pushed some more times. *Dear God, please save my baby. Save our baby, please God. She's just a tiny, little life, just getting started.* More breaths, more pushes on her little chest.

Within two minutes, the paramedics were in our front yard, on the lawn with a stretcher. Grabbing her off the floor, I carried her out to them and explained what had happened. "She stopped breathing!" I could hear the hysteria in my voice and struggled to regain my composure. "I've already begun CPR," I continued. "She doesn't seem to be responding, but she was just crying! She stopped crying, and I picked her up!"

I saw them do the same things I had been doing and, without anything to do, I began to panic. Tears welled in my eyes, tears of terror. I dropped to my knees right there on the damp cold grass and begged God, out loud, to save my baby.

Fear is not the word. There is no word bad enough for how I felt right then. *Please, God, don't take my baby. Take me instead. Take anything from me but my baby.*

Unable to resuscitate my little girl, the paramedics took her to the hospital. Quickly, we got dressed and drove over to the hospital. In my mind, I was going to the hospital to bring her home. I had to remember the diaper bag. I had to remember the car seat. Sunshine was confused when she woke up, and we didn't bother to dress her. She was wearing her favorite pajamas, the pink ones with feet and the bunny on the front. She was crying because she saw how upset I was.

"Come on, Sunshine. We have to go to the hospital. Your sister is sick. Hurry up. We have to go right now." It was the only thing I managed to say besides, "Oh my God," which is what I heard myself say over and over.

When we got to the hospital, they made us wait in the waiting room way too long. Then they only allowed one of us to see her at a time. Since Sunshine was only two years old, she was not allowed in, so one of us had to stay outside the room with her. When I walked into the room, I went from a state of panic to utter shock. My five-week-old baby was on a table, turning cold, with a tube in her throat. There was an impossible-looking IV tube sticking straight out of the front of her shin. They were able to get her pulse back, but she wasn't breathing on her own. She had not had any oxygen to her brain for quite some time. They were going to transfer her to Cottage Hospital in Santa Barbara, which was better equipped to handle pediatric emergencies. An ambulance to transport her was on the way.

We took turns with Halo until the very last few minutes before the ambulance came, when a nice nurse offered to help us with Sunshine. We spent that time with Halo together, trying to convince ourselves not to be horrified and scared. Kissing her tiny mouth and holding her little hand, I told her I would see her soon in Santa Barbara, where they would make her better. Then we would take her home. Turning to leave, I made myself believe that was the truth.

My mom, Bruce, Aunt Carol, and Uncle Frank met us at our house. We gathered some clothes for a brief stay out of town and made the hour-long drive to get to our baby. The prenatal intensive care unit waiting room was empty at 3:30 in the morning. It was my aunt's birthday, the twenty-first of December. I remembered that when I was pregnant with Halo I'd had a dream about naming her Carol. It gave me a sinking feeling to think that this was somehow destined to happen. The nurses gave us a general update about getting her stabilized on the respirator and said we'd be allowed in her room shortly. Time was swallowed into a vacuum, I guess, because I couldn't seem to hold onto it. In other ways, it also felt somehow drawn out. Waiting. Panicking. Pacing. Sitting. Staring. Praying. My bowels liquefied, and I kept throwing up little bits in the back of my mouth.

At last they let us in to see her. She seemed even smaller, lying alone on the table, hooked up to all her machines. There was a catheter for her urine, a tube going down her throat forcing her to breathe, that horrible IV sticking straight out of her leg, a gold heart sticker to keep track of her body temperature, and other wires that kept track of her blood pressure, pulse, and oxygen count. The respirator breathed for her, but her body convulsed and shook as she seemed to fight on every inhale. Her face looked swollen, and her pallor was waxy and flat. She looked almost colorless.

The doctor came in to speak with us. He specialized in prenatal intensive care. He shook Jevon's hand and then mine, looking us in our eyes, and seemed sincere when he told us he was sorry. He asked us to tell him what happened and assured us that we'd done everything we could. I would have loved to believe him, but in my heart I knew it was not true. *She never wanted to be put down*, I kept thinking, hearing her scared and panicky cry in my mind. *I even put her in her car seat, her stupid frigging car seat, when I would shower, so I could see her and make sure she was okay. She acted like she'd die if I left her alone, and now it looks like she actually will. It's my fault, and no one can tell me different.* I maintained eye contact while he told us she would have died if I hadn't administered CPR on the floor. He told us that I'd prolonged her life. Now we'd get to say good-bye to her, and that's more than most parents get to do when their children have SIDS. *SIDS? What did he just say?* Sudden infant death syndrome. Death. And just like that, everything stopped, and I felt waves course through my body, up and down my legs, torso, and arms, ending at my scalp. My blood turned cold. The doctor's lips were moving, but I couldn't understand what he was saying. I had to ask him to repeat himself, because nothing made sense.

He explained, "She is not sedated. The reason she is lying still, not responding to pain is because her brain is not functioning anymore. She went too long without oxygen."

I asked if he had ever seen a recovery from this condition before. He looked at me with obvious concern and pity and said, "No. It is SIDS. Sudden infant *death* syndrome. What we will do is have her checked out by a neurologist. He will hook her up to special monitors to check her brain function, then we'll know for certain what her diagnosis is. All you can do is wait. If you have any questions, I am here for both of you." The nursing staff introduced themselves to us and then left. And we were alone with our baby girl. I looked into Jevon's eyes, which mirrored my shock, pain, and fear.

I sat down and let it sink in. *Sudden infant death syndrome. What does that mean? Why does she have it? Why can't they wake her up? How can she be healthy one minute and dying the next?* My body folded in on itself, and I doubled over in my seat. I heard the sound of misery coming from someplace deep in my guts. After some time passed, I grew silent. The clock on the wall suggested the time, but I couldn't make sense of it. I stood up to hold her limp and tiny hand.

Her eyes weren't closed all the way, and she stared blankly out from under her eyelids. Her body still shuddered with each artificial expansion of her lungs. The machine made the only noise in the room as it sustained her life. Nothingness. My breasts were engorged, so I asked the nurse for a pump. *Maybe when she wakes up, she can be fed through a tube,* I thought to myself. The pumping relieved the pressure but not the ache. I filled up two little bottles within ten minutes. The nurse came in to say the doctor was going to take the awful IV out of her shin and put a new one in her groin. It would be best for us to go back out to the waiting room.

"I'll come get you when you can come back in," she told us kindly.

We shuffled out of the room, hand in hand. The floor moved under our feet, but we couldn't even consciously figure out how to make our legs move right. Our movements were awkward and mechanical. Step by step, we made our way to the waiting room, where I recounted the news to my mom, Aunt Carol, Uncle Frank, and my cousin, Sophia. Sunshine was at my mom's house with Bruce. I was again aware that my bowels were not working as they should, and excused myself to go back to the bathroom. It felt like a bout of food poisoning. I wished it were something so uncomplicated. Unloading like this would have been bad enough at home. Doing it in a public restroom with someone in the next stall was not only disgusting, it was humiliating as well. I was getting used to feeling like I was completely out of my mind. I lacked the ability to do anything but resign myself to my body's functions. It was terrible. I felt like my guts were coming out as loudly as possible, with another lady only a few feet away. Back in the waiting room, I watched Jevon's heart break more with every passing second. I couldn't accept the idea that I was going to watch our baby die right in front of my eyes, and I would be helpless to do anything about it.

The night trudged on, then gave way to morning, as we prepared to go back in to be with Halo. A nice man brought in a Dalmatian, a special dog who visited the hospital on a regular basis. At first, it made me feel pitiful and weary to be grouped with people who would need an animal's help to raise their spirits. Then she came up to me, and I felt my frown relax. Her fur was unbelievably soft and smooth. In my mind, I was transported to my easy chair at home, my lips brushing across Halo's hair, soft as baby-bird feathers across my lips. That was my heaven, and I was not willing to give it up. Not then, not ever. I felt my eyes become hot with a fresh wave of tears, and I swallowed hard. The Dalmatian looked at me with an innocence that only animals and babies possess. She allowed me to pet her for a minute or two and succeeded in making me feel better in the moment, and I was grateful. We made small talk with her human, and after a few minutes, they moved on.

Another mother took up a spot across the room. More time passed, and in desperation to think about something different, we made conversation. She was from Los Angeles and was there because her daughter, who lived in Santa Barbara, had suffered a major stroke. Her daughter was in her late thirties. The woman was baffled how something like this could have happened to a person so young. *At least you had thirty years with her,* I thought, envious and angry that I'd never even get to find out what color my daughter's eyes would be. *I'll never watch her learn to walk. I'll never hear her say Mommy. I'll never see her smile.* I kept my mouth shut while my mind kept going. I remembered to nod and show concern at the appropriate times. Nobody can know if anyone else's situation is better or worse. We were both terrified, because a mother losing her child at any age goes against nature.

Eventually they let us back in to see our baby. The neurologist introduced himself. He was older than I had expected, which made me feel better because, I thought, he must have had lots of experience. Maybe he had been in this line of work long enough to have seen a recovery from this condition. I asked him, and I was again disappointed. Electrodes were attached with goop to her scalp and then connected to a monitor. With a solemn but steady voice, the neurologist explained what the lines on the monitor meant. He showed us where the brain function would show up. We stared blankly at the lines as they made their way flatly across the screen. Halo did not respond as he ran a pen up the soles of her beautiful little bare feet. He opened her eyelids and shone a flashlight back and forth in front of them, searching for any changes in her pupils. I looked away at that point, because it was too much. His prognosis cemented our greatest fears. Although there was a minimal change in the dilation of her pupils, there was no other recognizable brain function. We had to wait and see if her condition improved in the next twenty-four hours, but in his opinion there was very little hope that she would survive even that long. I chose to hold onto the fact that her eyes were doing something. At the hospital in Santa Maria, her eyes had been fixed and dilated. It was a small improvement and just enough for me to hold onto. I prayed for a miracle.

We were only allowed two visitors at a time, but they allowed us to break the rules. I knew the reason for this was because we had a very short time to see our baby alive, but thankfully no one said that out loud. The visitors came in a few at a time. My mother, my aunt, and Sophia took turns coming in to hold her hands, rub her head, and touch her feet. Jevon and I stayed with her constantly. I stood right by her, always touching her and talking to her. In my heart, I believe she heard me.

"My love, look how pretty you are," I whispered in her itty-bitty ear. "You're stronger than this. You're a survivor, like your mommy. It's in your blood. Show these guys what you're made of. I believe in you, baby."

A couple of Jevon's friends came in then, one at a time while the other stayed in the waiting room with their three kids. Then Jevon's family got there.

Her breathing became more labored, and her tiny body shook and shuddered more and more with the effort of it. It was agonizing to watch, and I excused myself to go to the

151

bathroom again. I decided to smoke a cigarette. Outside, the weather was sodden and dreary. In southern California, we rarely have rainstorms. It was as if God's mood was mirroring my own. It had rained for five days straight. I couldn't remember ever seeing it rain so much there in my life. Mother Earth mourned, and the sky wept with me. Looking into the storm clouds, I could barely hear God whispering to my heart that He was still with me. Being away from Halo brought me anxiety, and I felt guilty before my cigarette was half smoked. *What if something happens? What if she flutters her eyes or moves just a little bit and I'm not there to notice? What if her heart stops?* My legs were wobbly and I had to stop walking occasionally, afraid of falling down as I made my way back to the NICU.

Something happened when I spoke to her. I probably wanted to believe so much that I was delusional, but I swore she heard me, despite the fact that the monitors showed no brain function. *Can't anyone else see how she seems to be trying?* Ever so slightly, she seemed to reciprocate my love when I touched her rose-petal-soft skin. *It's in my mind. It must be.* Slowly, the oxygen saturation on the monitor decreased. It should have been at a hundred, and it read in the seventies.

The doctor came in to discuss our options. He talked about the significance and importance of the oxygen saturation. He said there was a bigger respirator, and if they hooked her up to that, the number might go back up. There was also a chance that the change would be too much for her to tolerate. At that point, he asked if we would want to try to resuscitate again. *I don't know. I don't know anything.* He then told us about something he called "redirecting care," which focused on relieving struggle and pain if her condition continued to worsen. It called for administering a drug to relax her muscles, so that she wouldn't fight her own breathing, and morphine to help her if she in fact could feel any pain. Most likely, he said, she felt nothing.

"This is an aspect of science that we don't know for sure," the doctor explained. He was respectful and sympathetic with his tone and eye contact. "She may or may not feel pain at this point. It is a matter of how long you want to prolong her life."

"She's clearly struggling," I said, looking at Jevon but directing the statement at both men.

"She is, yes," the doctor said. Jevon silently nodded.

"We don't know what we want to do. We need to talk it over together and decide what, if anything, we want to do," I said, still looking at Jevon. I searched his eyes for a clue about what we should say or do. I felt empty and dumbfounded. I couldn't trust my own judgment.

"Of course," the doctor said. "Take your time. There's no hurry. We just want you to think things over and be prepared. Once her number drops to a certain point, her heart will shut down. We want you to advise us whether you'd like more aggressive action taken at that point or not. If you choose for us to redirect care, we will take her off of the monitors and allow you to hold her during the end of her life."

This is it. While I'm praying for miracles and living in fantasy land, my daughter is slipping away. Even if she lives, she'll be a vegetable. She'll never breathe again on her own. She'll never talk. She'll never speak. I've lived on the edge, throwing my life down the toilet, and God brought me back. I died and lived to tell it. I almost died time after time in different ways on different days. I've been reckless and irresponsible without any regard for myself. I walked the streets alone at thirteen years old. I slept on a tennis court, alone and scared. I've had unprotected sex, skydived, got behind a wheel on snowy nights and driven drunk, put a needle in my arm, and done countless other careless things. If anyone should be dying or dead, it's me, not a perfectly healthy and innocent little baby. Where's

the justice? Where's the sense? My God, I love and
respect you, but I question you! Why did your angels
look away from her while she cried herself to death
in the next room? What are you doing?

My guilt built along with the bile in my guts. We came to
terms with that fact that there was no hope. The only kind
thing to do was to allow her a pain-free escape from this
life. I wished it were me lying there, but it wasn't. She and I
belonged together, if not here, then in the next place. I didn't
deserve life. I craved the milky sweet smell of her breath on
my face. I craved it like I used to crave drugs. My body ached
with the need of her.

We smoked outside one more time. We went back in
by her side. We stood and stared. We sat in silence. The
machines inhaled and exhaled and beeped and hummed.
Sometimes the machines sounded an alarm for one reason
or another. The nurses would rush in and make adjustments.
I didn't stop talking to her, reassuring her that I was there by
her side, loving her, waiting for her to wake up and show us
all what she was made of. Her beautiful face looked puffier
and her stomach stuck out due to the fluid that was collecting
around her lungs. The doctor said her cells had begun the
process of dying. Her fragile body was giving up, and there I
was, talking to her, waiting for her to squeeze my hand, open
her eyes … anything.

Hours went by. I looked at the clock and noticed it was
evening already. A nurse brought me a Gatorade. People kept
telling me to eat and drink, as if it were me they were worried
about. *Can't they see I'm not the one dying here? How can anyone
have an appetite?* Halo's fragile condition did not improve. In
fact, she went downhill; her oxygen number was reading in
the upper fifties. They recommended that the priest go in
that night, instead of the next day as had been arranged
before. She was not likely to hold on through the night. The
priest showed up after some immeasurable amount of time

and gave a thoroughly bleak and depressing baptism. Last rites were read. Everyone was in the room with us. People were crying, and I watched them curiously. Somehow, I held my composure. My eyes burned, and my muscles shook. I was not tired, but I kept getting confused in my mind—wondering if this were real or I should pray harder or if she was not really as bad as they said—and then I'd come back to those gut-hollowing, ugly four words: sudden infant death syndrome.

It's over, isn't it? Look what I've done. She never would have died in my arms. If I'd held her, she wouldn't have died in my arms. All because I wanted to sleep. I haven't slept anyway! I can't believe how short-sighted and selfish I am. If only I had kept her with me, none of this would be happening.

The numbers continued their slow and steady decline, and the nurses told us it was time to say goodbye. *She is really dying. This is actually happening. My daughter is going to die now.* I looked away as they pulled out her tubes and disconnected her body from the respirator and monitors. They wrapped her precious little body in a blanket. *My beautiful and perfect baby, the girl who less than six weeks ago, was growing inside of me. My lovely little angel for whom I have tried to do my best. I have failed her. Put her down and left her alone, and now she is dying.*

When they handed her to me, I brushed my lips across her hair, so soft and downy. I looked at Jevon. "Sit with me. Sit with us," I said to him, and he did. I held her head and shoulders, and he held her lower half. We sat so close, there was no space between us. A minute or two of labored, short breaths rattled through her tiny lungs and out of her pretty little lips. She breathed. Then some time passed, and she breathed once more. I thought she was done, but one more breath came out of her. I kissed her cheeks. I told her I loved her and that I was proud of her. I looked at her face, so pale and lifeless, and told her how beautiful she was. I kissed the bridge of her nose. I rubbed her hair. I squeezed the bundle that was her body and finally broke down. An ocean of grief passed through me and out of my mouth, and I doubled over in anguish. When I looked up, everyone's eyes were on me. *Oh God, I'm out of control, making animal noises as I hold my dead baby. Pull yourself together.* I heard sniffs coming from snot-filled noses and felt utterly self-conscious and exposed. It was like one of those dreams where you look up and realize that you don't have any clothes on.

Awkwardly, I handed Halo to Jevon and got on my knees next to him. Time passed. I stood and kissed his head, fixed his hair, and whispered, "I love you, Jevon."

He turned his head to look at me. In his eyes, a deep chasm had opened up, with a sorrow that I knew mirrored mine. After a while, I asked if anyone else wanted to hold her. Both of our moms took turns holding her, then his sister, and then my aunt. The doctor wasted some more energy telling me what a good job I'd done to prolong her life. He assured me that I did everything right and far better than most people would have done under the same circumstances. I knew he meant well, but how could he honestly say those things? I guess he was just trying to make me feel better. It did little to help me, but it seemed to help Jevon. We both said thank you. I felt like a fraud. I was not a good mother. Even the nurses were in tears. People milled around for a while and then made their way out to the waiting room or back to their homes. I allowed them to hug me before I watched them walk out. Jevon and I once again were left alone with our daughter. They asked us to leave for a few minutes, and we did. They said they'd come get us after a bit. *Whatever you say*, I thought to myself as I shuffled out of the room to go smoke outside in the cold and rainy night.

Together, we walked hand in hand. My legs were shaking uncontrollably and I had to let go of his hand and stand still for a little bit. I had to tell my legs out loud "one foot in front of the other," and eventually I found the ability to follow through with the command. She was all alone, wrapped in a blanket, waiting for us when we came back in the room.

"Do you want to hold her again?" Jevon asked.

"No, I don't," I replied and immediately felt guilty. Swiftly, I turned toward her and lifted her up. That, after all, was where she belonged—in my arms. "Hey baby," I said awkwardly. "I miss you." Jevon stood against the Formica counter top, watching me as I looked her over. It was just the three of us for a while until a nurse came in with a pale pink box.

"Here's a memory box with a few little things to remember her by," she said. "Take as much time as you like. I'm so sorry for your loss." She spoke in a genuinely sincere way, and then she stepped out, leaving us alone once more. I dumped out one of the bottles of breast milk that was in the room and rinsed the bottle. *What a waste*, I thought, as I watched my baby's food make a cloudy mess in the sink. Sadly, I rinsed away the last bit with my free hand and made my way back to the chair.

"My love, what'll I do without you?" I talked to her as though she was still connected to that pale, lifeless body. She had started to cool down, I noticed, as I kissed her slightly parted and perfectly shaped lips. Jevon's lips. Then two officers in uniform showed up at the door. They said their names, but I didn't register them. *I wonder if they'll arrest me or not. I should be arrested for this. I know it is my fault. I deserve to go to jail.* I stayed seated, holding onto my baby. Too tired to be nervous, I absentmindedly nuzzled her little head and stroked her hair with my hand just like I'd always done. I listened as they asked us questions. We took turns answering. It was the same stuff we'd been questioned about already. Our answers were automatic. Then they talked about what came next. They said there would be an autopsy. It's mandatory, they explained. *So now, you are going to take my little girl away and cut her open. I just got done growing her inside my body, and you are going to take her apart.*

157

"Do I have to sign anything?" I asked.

"Nope, it's just standard," one of the officers replied.

So I guess all those tests they did, the CAT scans and MRIs and x-rays, didn't really mean squat. They don't really know what is wrong with her, and they have to try to get some answers. This is our last time with our daughter. These guys are going to stand, not sit, and interrogate us, while we hold our baby for the last time. Then we are going to leave her here, with them, and they are going to take her to the coroner's office to get cut open on a metal table. It doesn't matter if I say that's okay or not. Not that I want to argue, but what if I did? What if I have a problem with them mutilating my little girl?

I started to feel defensive and angry. To hell with those guys. I knew better than to argue. It was better to keep my trap shut. I knew what happened when I got mouthy with cops. After they explained things, I realized they were waiting for us to get up and go, so they could take her away. We said goodbye to her one more time and handed her to the officer who seemed like the lesser of two evils. When we walked out, I felt like I was leaving my whole world behind.

We spent that first night at my mom's house. His mom and sister got a hotel room nearby, which my aunt and uncle paid for. The night was unbearable. My breasts were so sore and engorged that I couldn't lie on my side. I lay only on my back; they still dripped down my sides. My body yearned for a baby who never needed to be fed again. The place where she grew deep inside me was a gaping void, and my insides contracted around it.

There was no conditioner in the bathroom, so when Jevon got out of the shower, his long hair was full of tangles. He sat down and tried to comb it out. Watching him struggle, my heart ached for him. Taking the comb out of his hand, I placed my hand on his shoulder. Silently, I combed the tangles out for him. When I was done, I kissed his forehead. I wished I could do more for him.

We lay down together in my mom's great big bed. She tried so hard to make us feel loved. She did everything she could, and I was grateful. I lay in the darkness and felt myself breathe in and out, in and out. It was torturous, and I was sick over the reality that my body was working, while Halo's was not.

The night crawled by, and when I finally drifted to sleep for a moment, I dreamed about my baby. She was lost, and I couldn't find her. She was not dead, but she had gone away from me, and I didn't know how to find her. I awoke to my own voice calling out. "Jevon! Where's Halo?" The darkness flooded my eyes. My breasts felt even more sore, hard, and swollen. They were leaking all over my mom's sheets. My whole body was covered in cold sweat. Even if I'd wanted to, I couldn't go back to sleep, so I tried to calm myself down and waited for the sun to come up. As I lay there in the dark before dawn, I thought about the previous day. Again, I remembered the dream I'd had while I was pregnant. I'd asked God to help me find a name for her and the name he gave me in the dream was Carol. It was too strange to be a coincidence. *So what does that mean? That this was fated? Was my baby supposed to die? How can life be so cruel?*

The next morning friendly voices made their way up the staircase and greeted us while we were in bed, both of us staring at the ceiling. "Ugh," I moaned, rolling over toward Jevon and wrapping my arms around him. I closed my eyes as I held him and wondered if we had to get up. Of course, we did. We smoked a cigarette, commiserated about a terrible night's sleep, and got dressed. Jevon's back had completely gone out, so he had to go to a last-minute appointment with my mom's chiropractor. After he left, I made my way downstairs.

The first face I saw was my sister's. She brought a smile to my face, and I immediately felt better, which made me feel guilty. Looking around, I saw Jevon's mom, sister, and brother-in-law. I got the feeling his sister wasn't happy to see me and that she put up with me because she had to. I could have been wrong, but I probably wasn't. She thought I was a home-wrecker. I guess I was. I sat down next to Michelle, and we made small talk. My sister always made me laugh and did so then. As soon as I laughed, I wished I could take it back. Jevon's sister sighed loudly and groaned as she walked out the door. I sensed her eyes rolling though her back was turned toward me. *I'm such an idiot. What's funny anyway? I should just shut up.* Feeling hated by her in that moment made the morning almost unbearable.

My mom made breakfast. Awkwardly, I attempted to recover myself by serving everyone orange juice. The day dragged on. Somehow, we managed to put together a nice service. More people showed up than we expected. It was beautiful and moving. Jevon and I stood up together and spoke in front of the crowd. A big part of my message was that even though we don't understand why these things happen, we should not get mad at God.

My mother bought a beautiful plot at the Santa Barbara Cemetery. It cost way more than anything we could have afforded on our own. The cemetery overlooks the ocean. The plot is in a perfect little place under a tree. The service was nice, but I don't remember a word of it. After everyone left, Jevon and I stayed to watch the men put the dirt on her little, white, casket.

We finally met with the detective who was on the case, on *our* case, more like. Shortly after Halo died, he'd called to "introduce himself." Luckily, Jevon answered the phone. The police wanted to meet with us, but they had to wait. We planned to call them as soon as we were back in town. We had just buried our daughter. We were doing the best we could. When we finally went back to Santa Maria, we returned home to a mess. The police had broken into our house and left a copy of the search warrant on our counter. Merry F'ing Christmas to you too.

Our landlords gave us a free month of rent, and Jevon's boss gave him a couple of weeks paid vacation. We needed to get away, so we hastily planned a road trip to New Mexico. Jevon had family there. We barely got through a Christmas that I can't even remember now. We got out of town as quickly as we could with Sunshine.

Our road trip was great. We drove to New Mexico and spent time with family, went to museums, and took a sky bus to the top of the highest mountain. There was snow up there, and we could see the entire city. It was beautiful. On the way back, we took historic Route 66. We went through a few real ghost towns, including one called Randsburg. It was so small that we saw a sign next to the fire station that read "In case of fire, yell loud, stay calm."

We drove through another ghost town, called Oatman. This place was really cool. There were wild donkeys everywhere. They were to Oatman what pigeons are to New York City. They seemed almost domesticated, the way people tried to shoo them away from their store fronts and porches. We even got close enough to pet one of them. I wished that we'd had more time there. Before we left, we went to a little jewelry store. Jevon bought me a beautiful handmade necklace. The store owner's name was Laughingbird. He had made the necklace Jevon bought. After we talked for a while, he asked where our daughter was.

"Right here," I said, pointing to Sunshine.

"No, the other one," he replied. "The younger one." I looked at Jevon. There were no other customers in the store. It was a small shop. There was no way he could have mistaken another little girl as ours, as nobody else had been there. I believe that he either glimpsed or sensed Halo with us. It made me feel better, knowing she was near me.

Our drive back was special. We felt so close and connected. We cried together, we laughed together, we talked together, and we sat together in comfortable silence. Being with Jevon was like medicine for my broken heart. It felt like he was my best friend. I loved him more than ever.

Getting back home was an adjustment, to say the least. I went to the store to buy a can of tomato sauce so I could make some Mexican rice, Jevon's favorite. It was the first full day that I'd spent alone since Halo died. I'd been lucky to have people surrounding me so much. It was already January 12. On the short walk to the store, I apologized to Sunshine for yelling at her for something, I've forgotten what it was. She said it was okay, and I could tell that she meant it, like she always does, but it was not okay. You'd think I'd be sweet as syrup to her after losing Halo, but I was not. Sometimes I was nice, and sometimes I was a total jerk for no reason at all. She was such a good girl, always loving, always trying to make me happy. She really did make me happy. I had to work much harder to show her how much I noticed her goodness. I'd gotten off track. I did that often during those days.

The store ... yes. The little store, right down the block. The staff had seen me walk in there quite often since being pregnant, and they'd seen Halo. There were only a few checkers, and they were all nice to me. We hardly talked, since they spoke Spanish and didn't realize that I do too. I hate to be a show off and prefer keeping to myself anyway. Sunshine asked for a yogurt, which I got for her, and we also got a quart of milk along with the tomato sauce we came for. At the checkout counter, the girl asked where my baby was. Looking her in her eyes, I said, very matter-of-factly, "She died." The girl looked at me, confused, and I decided to tell her in Spanish and stop being weird about it. But then my mind went blank, which was also something that happened quite often back then. "Yeah, you know, dead," I said in an ineffective attempt to help her understand. I tried to figure out how to make her get what I was saying, and pictured myself with my hands around my neck, tongue out, eyes rolling back to convey death, but I was spared this embarrassment when she called the manager over.

"My baby is dead," I told him flatly. I was thoroughly tired of this conversation.

"*Se morir,*" he told her, not taking his eyes off me. "I'm sorry, ma'am," he said to me, with sadness. "My wife, she have two babies, a boy and a girl, and they both go. It's okay. They with God." He was sincere, but I couldn't agree that it was okay.

"Yeah," I mumbled. He gave Sunshine a little bag of chips and a piece of candy and sent us on our way. I just wanted to get wasted.

And I did. I got trashed. It was horrible, and I was a mess all over the place. I looked and acted as badly I felt on the inside. I took every word that Jevon said too personally. I went inside myself. I moped, wallowed, and wailed. After I put Sunshine to bed, I dragged myself out to the couch and listened to the "funeral playlist" on the iPod. I sat on the opposite side of the couch from where Halo had begun the process of dying, and I went deep. It was pitiful. When I went to bed in the early morning hours after exhausting myself, I found an empty bed where Jevon should have been. I realized again that drinking wasn't for me. Maybe quitting didn't have to be forever, but it certainly wasn't a healthy option right then.

On Sunshine's first day at preschool, I had to get out. Being around the house was driving me crazy. Being preoccupied with cleaning and re-cleaning the house began to wear on me. The grief counselor said I was displaying classic symptoms of obsessive compulsive disorder. I knew it had to be something like that. Words from movies or conversations stood out in my mind, and I found myself spelling them over and over again. I spelled words and mimicked typing them out on a keyboard that wasn't there. I was constantly tapping away at nothing, like I was playing an invisible piano. The therapist said that when I started doing these things and they bothered me, that was a good indicator of my stress level and I should do things to counteract my anxiety. One thing I wanted to do was work. More than providing us with an obvious financial gain, working would distract me from my own mind. Unfortunately, our economy was in a serious slump. Luckily, the government still funded childcare for women like me who were trying to go back to work. Although I hadn't started a job yet, I'd had an interview and a call back.

The first place I sent my resume called and asked me to do a test. It turned out to be a very interesting test, which I assumed created a personality profile. It consisted of a bunch of words with which I had to rate myself, using a score ranging from one to five. One meant strongly disagree, two was disagree, three was not sure/neutral, four was agree, and five was strongly agree. The words were in alphabetical order and started with *abstract*. I put four for disagree, because I did not believe I was abstract. Who would actually agree that she is abstract? I agreed that I was tidy. I disagreed that I was self-effacing. I strongly agreed that I was parenting (I'm a mom, so this seemed pretty obvious) and strongly disagreed that I was micro-managing. Agreed that I was punctual, disagreed that I was a natural sales-person. Strongly agreed that I was sympathetic and that I was trusting. It was interesting, and I found myself mulling over my answers, wondering if my results were favorable. I asked myself, *Am I really changeable, or did I answer that too quickly?* At least I'm sure I answered the intimidating question right: strongly disagree.

Taking Sunshine to school was more fun for her than it was for me. I had to do a mandatory orientation for the government-funded childcare program in which I was participating. Since I still had no car, we rode over to the school on the bike; Sunshine was in the trailer. It took eighteen minutes to get there. When we walked into her classroom, we looked around and saw the other kids playing with building blocks on the floor. I was feeling anxious, but Sunshine spread her little wings. She walked right into that room in her new outfit, pink fuzzy jacket, and Dora the Explorer backpack. I stayed by the door with a forced smile, trying to look natural and happy for her. I remembered how socially awkward I'd felt at her age. Watching her smile and stand up tall, turning to wave goodbye, I had a new respect for her; she was an independent and gutsy kid. I signed her in, thinking about all the things I'd said about Sunshine on her enrollment papers. She had no health problems, no behavioral problems, and no allergies. She was happy, well-adjusted, enjoyed learning, ate everything she was given, and was an all-around great kid. I walked away feeling my heart tug me back toward her, envisioning myself saying, "Never mind, we're going home now." Instead, I pushed open the door and waited until I was out of sight to break down and cry.

It took me about two hours, two long, boring hours in which I had all the time in the world to review all the dreams I'd had lately: Sunshine getting run over by a truck right in front of my eyes, while I reacted too slowly to stop the tires from crushing her little body. Or the freeways all turning into water slides, and Sunshine going ahead of me, sliding too fast and getting away from me, just far enough out of my reach so that I had to watch, helplessly while she drowned. I prayed that she would be herself, outgoing and full of life, and enjoy her day. That way, I would be the only one who felt miserable about her being away from me.

She made me proud. Right before lunch time, I walked in the classroom tentatively, not knowing what to expect. What I saw was my sweet little girl, making me a Valentine's Day card on a big cutout pink heart with globs of glue all over her precious little fingers.

"Hey, Mom," she said when she finally noticed me. This time, my smile was authentic as I looked at her, not wanting to rush her art project. Sitting down next to her, I helped her finish up.

On the bike ride home, she filled me in on her new friends and how much she liked playing on the slide. Looking up into the cloudless sky, I smiled to myself, realizing that somehow I was moving forward with the wonderful and cheerful child that I still had. I was not paralyzed every moment in grief. There were moments of absolute despair, periods that stretched on in a seemingly endless gray and dull expanse. Then there were these moments when the sun seemed to peek inside me. In contrast to the bleak and exhausting state I had been getting used to feeling, those moments of fresh air felt surprisingly refreshing. Maybe I'd go back to feeling bad again minutes later, but I thanked God for those brief moments of reprieve. They helped me to remember that somehow I'd get by, because it was not all bad, all the time.

August 2012

I had a dream in which someone asked me to finish this book. I'd been dreading sitting down at my computer, because so much had happened since the last time I wrote. I didn't know how to begin. Sometimes, writing about a hard experience leaves me irritated at best. The reason I hadn't written for so long is that I was separated from my computer. I did, however, journal on paper.

I guess there is really only one place to start. It was springtime, and Halo's death still had me in a funk. I was trying to get through the only way I knew how, which was to be completely honest with Jevon about how I felt. By the time Jevon got home from work, he was not in the mood to listen to me talk about her. Our communication slowly deteriorated. The trip to New Mexico turned out to be the best time of our relationship, and it never got that good again. Our connection to each other fell apart. We were tense, and we were broken. Jevon was drifting away from me, and I eventually stopped caring. I listened as he talked about work until I couldn't understand the words he said. Work was all he talked about. Other than that, we spent a lot of time bickering or in uncomfortable silence. I watched as our relationship blurred around our drinking. We drank every day. We drank and argued and became strangers to each other.

To try to get out of my head, I decided to get a job. I got the first job I applied for, at a self-storage place. It felt good to get out of the house and to have a little bit of income. A month later, I enrolled myself in college for the first time in fourteen years or so. I was starting in the summer semester, so I decided to take only two classes to begin with. My hope was to get too busy to feel sad.

By July, I was taking midterms and getting perfect scores and doing well at work. I didn't have time to cry too much, stagnate, or drink all day. Still, my relationship with Jevon was in a steep decline. Our fights were irrational and full of jealousy. The day I brought home my first midterm with a perfect score, he didn't say one positive or congratulatory word about it. Instead, we fought because he wanted to know who lit my cigarette at school. We fought about it all night long. The fight that we had the most was about my job. I had a wonderful situation. I worked only with women. I thought that would have made it virtually impossible for us to fight over jealousy or insecurity issues, but it didn't. I can't believe the time we wasted fighting over such nothing. It's amazing the energy we expended, the mean words we said in retaliation, the anger that built up.

Then one morning things changed. It was right after the midterms, but before the finals. My cousin Aaron (Auntie Carol's son) came to me in a dream. It was early in the morning; Jevon was out of town for a couple of days on a job with his boss. I didn't have school and wasn't scheduled to work until the afternoon. I don't remember what Aaron and

I talked about, but I had one question I needed answered. I asked, "Is Jevon cheating on me?"

After hesitating briefly, Aaron replied, "Well, I have to be honest ..." Predicting a devastating answer, my heart rate sped up fast enough to jolt me awake. I was unable to get back to sleep. I toiled over it all day. That night, as soon as I fell asleep, Aaron was there, in the place between dreaming and being awake. He told me that yes, Jevon had cheated on me in the past, but that he wasn't currently cheating on me. I waited until Jevon came home to confront him, and he admitted to cheating on me. He said that it had happened in the beginning, before we lived together at my dad's house. He said it had been a one-night-stand.

Sometimes when I hear terrible news or someone hurts me really badly, it takes a few days for it to sink in. This was like that. I was relieved to know that it had happened so long ago and that it wasn't a relationship but a one-time thing. I don't know if I believed it happened only once, but I knew it had been over for a long time. He said it happened when he was still going back and forth between me and Patty. He reminded me about a conversation we'd had back then, about how having two girlfriends was too much work. I'd asked him at the time if there had been someone else, because I had a feeling about it. Of course, he'd denied it, and I remember saying how impossible it would be to keep three women happy. In a way, I guess I was right. None of us were happy.

Three days after this conversation, I went into a tailspin. I've speculated about knowing versus not knowing something. Is it better to live in the real world with all the facts at hand, or is it better to know nothing and live blissfully in ignorance? I still don't know the best way to live, but I do know that if you plan on staying in the relationship, it sucks to know. The thoughts that crept into my head told me that my whole relationship was a lie and that I deserved it. It was my fault that his family broke up. I'd hurt Patty, and I'd hurt his son.

This was what happened to people like me. I shouldn't have been surprised that he'd cheated. He cheated with me. I mean, of course I knew he was capable of it. *Duh.* He wasn't ready to commit to me after coming out of such a long relationship. I could relate to that. I remembered my feelings back when he said it had happened. *I knew it.*

Not only could I *not* let it go, I started to dissect and analyze it. Did they make out? Was he too drunk to use protection? Did they cuddle all night? Were numbers exchanged? Was there oral sex? And on and on I went in my head. Of course, the answer to all of those questions turned out to be yes. It made me insane with rage. It was a smack in the face. My ego was trampled. I kept thinking about the times he'd mistreated me due to his own jealousy. In the delivery room, after Halo was born, he got mad at me for texting. I had only been texting my brother. I was so hurt by that. Why did he want to make me feel lousy when my vagina was still inside out after delivering our little girl? My birthday at my aunt's house had been ruined when he sat in his truck, drunk all night, because he thought I was flirting with Julia's boyfriend. It became a weight that was impossible for me to carry, and the righteous indignation made me scornful and hateful. I was murderous and insane. I even told him that I could get away with murder if I killed him. He'd pushed me over the edge. I probably could have gotten off on a temporary insanity plea. That's how furious I was. No matter how much I hated him during that time, I never "got back" at him for cheating. It wouldn't have made me feel better; it would have only complicated things and made me feel worse. No matter how bad I felt, I couldn't shake the knowledge that deep inside my heart, I still needed him to love me.

Very soon after finding out about the infidelity, we were drunk and fighting, and I admitted that I was on the verge of a relapse. He told me I was stupid and that I should not threaten him with that. It wasn't a threat. I was being honest.

I needed help. I needed him to stop being mean to me. I couldn't go on like that anymore. He walked away from me while I was talking, turning his back on me again. The very next day, I went to my dad's house, called my connection, and put a needle in my arm. It was the first step in my dance with death, and I took it to extremes.

There was nothing like that first high. It was like I could actually feel my brain shorting out. The connections didn't quite get where they were trying to go and the little synapses seemed to fire at the wrong times. My eyes glazed over, and I got stuck in a facial expression or a thought, but I couldn't help it or stop myself. To the average person, I'm sure this wouldn't sound like much fun, but for a person in a place of emotional anguish, it was blissful. Not to mention that the immediate body high took me away from myself. My lungs constricted and my throat got tight, making me cough once or twice. My scalp tingled and so did the skin on the backs of my thighs and butt cheeks. The skin on my face and chest turned red like a sunburn, and then the blood rushed to my crotch. The effects of the stimulant reached my bowels.

Even writing it down nine months later, that sensation is so intense, just thinking about it makes me have to go. My face even tingles. It scares me that it is so easy to remember.

Part 8

"No temptation has seized you except what is common to man. And God is faithful; He will not let you be tempted beyond what you can bear. But when you are tempted, He will also provide a way out so that you can stand up under it."

—1 Corinthians 10:13

2012

The following entries are from my handwritten notebook. I wrote in my journal every day for six months while recovering from my relapse.

It has been about a year since I've written, but it feels like far longer. I was so sure I wouldn't relapse, even though I was grieving for my baby. I did surprisingly well for so long. I remember those days, filled with silence, grief, torment, longing. We were so lost. Thinking back, I'm shocked it didn't happen sooner. I'm glad it didn't, because if I had done it earlier, we may not have survived. As it was, we barely did. I was at home, trying to fill the days with something, anything, to fill the emptiness that was my heart, body, and mind after she died. When I started working, even talking to strangers helped me remember myself in the small ways. *This is how to have a conversation. This is how to smile. This is how to interact with a person who knows nothing about me.* Time went by, but life at home stood still. Jevon went completely inside himself. The distance between us grew as he pulled himself together each morning and went on his way. By the time he got home, he just wanted to be normal and have me listen to him about his day. But by the time he got home, I was ready to talk about something that mattered to me. Or just cry. Or both. My topics of discussion were never lighthearted or easy. They were deep, needy, and dark. The best friend I had always found in him was gone. He didn't want to see me cry. He didn't want to hear about pain, longing, or my broken heart. It began to feel as though he had gone on without her. He was moving on, away from her and her memory, and therefore away from me. I stopped talking to him, trusting him, and held my precious memories of her inside myself. Sunshine became my only friend, and she was three, and hardly able to have an adult conversation. Everyone stopped calling. After that, when they did call, I found myself ignoring the calls. I didn't want to hear them say the things they were saying to "make me feel better." For instance: "Pull it together." "You sound like you're getting over it. That's great!" Or my least favorite, "She's in a better place."

The truth was, as well as anybody thought I was doing and as hard as I was doing to meet their expectations, I was completely and totally miserable. I was a big huge faker. What did I want to hear? I don't really know. Commiserating would have been kind of good. Something like: "This is the worst! This is horrible and totally wrong! I hate this! I miss her!" Yes, maybe that's it. I wanted to hear someone else say, "I miss her too." Still, it quite possibly wouldn't have made me feel that much better. I was in a hole.

What I wanted, what I needed, was my best friend, and he was in a hole too. But his hole was far, far away from mine. He was lost in his own sad, fallen place, a place I could neither get to nor understand. Time dragged on again. The days felt like weeks or even months. I thought things would never change. It got worse by the day, the separation of my love from myself. People talked about a "new normal" that people get to after the death of a child. If this was our new normal, I didn't want it. I prayed for change. And this is a very dangerous prayer to pray. Change is exactly what I got.

I couldn't figure out how to make things better. I was really trying. I was doing all the right things. I was working, making money, doing great in school. I was making it so Jevon wasn't responsible for my happiness. I was making good choices. Heck, I was even making my mother proud (which isn't an easy thing to do.) So why couldn't he appreciate me? He didn't see who I was anymore, and I didn't see who he was. We didn't want to see each other. We just did our best to tolerate each other, and each night it felt like we found another way to pick each other apart or cut each other down. I could indulge in some petty and ugly remarks here, but I won't. Let's just say that we both said many mean things. We weren't there for each other when we needed each other the most. From my perspective, I was trying hard and doing well. Even when I asked the simple question

"How are you?" it would upset him. Nothing I did seemed right. From his perspective, he was working hard, which was all he could manage, and the last thing he felt like doing was talking about his feelings or hearing about mine.

I didn't even like him anymore, and I doubt he liked me. We were always fighting, and he was always accusing me of flirting or cheating. I had never been as loyal to anyone as I had been to Jevon, which was the ironic thing. We argued ourselves sick. After he admitted to the cheating, I relapsed immediately. I felt everything in my life was a lie. On top of it, I felt I deserved it all. I broke up his family. I killed my baby. I hated myself. I needed to escape.

The needle went in, and the warmth spread, and it felt really good for about two minutes. Then the paranoia set in. Only this time, there was like a whole part of my brain that felt sideways. It wasn't the same high. It wasn't the same at all. My theory about this is that the grief worked some kind of chemical malfunction inside my mind. I became everything that I had made fun of about other people who got high and acted stupid. I had always called those people weak-minded. Now I was just like them. I became delusional and the fear was perpetually fueling me into anger and agitation. It wasn't your average boogie-man kind of fear. This wasn't even a sleep paralysis nightmare kind of fear, which is pretty bad. This was absolute terror and it was all-consuming. I was scared of everything. Jevon finding out, anyone else finding out, God, the devil, the house, him cheating again. Yes, especially that one. Wow, going back here is so bad for me. Let's just say this: I behaved badly. I went right back into a daily habit and became impossible to deal with. Now I became the one who was always accusing him. I must have made him so mad. I seriously thought that he was cheating again. Every day I made up some new theory in my mind about it. I confronted him. I physically attacked him. I insulted him. I degraded him. I wanted to punish him. We punished each other. We picked on each other a lot. We physically, emotionally and verbally abused each other. It was really bad and then it got even worse. One day we started to get high together. More on that later. For now, I have to stop and think about something else.

Instead of writing about any more past issues, I'm going to focus on what I'm grateful for. Writing about our past has a way of really making me mad. I'm not far away enough from it yet. The way I get through this is by focusing on now. Luckily, my drug-addled brain is good at selective memory. Here's what I am grateful for: I once made a list of everything I want in a man. Then I made another list of everything I need in a man. Jevon turns out to be everything on both of those lists. Over the years, I've found that I've finally gotten something that I've always wanted and never had: unconditional love.

Last week at counseling, my therapist asked me what would happen if I decided to use drugs again. What would I lose? What would be the extent of the consequences? She specifically asked if I would lose Jevon. After considering that for a moment, I realized that no, I wouldn't. There's nothing that could tear us apart. "No, I wouldn't," I told her. "We're unconditional." It would devastate our relationship and hurt him very deeply, but I know we'd get through it.

It was a definite lightbulb-going-on-over-my-head type moment. I feel incredibly fortunate to have found a love like this. Although our history isn't mistake free, we certainly know what not to do. Our love for each other is stronger than ever.

How I got here: On the night of October 1, we decided to get loaded together. Like, really loaded. As in with a needle in the arm kind of loaded. We got a teener, and I made it up for us. The night went straight to hell from there. We started in on our weird accusations at each other. It was the same stupid fight we always had, except I was doing it all right back at him. Before this night, he had admitted to cheating not just the once, but also another time, with someone else. Another one-night stand, he said. By this time, I was insane with rage, grief, paranoia, bitterness, and even hatred. On this night, after we got high, I decided to try to trick him into admitting more things. I had a feeling that there must be more dirt for him to admit, and I wanted to hear everything. I wanted to know how much he hated me. I hated myself so much. I felt our whole relationship was nothing. It was built on nothing and remained worth nothing. I felt I deserved to be hurt anyway. He had never loved me, and I just wanted even more proof of that. I actually snapped that night. I started to hear words he wasn't saying and envisioned pictures in my head of things that weren't even happening. It was like a complete loss of reality. My mind stopped working right, and I had what I think is called paranoid psychosis. The sickness was far beyond what I'm capable of describing here. My thinking was totally beyond reality or shred of sanity. I actually thought I heard him admit to having sex with his boss's wife! I swear I thought I heard him say this. It was so real that I had to pack up all mine and Sunshine's things at five o'clock in the morning.

At six o'clock, I got Sunshine in the car to drive to Santa Barbara. I was committed to taking care of Rose, who was living at my mom's house at the time. My mom and Bruce were in Vegas for a few days. What was I thinking? I wasn't thinking. I guess I thought I could handle my dope. It had been a long time since I really could handle my dope, or even my sober mind. I was losing it big time.

I took Rose to church, and I sat outside in the car and waited in the parking lot. We went shopping. I was so lame I even shoplifted in front of my poor little thirteen-year-old daughter. I was so irresponsible. Rose was very easily influenced, and I was swearing and breaking laws. I'm embarrassed to admit these things. Instead of thinking about Rose or her best welfare, all I could think about was Jevon and all his shenanigans. After choking down some cheeseburgers, we went back to my mom's house and tried to turn in for the night. No sleep was to be had. I'd gotten too far off the ground to come down yet, and my psychosis started to come back. The thing about it was that the drug had never affected me this way before, so it felt totally real to me. All my thoughts felt rational, and I trusted myself because I'd never had a meltdown like this in my life. I hadn't used since I had been with Rose, but my high was getting weirder and weirder. By four o'clock in the morning, my brain was fried. Jevon and I were texting back and forth a little bit, but my brain was too confused to understand what he was saying. I had to ask Rose what she thought about the texts. Then, Jevon stopped returning my texts, and I had an overwhelming feeling that Jevon had killed himself. What's worse is I thought that his spirit was somehow communicating through Rose. I stopped being able to think normally about anything.

I was so seriously insane at this point that I felt I should keep Rose out of school and drive clear back to Santa Maria to check on Jevon. I really thought I would walk into the house and find him dead on the floor or hanging from something. Instead, what happened is I got into a car accident. I got into the wrong lane of a construction zone on the highway and didn't react fast enough when a steamroller backed into me. Then, afraid of getting in trouble I sped away and ended up in the center of the highway with a car that was smoking and looked ready to explode. My goose was cooked. Police got there soon, and what I figured was going to happen was that I would go straight to jail. They checked my license and talked to me for a while, and somehow, I pulled it off. They actually gave me and Rose a ride all the way to Santa Maria. I decided not to go by my house to check on Jevon, because things had gotten too far away from me. I was starting to realize my mind was not thinking right. I had too many crazy thoughts and had made too many stupid mistakes, and I needed to calm down. So we went to my dad's house.

Within a few hours, Aunt Carol and Uncle Frank were there to pick us up and take us back to Santa Barbara so I could keep taking care of Rose at my mom's house. Unfortunately, my high was still messing up my thinking, and I hadn't gotten enough sleep or food to ground myself. We never made it to my mom's. I ended up having even more crazy thoughts at my aunt's house and then split from there, taking Sunshine with me, leaving poor Rose behind taking a nap. For some reason, I was thinking that they were in on some crazy scheme with the police or something. Truthfully, I can't remember all the things I was thinking, but I know for certain my thoughts were all bad. From there, I went to my grandmother's house, where I had a major nose bleed and cried for an hour, worrying her nearly to death. Finally, I had a solution. I would call the same domestic-violence shelter I had stayed at before, when I was pregnant with Sunshine, and figure it out from there. I knew Jevon and I needed a break, and since he had sent me another text by that time, I knew he was okay. We just needed a break.

I did something that is really, really stupid to do when you've been on the verge of mental collapse after shooting crystal meth into your veins. I called the police. See, the police are the only ones who can refer a woman to the shelter since they have to determine the validity of an abusive situation. I couldn't just show up over there. Jevon and I had been in a big fight a day or two before that, so it wasn't a lie. I knew I needed space and time away for at least a little while. Thinking I was coherent enough to deal with this situation, I sat there and waited. Within twenty minutes or so, they came. There were two of them I think. One officer talked to me, and the other one talked to Sunshine. Before I knew it, I was in handcuffs. I was under arrest, they said, for an old warrant from 2009.

What I still can't understand to this day is why I was under arrest. What warrant? I had just been in an accident where they looked at my license and presumably ran my information. If there had really been a warrant, why would they not have arrested me earlier on in the day? Or how about during my police interviews after Halo died? It was bull, but when you are the one getting arrested, it doesn't matter what you say. I knew it made no sense, but it didn't matter. I was going to jail.

When they took me away, the worst part was the look on my little girl's face. It didn't matter that I'd spend time behind bars or that I had embarrassed myself. I hated that I had hurt and upset my grandmother. But it was what Sunshine was having to go through that was the worst. I asked if my grandma could watch her for the night. I wanted to know what they were planning on doing with Sunshine. I said there was family in town that could take Sunshine.

"You know we can't do that," the officer replied to me. At that moment, I had a bad feeling that she was going to become a ward of the state. The afternoon turned into evening as I got taken to the police station. The arresting officer on this case was one of the dirtiest cops I have ever met. On my police record, they must show that I have a child who is deceased because he accused me of murder on the way into the station. It wasn't just an insinuation. He actually accused me killing my own child. *Soft spot!* After two nights of no sleep and having eaten only one cheeseburger in so much time, I was finally starting to come to my senses just a little bit. The reality that was flooding in was very, very bad. Let's just say that it was the come-down from hell. *Oh my God*, I realized, *I've just lost everything I have from one high.* My car was wrecked and in a tow yard some place; I ruined things with my boyfriend; I said some incredibly disgusting and rude remarks to Jevon's boss about his wife. I also texted the wife some ugly and terrible things, possibly losing him his job. I pissed off everyone in my immediate family, I let down Rose big time, and worst of all I've probably lost Sunshine to the system. Who knows if I'd ever get her back! Suddenly I realized, everything that could have gone wrong had gone wrong, and it was all my own fault.

When I was taken in, they told me I had a choice. I could take a drug test, and no matter what the results were, I'd have no charges. (What I didn't really think of is that if I hadn't taken the test, I would have still had no charges. I had no drugs on me when I was arrested and hadn't done anything illegal.) Here's something else I've kicked myself for a hundred times. I took the test knowing I was still dirty and knowing the warrant was bogus. They would have had to release me the next day regardless. Why I peed in that cup is beyond me. But I did. The reason they wanted the test wasn't to charge me, but to have evidence as to why they weren't going to allow my child to be returned to me. I may not have had drugs or paraphernalia on me, but what I did have was a little over $2,000. It was money left over from a generous gift that my biological dad had given me back in September. By the time they "realized they made a mistake regarding the warrant" and released me the next day, two more bad things happened. They gave me back only $1,000, and I found out that Sunshine was gone, and there was nothing I could do about it. Apparently that nasty cop who arrested me "counted the money wrong," and kept $1,000 for himself. I could file a complaint, they said. But who was going to believe a drug addict against a cop?

I got a cab to my mother's house at that point, feeling utterly defeated and completely humiliated. I was angry at so many things gone wrong, but most of all, I was angry at myself. When I showed up at her house, she told me right away that they had offered to let her keep Sunshine, and she had refused. I felt the familiar sting of betrayal. She explained that she knew the people that had taken Sunshine in. They weren't close friends, but they knew each other somehow. *Whatever, she is with strangers. They are strangers to me.* My feelings went into a rage as I looked into my mother's eyes. What kind of a person lets her grandchild get put into foster care? It didn't matter to me that she was taking care of Rose at the time. Sunshine was a baby and needed someone she knows to stay in her life. She was my innocent little girl, and she was paying the price for my mistakes. She was lost and alone in a strange world with strangers. It must have been absolutely terrifying for her. Thinking about it now makes me feel sick to my stomach. My hands are shaking, and my heart aches for what she must have gone through.

The night was down the tubes. I told my mother I would never forgive her for turning away her own granddaughter. There was nothing I could do about it but feel mad. The next day, I went back up to my dad's house in Santa Maria. It took less than a day for me to contact Jevon and go back home.

The house was in shambles. It was an awful mess. I brought my clothes in but hadn't the strength or ability to put them away. All my things either went on the floor or stayed in the suitcase in the room. We ate a little bit, slept a little bit, and talked a little bit. The fight was mostly out of us, but he was looking at me funny, trying to figure out what the heck had just happened to our lives. This began a new chapter for us. Everything I had said in anger came back to bite me. During my high, I had told him that it was fine if he screwed his boss' wife, because I had been with his boss. I wanted to make him mad enough to admit something else. I had been so sure there was more for him to admit. This ended up being a huge mistake. It ended up being something he never really seemed to be able to let go of.

It was a hard and lonely time. Jevon and I hated each other more than ever, and when Jevon went to work, his days were filled with misery instead of the escape of busyness. At home, I was alone and had no purpose whatsoever in my life now that I had no babies to take care of. Finally, someone told me that I would need to make an appointment with Heather at Project PREMIE. Again. I made an appointment right away.

One thing that sticks out in my memory is that while I was trying to tell Heather what had happened, I was unable to articulate myself. All my thoughts and ideas were confused, and my words were muddled and didn't even make sense to me. My brain had stopped working, and apparently it hadn't started working again. I couldn't do anything but sit there pathetically and try to answer her questions with the shortest answers possible. Inside I felt like such a loser.

I would start attending the program as an outpatient, which meant showing up for random testing and group five days a week. Again. It was just like the last time, only more embarrassing. My life had ended since I'd gone to this place. Couldn't they see that? I'm sure Heather could see something majorly wrong had happened to me, but she had the common decency not to tell me I seemed to be ruined. Lots of ruined girls cross her path.

I became pregnant again. When I told Jevon that I was pregnant, he laid down on the kitchen floor with a look of horror on his face. It was not the reaction I had anticipated. The pregnancy lasted about five weeks. My cramps came on hard, and I went to the emergency room so that they could tell me everything was going to be okay. That was not the answer I got. When I miscarried, it was very painful physically and emotionally—not just because it was another death of a baby, but because Jevon was totally disconnected from me, and I felt so very alone. When the blood clots came out, I was in the shower. I couldn't just flush it down the toilet or put it in the trash can. I had to hold it in my hands, crying as the hot water beat down on my back. Blood mixed with the water and went down the drain, but I had a clump in my hands, and I was going to take it outside in the dark of the night and bury it in the grass. I knew it was a weird thing to do, but it was what I felt I had to do at the time. There was very little ceremony, but it was good to know that the life that had lived was not going to go into a garbage heap or sewer some place.

It didn't take long before I realized I had a chance to get Sunshine back, but it would take a long time and a lot of work. I was ready to put in the work. No matter how depressed I felt or how shattered my ego was, I was up for the challenge. In my mind, there was no other option. There could be no other way. It was like I had to get Sunshine back or kill myself, because there would be no life for me to live without her.

So the journey to redemption began.

It didn't take long for everyone involved in my case to recommend to the judge that I needed to be an inpatient in rehab. It was not what I wanted to hear. I was addicted as much to Jevon, our fights, and our dysfunction as I had been to the drugs. Well, not quite that much, but almost. I felt we had been through hell. Even if we were continuing to put ourselves through hell, it was important that we got through it together. Our fights weren't as bad as they had been when we were getting high, but they were still pretty bad. There was hitting, chasing, bruises, bites, and endless yelling and mean words. Our life together had deteriorated to the point that I didn't know how to fix it. What I thought would fix it was to have another baby. Because if I got pregnant, it would take away the pain that I had in my heart from missing Halo. I thought I could fix it all with another pregnancy. That was the best plan I could come up with. It's sad, I know. I just didn't get it. I was sick in my heart and sick in my mind.

Making me be a resident in program was going to totally ruin my plans, but there was no way around it. In order to get Sunshine back, it was the sacrifice I had to make. Finally, we had another fight at home bad enough to make me realize a new truth. Moving into that place was not only the one way to get my daughter back, it was the only way to get my life back. We weren't living anymore. We were barely surviving.

My caseworker told me that because of the domestic violence, I would most likely not be able to come back home after my case closed, so I hastily made a decision to get married. Sure, it wasn't the best time, but I knew that Jevon and I were going to get through this together, eventually. I believed in him and I believed in us. So we drove to Las Vegas on December 18 and got married. When we got back, I found out that I was pregnant, again! Hey, maybe life was looking up. We weren't fighting too much, as we were living each day as though it was our last one together. The future was wide open but scary, and all we had was the present.

On January 3, I moved into the house. It was one of the scariest and saddest days of my life. I felt overwhelmed, terrified, beat up, and utterly alone. I went in with a bad attitude, telling myself every step of the way that it didn't matter if people liked me. I didn't care to make friends. I dressed in nothing but all black clothes because it was what I felt I needed to do to mourn my Halo. Inside me was a grief so wide and deep that I felt I needed to outwardly show my desolation. Not that anyone cared or saw anything but a drug addict in me. I allowed very few people into my world to share my real life or my real feelings, let alone the reason for my black wardrobe. Each hour that passed in those first few weeks was an eternity. My roommate snored louder than most men I've heard, and my nights were sleepless. I went out to the couch to try to get a little sleep and got in trouble for that. Adding to my misery, my roommate had just had a new baby. He was a beautiful little boy, but like all babies do, he cried. His cries tore my spirit in half. His presence did nothing but make me think even more about losing my darling girl, and I felt a deep need to run away. There was nothing I could do to get away from the feeling of needing to get away from my room, my roommate, and my roommate's baby. After trying to move rooms, and being turned down, I finally broke down in my drug counselor's office saying that there was no way I could continue to tolerate being in the room where I had been placed.

That's where I pick up now, in my new room. I am upstairs in a room with a new roommate. She is the scariest girl who lives here. But I count my lucky stars to be in her room. She is at least ten years younger than I am. She has a little boy who is two, and another boy on the way. I'm glad for the move but feeling ungrateful at the moment. Today, I got a "check." Getting a check means that your get free time taken away. For the first thirty days there is no free time at all, so any checks that we get have to be taken off of the free time we are waiting for. So I'm starting off in the hole. Reasons a person can get a check are: not doing chores, not being on time, not cooking the right dinner, not making it to group in the appropriate clothes, not being punctual, not being appropriate at the meetings we go to, etc. There are many, many ways a woman can get a check, but the reason I've gotten one is because while I was out this afternoon, the girls dirtied the house to the point that everyone who lives here got a check. Ooh, it's frustrating! On top of that, I went to my appointment at Child Welfare Services today and met with my worker, and that didn't go as well as I had hoped it would. Next, I went to the doctor to get my first ultrasound, and the doctor told me that I will most likely lose this pregnancy too. "There is about an 80 percent chance that it's not a good pregnancy" was exactly what he said. Screw him. I hate him now. He doesn't know anything.

To top off my day, we are supposed to go eat hot dogs with the Sheriff's Treatment Program people. At the doctor's office, I'd asked Jevon if he wanted to eat hot dogs with us. Free food is good, and I usually like being around him these days. He came, but he reeked like alcohol, which was a total downer, not to mention embarrassing. Today is just not my day. One of my biggest problems is wishing I could have a drink, and he knows that. Then he started in on the phone. He has my phone, since I'm not allowed a cell phone where I am. All he wanted to talk about was whose number this is, or what this or that voicemail is about. I did my best to explain and even called my voicemail on speaker to let us both hear the messages out loud together. After all, I have nothing to hide. Still, it wasn't enough. He wanted to listen to a message that was nothing but a couple of seconds of static over and over. Then he wanted to hear the envelope information to try to figure out who it was. Most likely, it was a wrong number, but to him it was some kind of "evidence." It was also, apparently, reason to treat me badly and ruin what little time we had together.

Here I am in virtual lockdown. I have no free time to do anything I want to do, I get very little sleep and can't enjoy anything in my life right now. And all he wants to do is *this*. Meanwhile, he is at home, doing whatever he feels like, drinking and God knows what else, and he wants to hassle *me*. The nerve. To make matters worse, he is acting mad at me because a cop is calling him to set up an interview.

Before I came into the program, a cop came by our house to follow up on the domestic-violence incident that I had mentioned to the arresting officers before. Yes, there was a fight. There were many fights, as I have said. But when that cop came over, I told him it was just something I said because I needed a place to stay. I even went so far as to say that I made the whole thing up and that I was on drugs and mad and didn't know what I was talking about. The cop was at the doorway of our house for about five minutes, no longer than ten. When I told Jevon what I had done and how I had gotten him off the hook, he got upset with me. He actually accused me of giving this cop some kind of sexual favor in return for his charges being dropped. That was ridiculous, of course, as there never were charges against him. Anyway, Jevon took it all wrong. He made my attempt at being a good wife, trying to get him out of trouble, look whorish and cheap.

Back to my evening of cold hot dogs and never-ending questions. He decides, of all the times, to bring this up again. This may be the first time I'm writing about this cop issue, but I will tell you what.

It has been beat into the ground for me. We've had hours and hours of wasted time explaining the same conversation that I had with that cop. The thing he kept going back to is how I managed to "get him off the hook." It is so irritating and frustrating to answer the same questions over and over and never be believed. The end-all is being called a whore about it, especially by a cheater. Now I'm mad. The more I think about it, the madder I get. I don't want to do any of my chores tonight. I had been feeling so much better lately, maybe it was time for me to have a down day. My feelings fluctuate pretty often between the detoxing, new surroundings, new routine, less sleep, and hormones. Guess it is okay to feel bad, get mad, and let it all get to me sometimes.

That last journal entry was pretty nasty. I want to try to stay away from trash-talking or letting myself feel too sorry for myself. Jevon and I have certainly had our times of trouble, and I've gotten burned out on him. If I want to look at things in a negative light and let him get under my skin, it's easy. It's also important to look at the bright side. He is holding down the fort. He is going to Alcoholics Anonymous meetings and Narcotics Anonymous meetings when he can. He is providing me with a place to come home to. He is there for me when I want to call him, and he brings me things whenever I ask. Most women in this place don't have a man who is there for them at all. What I should be doing is seeing the proverbial glass as half-full instead of half-empty. There is always something to be thankful for, and I want to try to find it.

When Jevon goes to the meetings, he doesn't just sit there quietly anymore. He has started to open up and make friends in the rooms. A lot of men like him, and I can see why. He shares from the heart and has a directness and honesty about him that most people can respect. He looks you right in the eye when speaking and tends to keep his voice low and quiet enough that people find themselves trying to listen instead of being forced to listen. I like sitting next to him and hearing him share. I also like to see people's reactions to him after he talks. A lot of times men will approach him afterward and introduce themselves. Quite often, the things he shares are things he never talks about at home. For instance, at home, he rarely ever brings up Halo. But in the meetings, he brings her up a lot, which makes me realize he does still think about her. In my heart, I know he must, but when I'm the only one talking about her and arranging her birthday or death-day events, I think I'm the only one grieving or remembering her. Not so. It's good to feel we have this in common. In a sadness this vast and deep, it helps me to know that my memories of her are shared. It's also comforting to know that we still share something so sacred together.

I'm struggling now because I'm sure that there is no hope for this little life growing inside me. The pregnancy is not developing as it should be. It has been almost twelve weeks now. I'm scared because I'm bleeding now, and I know that things aren't right. The blood started out dark brown and spotty at first and then got heavier. I went to the doctor for the second ultrasound, and he said the baby has not grown. He couldn't find a heartbeat. Now the blood is coming out bright red, and I am hurting. I've had five miscarriages in my life. This will be the sixth. I know that this isn't over yet, especially given how far along I am. Hopefully this baby will come out on its own; otherwise I will have to have an operation called a D&C, which is where they go inside and pull the baby out by force. I am hoping I won't have to go through that. Either way, I am having to trust that God has this situation in His control and that no matter what happens, He will get me through. My own strength is failing. I have so little left.

My visits with Sunshine are three times a week. I go to Santa Barbara on the Greyhound bus, which is very unpredictable and difficult. Child Welfare Services pays for my tickets, but what they can't do is make sure that the busses are on time. More than once, the bus got to Santa Barbara so late that I had to stay there and wait for the last bus to bring me right back to Santa Maria without even seeing Sunshine. It takes a whole different bus forty-five extra minutes to go up State Street to the street where Sunshine's school is; then I have to walk about fifteen minutes up a hill to get to her. If the bus is too late, there is no point in trying to get to her because if I miss the last bus coming back home, I'll be stuck in Santa Barbara all night. And I can't just not go back to program. I'd get kicked out or worse. Better to disappoint my girl in the short-term and not the long-term. The problem is I hate to disappoint her at all. It is the worst feeling to know that she is there, waiting on me, and I've failed her, again. This has happened three times now, and it kills me to think of it happening again.

I had to do the D&C. Somewhere in the back of my mind, I thought that when they gave me the anesthesia, I would get knocked out and go to the place where Halo lives. I was wrong. When I woke up, I felt stripped of everything left inside me. My body had been emptied out, and even if what they took from me was lifeless, it was my baby. When I opened my eyes on the table, I cried inconsolably. I sobbed loudly and embarrassed myself. My heart is broken, and my body aches. One of the worst parts of this day was having to come back to the recovery home. This is not where I belong. I want to be home in my own bed. I want to be in complete silence, not here, with the constant sound of children running around, none of whom are mine. I want to be away from this incessant madness. I need to be away from it more than I need food or water right now. And yet, here I am. I told my Child Welfare worker that I can't do this anymore. We talked on the phone earlier. Her response was, "Just hang in there for the night, and I will come and talk to you tomorrow." It was good advice. If I can get through this night, I can get through it all. Period. I'm stuck with the hardest chore this week. I'm on "kitchen and dining room floors," which means sweeping and mopping. It was never as hard as it was tonight. There was a lump in my throat the whole time, and I couldn't even stand up straight. I shuffled through it and felt incredibly sorry for myself. Nobody asked how I was or offered to help me.

I just want to have another baby. Clearly, this isn't the right time, but when are we ever really ready to have kids? I know from the past that even if you think it isn't the best time, the baby will come along and make it the right time. I am asking God for a baby. On the bus ride to Santa Barbara, I see cows in the fields with their babies. I envy those cows the simple act of being able to have a baby. How pitiful to be jealous of cows. I have said a million prayers and I know He hears me. It's only a matter of timing. It simply isn't up to me, and I have to learn to let go, trust God, and appreciate what I have today. I think I can do this.

As the month comes to a close, I find myself feeling a little bit better. The first month was by far the hardest. With no free time, it's hard to be constantly surrounded by women who are as moody and irritable as I am. Few of us ever smile for the sake of smiling. Everyone snaps at each other, gossips about each other, finds every excuse to pick a fight or hold a grudge. Instead of risking saying the wrong thing, I find it's smarter to keep my mouth shut. Better to keep my nose in a book than in someone else's business. My favorite thing to do is read, so I always have a book with me wherever I go. While it was hard to get into a routine here, I have finally got it down.

This is my last weekend on restriction. All I have to do is get my rent paid, and I can go home next weekend. I may have to ask my dad for money. The first two weekends off restriction, we get to have one day away. After that, we get two days, but we still have to be here overnight. Back Saturday night at nine, then leave the next morning after chores are done at nine. Eventually I will be allowed one overnight at home a month. I can't wait!

Jevon bought groceries. I gave him a list of the things I'd need to make spaghetti, and he went and bought everything. We each make dinner once a week here. Sunday is my day, and he went to the store for me to get everything we need. I saved some leftovers for him. Hopefully he will go to a meeting tonight, and I can give them to him.

If I had one wish, it would be that I wasn't a drug addict. I want that above all else, even winning the lottery, because it would reverse every failure I can't undo. Behind every act of selfishness that made it hard to look in the mirror, there lies my addiction.

Sunshine is coming to visit me! I get to put her to sleep and read to her and cuddle her! I am thrilled! It's going to be so amazing to be able to spend time with her and not have to turn around and walk down the hill, get on two busses, and come back to this place alone. Oh, I can't wait!

I saw my ex-drug dealer the other day. He was driving. Kinda awkward, but not too big of a deal. What was really bad was how I felt about seeing him. Inside I was thinking, *Just one more time!* How can I be this way? I know I don't want to use, but I feel the need to do it anyway. The other night, we watched *Intervention* together, and there was a girl who was totally miserable and disgusting. She was out of her freaking mind. They showed her fixing up her dope, putting the needle in her arm, and it was sickening. So why did I want to get high so bad when I saw it? It was so bad, in fact, that I cried myself to sleep afterward. I needed the drugs so desperately that all I could do was cry about it. The only thing that helped was praying. I just kept saying the same simple prayer over and over. *Please God, take it away from me. Please God, make it stop.*

Being in program means being all over the place emotionally. After tuning out some of my feelings on drugs for a while, they came rushing back in, magnified. The feelings aren't all bad though. This will be my first full weekend back home. I should be excited, but I'm worried. Jevon says he found some needles in the house. I always thought we were very careful about disposing of needles. I've always been so worried about having that stuff in the house that

I threw them away all the time. Maybe we really did misplace some, but I don't think so. Who knows, but one thing I know for sure is that I would never hide a bag of needles in his son's room, and that is where he is saying he found them. When he confronted me about this, he acted like it was something I had done. It's so obvious to me that it was just another one of his things he did while high that he can't remember. I wish I could be like that! It would be so great to zone out and totally have no idea of all the dumb things I've done while loaded. No such luck. Jevon, on the other hand, doesn't remember most of it. That's his story anyway. I should be so lucky to forget. What this means to me is that he just outed himself and has done drugs behind my back. I guess it doesn't really matter since I've done plenty of drugs behind his back. That's been the only secret I've had over the years. It's never been all the devious and slutty things he has accused me of—just drugs, always only the stupid frigging drugs. Maybe I should call him out, but I probably won't. The thing that irritates me about using drugs behind my back is the hypocrisy. He used to get so mad at me when I got high without him, or in secret, that he used it as an excuse to cheat on me. Now I'm supposed to just accept it because the roles are reversed. Kind of like if he cheats on me, I am supposed to forgive and forget. If I cheat on him, he would never be able to forgive me. I'm making a big deal out of this, and it is silly because it shouldn't be a big deal. We are both clean now, and we are both trying. Live and let live. Focus on today. Be responsible for myself. Clean up my own side of the street. I listen to and repeat a hundred one-liners at group and during the meetings I attend. They are a lot easier said than done.

Tonight was really fun. We broke rules together. Not any big rules. Nothing that would compromise my Sunshine. It was just a little rule that was meant to be broken. Now we all have a little secret to share about going outside the front door after lights out and having a cigarette together. I'm starting to like my house mates. They are all so unique and funny in their own ways that it wouldn't be as cool or entertaining if even one of them wasn't here. The only problem I've had is with my new roommate, Bertha. She just moved into my room and already she is starting problems. I found a bag of dope on the floor in my room while she was out, and I flushed it down the toilet. It wasn't an easy decision, but it was the best thing to do. After that happened, I pulled her aside and told her that if I found drugs in our room again, I would tell staff, but that I was handling it my own way the first time. Why would anyone want to bring drugs in this place? What a bust. Bertha is lucky, though, because her son isn't in the system. Her mom took her son for her, so if she screws up, she just goes to jail, and nothing bad will happen to her son. Well, nothing but being let down. But he won't be taken away from her. She is one of the lucky ones. It makes me resent her because even though she is so lucky, she doesn't appreciate it. Most of the girls in here are like me. Their kids are in the system, being taken care of by strangers. Most of these girls have parents who can't qualify to be temporary foster parents because they have bad records of their own. It's so sad, generation after generation … drugs, violence, abuse, and brokenness.

Next time I ovulate is March 19. That's the Monday after next weekend. Maybe I can go home and try to get pregnant on that day. Next weekend I'll be with Sunshine. She'll be here from Thursday the fifteenth through Saturday the seventeenth. Her birthday is on Sunday the eighteenth. I guess I should just feel happy that I get to have a birthday party with her, even if I don't get to spend her actual birthday with her. I want my baby back now, not later. Having her a little bit at a time is okay, but it is terrible to give her back. It's painful for me, and I know it is probably even more painful for her. I feel as though I deserve to go through the pain. I'm the one who got high. She doesn't deserve any of it, though! She is so sweet and innocent. The guilt I feel is like a hand strangling my neck and a huge weight on my chest. It makes me feel like I weigh a thousand pounds, and everything I do takes way too much effort.

I have a lot of workers to kiss up to and a lot of appointments to get to, on time every time. There's the Child Welfare Services worker, the children's therapist, there is a CASA (court-appointed special advocate) worker, my couple's therapist, my individual therapist, Sunshine's attorney, and the judge I see in court. In addition, there are all the staff members here. We have a director, three group leaders, an on-site house mom, a daycare person, and a transport person. There are also all the staff members at Sunshine's school who are mandated reporters. They all think I am a bad mother; otherwise I wouldn't be in this situation. They watch every move I make and listen to every word I say. The foster mom is the woman who runs the school that Sunshine goes to. She is both kind and intimidating at the same time. It's hard being under a microscope constantly. It's so much freaking pressure! If you ask me, no one should ever have to be on best behavior for this many people constantly for this long. My little girls are truly the only ones I would do this for.

Journaling has been taking a lot of emotional and mental energy. Sometimes when I get done writing, I feel worse instead of better. Sometimes when I go to bed at night, my only prayer is "help me, God, I am in despair." I've been praying for mercy. Somewhere inside me, I know that this path is the one I chose, and this is something I must conquer. I also don't think I knew how horrible and impossible it would feel to get to the other side of it. I need relief; I need to be able to breathe again.

While writing this, I am reflecting. I do experience joy. Every single day there is a reason to smile. Even if it is laughing about an obnoxious thing one of the girls said, or smiling because the sky is clear while I am having my morning cigarette. Sometimes a dove will land on the phone wire, and I think maybe Halo is sending me a sign, which brings me a small comfort. There is always beauty waiting to be noticed. God's loving pull is always there throughout this vast universe. Look, there He is, even in the tiniest details. The breeze blows, the leaves rustle, the coffee tastes good.

I'm happy today. I can't really name a specific reason why. For three days I've been crying a lot. Happy tears. Something is happening inside of me that I don't understand. I will try to explain it. My heart feels full of love and gratitude, and my mind is less restless. I can feel a calm in my soul that feels subtle yet profound. My grief doesn't hurt as badly. It has become bearable. Once more, I am capable of seeing the world around me as a place of wonder and beauty. My life hasn't changed. I'm still in a recovery home, living with a bunch of loud and moody females. I still have a CWS case. I still have one daughter in foster care, one daughter I haven't seen in years, another daughter who is troubled, and another in the ground. I have let them down. But instead of this failure being what defines me, it is the fact that I am still standing that I want to focus on. Hey, I'm not done yet! Maybe this is one of the greatest opportunities of my life, because I can finally show myself what I'm made of! When I get through this and get my daughter back, I will know who I am. I want to make myself change. I want to change how I talk, how I think, and how I treat myself and others. I pray all the time that I can be a good mommy. Maybe this is life's way of giving me the chance to prove that I am. If I get through this, I will be a good mother. I will be someone my kids can depend on and look up to. It's not going to be about how I got here, but how I picked myself up and made it through! I will regain my dignity. I will get Sunshine home and never let her go. I will get close to Rose again and apologize for letting her down. Maybe even someday, I can see Payton again. It's never too late. I met my bio mom when I was eighteen, and that wasn't too late. It isn't over for me at all. I will never give up. I will never stop trying. I am seeing the future and for the first time in forever, it looks bright! Only God is able to orchestrate a symphony of redemption so complex and perfect. It is exactly what I needed to get my *self* back. I've given up way too easy in my battles in life so far. I know in my heart that I should have never let Walter win the fight for Payton, but I didn't believe in myself enough to fight him. I gave up way too easily in my battle with drugs. I was totally prepared to die with a needle in my arm, hoping to never have to live a sober day of life again. Looking back over the years, I can see time and time again when I have allowed my life to run me and never stood up to do anything about it. It looks like my life has presented me a set of circumstances that I must fight to overcome. I must succeed. I can and I will! There is no other way.

When Halo died, I asked Auntie Carol for some words of advice. I knew she had gone through everything I was going through, and that she would know exactly what to say. Here's what she told me:

"It is what it is," and "the sun will come out tomorrow." I could totally understand "it is what it is." I liked that one. But the sun will what? Oh, come on, isn't that from *Annie*? I didn't like it. I may have even rolled my eyes. If I didn't, then I certainly rolled my eyes inwardly. For the first time, though, I'm starting to understand what she meant. The sun is coming out. The sun will rise, no matter what I do. It did it today, and it will do it again tomorrow. Regardless of whether I was capable of opening my eyes to notice, the sun certainly has risen. The world doesn't stop, though it feels like it should when a child dies. We can't take a break when we make an utter disaster out of our lives. The sun is shining through the fog I have lived in for too long. I will point my face toward the warmth and light and appreciate today.

Tonight we're watching *American Idol*. We can always agree to put this on the TV. We like Phillip Phillips. This isn't home, but that's okay. This is where I have to be, so I may as well try to enjoy it. When I get home, I will be a better wife, mother, and human being in the world. It is what it is, right? So it must be okay. I'm not hating it nearly as much as I did in the beginning. It's not really all that bad here. There is always something to like, if I want to see it. Let me think … I like that I'm finally starting to surrender. I like that even though I am mad at myself, I can still see the good inside me too. I'm glad for my many imperfections, because they inspire me to continue to grow. I appreciate the food pantry where we get free food for this place. I'm grateful that my girls still love and believe in me, despite the many reasons not to. I'm grateful for my marriage. I'm grateful I have a place to go home to. I'm grateful for God. It is because of His quiet voice inside my heart that I am able to see any positive about my life at all.

God says that if I ask, He will answer. Maybe I ask the wrong questions. Maybe I am focusing on the wrong problems. Maybe if I get underneath the drug, there is a root to the problem and I can actually recover not just from the drug addiction, but also from my need to feel different.

When I went to the Santa Barbara Rape Crisis Center, I learned that I am not a victim, I am a survivor. As it turns out, I am a survivor of a lot of things. Some things were out of my control, but most things are consequences of choices I made. These days, I'm dealing mostly with things I can't blame anyone for but myself. How do I make peace with these things? How do I put to rest the other things that were not my fault? I've gone through my life thinking the past is in the past, and there isn't anything I can do about it, so I may as well stop thinking about it. I've tried very hard to act like none of it is a big deal, to just get on with it, as my mom would say. But I'm haunted. This stuff is still taking over, and the worst thing is I'm making even more wreckage as a result of not dealing with the old stuff. I want to move forward, and I want to finally do it the right way. I need to heal.

I feel sick today, like sick in the head. I went to a meeting tonight and held a little baby girl. She was feverish and fussy, but I was able to get her to sleep. She is beautiful, but she is not my baby. My thoughts were disturbing. As I looked at her, I could see her pulse as her soft spot moved up and down on the crown of her head. I was reminded of the mortality of being human.

My thoughts drifted to the reality of what my daughter looks like now. Probably, by this time, she has no skin left on her face. Perhaps her tiny little perfect hand reveals the fragile bones beneath. These thoughts are repulsive to me, but they come into my mind. My face must look ugly as I contemplate what is left of my little girl. Is my smile a mask for the ugliness that goes on inside? Or is the sad and mournful face a mask for the person underneath even that?

When the baby's dad came back to take her from me, my immediate feeling was wanting to get loaded. Looking down at my empty arms, I saw them as useless. I could feel the hot space left behind where she was. I looked down at my arms, the plump veins pumping underneath the scarred skin. I'm sure all my veins work again by now. Even the one I used the most, the one tough with scar tissue. The left one is my go-to. I know I could jam a needle in that one, especially a brand new needle. Oh, what a horrifying, selfish and disgusting fantasy. When will I stop being this way?

All I could do with that, after obsessing for a while, is share my thoughts in the meeting. To avoid pity or worry, I left out the morbid thoughts and simply expressed my craving. I want to feel the flesh give way and succumb to the needle. I want to feel the immediate rush as the drugs hit my brain. I want my lungs to tighten up, and I want my vision to go wrong. I want my skin to get goosebumps and I want to forget. I want to get so sick and stupid that I forget. Forget everything forever. I want everything to stop making sense and to feel warm and away from myself. Just for a minute. But I won't. *Just for today,* I tell myself, *I won't. Deal with tomorrow when that comes. God help me.*

I imagine this life. My recovery, my CWS case, where I live, and all these other women I live with. I see my beautiful Sunshine's little face every time I say good-bye to her. I know there is absolutely no way I can allow myself these thoughts. I can't play out the fantasy and remember the high. Instead, I have to see the tears running down Sunshine's face, holding onto my sweatshirt, being forced to turn and walk away from her, leaving her with her foster mother or some teacher at her school. If I try hard enough, I can feel her hot little face, smell her hair, feel the snot and tears on my skin. I must stop myself from thinking about the drug. I must force myself to stop and think of her. Only her.

I'm getting ready to take a two-day weekend. I've got my meeting card filled out, my dinners were right, I bought meat for the house, I cleaned my room, I did my extra cleaning chores on Wednesday, I haven't broken any rules, and I've made all my groups, meetings, and tests on time. Yay me!

I get to have Sunshine this week. Yes, the whole week. I'm really starting to see the results of all the work I've put in. Now, instead of seeing my caseworker every week, it is twice a month. Same with court, twice a month. Having her for that long is really great. I love turning in early with her and cuddling in our tiny little bed. There is a trundle under us, but I love the cuddle time. We really do have fun together. Even in this place, we manage to have a great time.

I really wish staff wouldn't hang out in this house so much. I'd love to have a snack before dinner. I feel like such a child. Guess that is what happens when one makes a mess out of her life this much. If I can't be a person who can handle making decisions for myself, then I don't get to have the freedom to make any choices in life at all. Not even the decision to have a snack before dinner. Consequences are such a drag. It would be nice if they could focus on big-picture stuff and not nitpick so many little things.

I am looking forward to going home this weekend. At home, I can go to bed and stay in bed. I don't have to be constantly monitored. I may get interrogated, but at least I can talk back without getting my visit with Sunshine taken away. I can go to bed when I want, read when I want, shower as long as I want. I can smoke late or use swear words or have a snack when I feel like I want one.

The smell of dinner is wafting throughout the whole house. It's pork scalding in Crisco. *Gross.* The girls are all in the front room, because nobody is allowed in the kitchen when one of us is cooking. So many rules. Anyway, I can hear the kids outside screaming and laughing while their mothers are in group. Group gets out at 4:30 p.m. and that's when dinner has to be ready. Hopefully the cook is making rice or bread too. Some of these women really can't cook to save their lives. I'm talking about burned Tuna Helper for dinner. *Sigh* ... This is only temporary. I just have to keep remembering, it is only for a little while longer.

Finally I think I may be getting to a point of acceptance about not getting pregnant. I know that I will have another child. I've asked God for this, and I know that I will eventually have a baby. It just isn't happening now. It isn't going to be according to my timing. It is obviously not in my control.

Last month I really thought I was pregnant. I thought it so much that I even gave myself morning sickness, which just turned out to be crazy sickness. Seriously, I even threw up about it. It was so awesome to throw up until I took the test and it was negative, and I realized I was just creating the whole thing inside myself because I wanted it so badly. That's sad, so sad that it made me really mad. Boy was I mad! I was so mad that I waved my fist in the air at God and stomped my foot. I even missed church, all because I wanted something now and not later. I realize I can either live my life in a state of expectation and anger, or I can live in acceptance while I wait. It makes more sense to wait and learn patience while my life changes for the better.

Jevon fixed my car. It was a relatively inexpensive fix. It's so great to have a car again! It's parked here at program now, and I get to drive myself and other girls to meetings. Best of all, I get to go pick up Sunshine in Santa Barbara. I had her for a whole week last time, and now I get to have her for an extended weekend. Yay, I'm so excited! Everyone on staff says this is a good sign, because people are trusting me more and more, but they also say that I won't be able to get her back completely until I get out of here and go back home. It's hard not to get my hopes up. I just want this to be over already. She is all I think about, all the time, every day. Instead of guilt-ridden thoughts bringing me misery, I'm thinking about the positive and how things are changing all the time to build a brighter future for us both.

Still, when I take her back, I go right back to feeling down in the dumps. That's all normal I'm sure. We all go through it. I can see it on other girls' faces in the house or in group when they talk about their kids. It's awful. Things are changing though, and I try to focus on that. Court is now only once every three weeks, and I see my CWS worker only once a month. We've stopped doing family therapy in Santa Barbara, and my individual therapist and I only meet twice a month. She's my favorite. My couple's therapist is the absolute worst. I dread having to see her. We go twice a month to that too, but it feels like far too often.

With all my appointments slowing down, I have a little more free time to read or relax, which is nice. Time alone during the day is good, because sometimes I can get a little peace and quiet, which I've missed since I have been here. I wonder if Sunshine knows how much I've changed. I wonder if she realizes that she has been the reason for my change. I hope that someday she will realize how important she is to me and the great freedom from drugs she has helped give me. I hope that someday she will know how deep and profound my love for her is. I hope she will always know how special she is. She has been the catalyst that I needed to get my life back to where I wanted it to be. It's true that if people give up drugs, they do it for themselves. But in my case, I needed to love her enough to quit before I had the strength to do it for myself. She is my hope, my future, my inspiration. She is a total love. She is beautiful inside and out. Without her, I would be utterly lost. I would have given up on myself and everything else had it not been for her sweet little everything. She is the rainbow at the end of a storm, the dawn at the end of a dark night. I'm so lucky to have her to look forward to.

My moods are still all over the place. How can I be at peace with all things in the universe one day and then seriously want to kick somebody's butt the next? What is really going on? I think maybe I'm still madder at myself than at anybody else. I really do still feel angry at myself sometimes because, yes, things are changing, but I want them to change faster. I need to get out of here so bad! These girls can be so irritating sometimes. It's probably mean, but I admit I do judge them. I can't stand when I see girls hit or be mean to their kids. After everything they've put their kids through, some think it is acceptable to hit them too. It takes a lot of nerve to do that in front of other people. Imagine what they do behind closed doors. I'm probably being negative. I know I'm just grouchy right now. I would rather drive myself off the San Marcos Bridge than ever come back here. I. Will. Never. Let. This. Happen. Again. I just have to keep hanging on and count the days. I've got sixty days left after today. I can and I will finish this thing. Nobody is going to make me fail but myself. I can do this.

Sometimes I feel like I have set out to swim across an ocean. I've been swimming for months now, and I'm past the halfway point. If I turn around, it will take longer to get home than to keep going, so I must keep going. But I am wiped out, spiritually, physically, emotionally, mentally. I want to give up, but I can't because I know I will die. Am I just treading water? Am I making progress? I must be, because the sun keeps coming up every day, and I haven't failed yet, despite my own flailing and fear of drowning. I am going to keep on going. One of these days, I will feel the stability of land again under my feet.

Jevon and I seem to be drifting together again. The trust may not completely be there, but I feel that it could be. It seems like we are working toward that. I feel connected to him again, and I feel like it is more beautiful and meaningful than it was in the past. He has let up on me about the past, and I don't bring it up either. I don't ask questions about his past things or throw them in his face. I really want to move forward. If we can get through this, I will know we really have something special. In fact, I realized something about being unconditional. How do people ever know that what they have is truly unconditional unless it has been tested and ended up proven to be so? I have high hopes, and I'm not giving up on him. Until recently, I've had a secret thought in my mind that told me I would get loaded again when I get out of here. Lately, though, I am starting to see a future without drugs in it. I am actually realizing how good a real life can be. I am hoping that this life and future will include Jevon in it. It will really be something incredible if we can pull through this together and be committed to something better, together. It usually doesn't happen with people. In here, I see couples all the time who want to be together, but who are unable to make the decision to be clean at the same time. There is no way a relationship can work when one person is using and the other isn't. It is simply impossible. When a person is clean, everything changes—from how you spend your time to how you spend your money; what you think about, your focus, your friends, your spirituality, attitude, appetite, and hobbies. And if one person is ready and the other isn't, it isn't realistic to ask the other to quit and expect them to be able to do so. It is a very personal choice that nobody can make for you. Hopefully, we are both at that crucial place individually, and are making the choice separately; then we can come together and make a better life for ourselves as a family. It is an exciting thought, because when one person makes the choice to get clean, it is a miracle; when two people do it, it is another. But if two people do it at the same time, well, I don't know what that is. Amazing. Unheard of. It's a lot to wish for, and for now, all I can do is focus on what I am doing, and when I get home, we can focus on what we are doing together.

I'm feeling pretty lucky. Sometimes in group, I hear other women's stories, and realize that my story isn't really so bad. See, it may have begun badly, but it is all turning around. I felt really bad when I first came here, but in the last few months, changes have been happening so often that I really feel things are moving along. Sure, some days are still bad, as I have expressed, but the big picture is getting brighter all the time. There's one girl who is missing teeth in the front and has a crazy two-tone hairdo. She lost her kids, and she thinks they may never let her have them again. There was more than just drug abuse; there were other kinds of abuse. She has no idea who they are with, and there is a huge probability they will grow up never remembering her. There's another girl who used during her pregnancy and tested dirty at the hospital when her baby was born. She never even got to hold her child. They took him immediately. There is no hope or light in some of the eyes of the women in here. It breaks my heart to think about what they are going through. Some of the other women here have no safe drug-free environment to go home to. Their families or husbands or boyfriends are still high. Or they were homeless. Or since they came in they have lost everything. So after this is all over with, they still have nowhere to go except the transitional shelter. That would be so hard. I am endlessly grateful I don't have to do that. There is always a reason to feel lucky. Right now, I can definitely see mine.

Every week, things get better for me. I smile and feel more outgoing. My laughter comes easier. I know that my life is starting to put itself back together and that all the treacherous hard work is paying off. All my despair, loneliness, and heartache has been worth it.

It's Thursday. I like Thursdays because the hard work of Wednesday's extra chores are over, as is the bulk of the week. I even get to go and spend a couple of hours at home on Thursdays. Free time is from 2:30 to 4:30. I like to go home and shower there. It's so nice to be able to take my time and use my razor and not have to walk the hallway in my pajamas, carrying my towel and soap and all that. I love the quiet of my time at home. Usually, Jevon is still working, so it is my own private time to just relax and enjoy the silence. I don't even turn the TV on. I get to just *be*.

Today I worked steps four and five. It took me a month to get step four together because that's all about writing down your resentments. Getting together with my sponsor and completing steps four and five took a couple of hours. It wasn't nearly as bad as it was cracked up to be. I've seen girls totally come undone after doing it. I feel much better. I even feel physically lighter than before. It was good. Maybe I am beginning to work through some of that old stuff I have been wanting to deal with. It's weird how much I dragged my heels to do this. It didn't actually take a month to write down my step four stuff. It took a month for me to overthink it and toil over it. Once I finally decided to get down to it, it took me about fifteen minutes to get it all down. So dumb. No tears had to be shed. It's not like any new information came out. It was just the same old stuff. Stuff that is always on the tip of my tongue anyway.

Step five is all about seeing my part in every resentment I have. For someone like me, who is always second-guessing myself and seeing the negative in everything I do, that was fairly easy. I had already done that in my mind over the years. What was really important was having a sponsor to go over these things with and give me a realistic point of view. For instance, I'm still resentful about that dirty cop stealing $1,000 from me. But if I hadn't gotten high and arrested, there would have been no way that he could have gotten his paws on my money. After all that, we looked at the underlying character defects that are causing me to behave badly. Then we observed the repeating patterns.

There were some pretty clear patterns that I really didn't see until today. Outside perspectives are great for noticing the obvious things that a person can't recognize. I had a few "aha" moments. Then it was time to burn the list of resentments. I love burning things like papers, memories, pictures, whatever. It feels so good.

(While entering all this stuff from my journal onto my laptop, I had so much fun burning the pages. Every single day, I took the pages I had transferred, and crumbled them up and burned them. Sunshine also enjoyed watching the pages burn. My all-time best in one day was thirty-two pages. While the smoke drifted up into the sky, I prayed. My prayer is always "God, please take it away from me. I don't want to hold onto these memories or my pain from the past any more. Please God, remove it all from my heart and mind." Every day after my little ceremony, I felt better. My neighbors must think I'm nuts, standing out there in my yard, laughing or crying or whatever I'm doing, holding a hose in my hand, just in case.)

I did it. I admitted to God and another person the nature of my wrongs. I owned my stuff, and I kept no secrets. A huge pattern I could see was how much I resent myself. I hate that I didn't fight Walter harder to keep Payton. Realistically, I can thank him in a way for doing that, because had it not been for that experience, I would not have had the fight inside me today. But still, I failed my girl, and I hate that about myself. I can't forgive myself for that, because I have a beautiful special little girl who is so loved and is growing up every day without her mommy. She will always feel rejected in some way by me, and that is my fault. I should be there for her. He won't even let me talk to her on the phone. I can't stand the situation the way it is. Another thing I can't forgive myself for is Halo. I know that she would never have died in my arms. It is my fault she died. Maybe that's why I hated what that cop said so much, because in my heart, I do think it's true. Did I intentionally hurt her? Of course not. Had I known she was going to die, I would have never put her down. But I did, and she died, and it is my fault. I know that. I'm also upset with myself for not making Rose live with me. I let her choose to go with her dad, and now we aren't close at all. I don't even really know her. Now she has seen me at my worst, and I feel again like a terrible mother. Oh, it hurts so badly to have always wanted to be a mom, and then to be such a letdown to my girls over and over again.

Like I've said before, I feel now is the time to turn that all around. I want to prove to my girls and to myself that I am a good mommy. I need to make a comeback, and I know I am the only one who can do it. It is already happening. Still, the past can bring me down if I let it. Maybe now that I'm actively working my steps and putting a lot of effort and honesty into them, I can unburden myself and work toward forgiving myself for my wrongs.

At least I still have my mind. Well, at least I think I do. There are some girls in here who have done one hit too many. You can just tell. Their eyes aren't quite right. Something inside is kind of sideways, and I'm not sure they can get that back. I think about when I first got here and how I could hardly even talk to Heather that day in her office. Maybe we do get it back sometimes. It's like the luck of the draw. Some do, some don't. I'd much rather be sane and aware than a crazy person. I see so many people wandering the streets around here. This town is riddled with homeless meth addicts. There is one girl in particular who is really tall and thin. She sleeps at the park or sometimes I see her hanging around a cheap hotel. She wears these super-high platform shoes and a ski mask over her face even if it is hot out. One time I saw her at a grocery store, and she had nothing but eight containers of cream cheese in her cart. What happened to her? Was it one hit too many that put her over the top? Was she predisposed to mental illness? Did somebody hurt her so bad that she broke? That could be me, but it isn't. Here I am with the ability to face the music, and the capacity to follow through with changes. I really am lucky in a lot of ways.

We went to couple's counseling tonight. Usually our couple's counselor is such a bore, but today felt different. We both opened up to her. We talked about Halo. She told us about the five stages of grief. We did grief counseling with a wonderful lady at Hospice after Halo died, so I've heard about the five stages. I also know them from personal experience. They are denial, bargaining, anger, depression, and acceptance. For me, the guilt around her death keeps me stuck in these stages. Sometimes I feel more than one at a time. Sometimes I vacillate between all of them—all, that is, except acceptance.

Hearing Jevon talk about Halo is always good for me. Hearing his feelings about our beautiful little angel and watching the tears well up in his eyes softens my heart toward him. It also helps when I can look at his coping mechanisms and see some similarities to mine. I like feeling that we have things in common that way, since it felt like we were separated for so long. Hearing him talk about where he was back then is also a good reference point for me, because I can see how far he has come. He is changing too, and I feel very proud of him. I have so much love for him. This is a good sign. It's not like we are stuck. I truly do feel my heart opening up to him again. I can feel myself starting to trust him more. He still shows up to meetings, and he always makes it to our appointments. He is working and totally doing the best he can to be supportive and present for me. We've only been together for four years so far, but we've made up for the short time in content and intensity. If anything, it has been intense.

Mother's Day was great. I went into it with a poopy attitude but was really pleased with how it panned out. My mom invited Jevon, which made it even better. We went down to Santa Barbara with Sunshine, because it worked out that I had her that weekend. When we got there, I gave my mom a quick haircut and then she took Sunshine for a walk. That gave me some time to have Rose all to myself. We took the scooters and rode them to Giovanni's Pizza, which is right down the street. It had been years since I rode a scooter, and it was really fun! I was a little shaky at first, but I got the hang of it. We laughed a lot. It felt good to laugh at myself. It was a typical clear and perfect day in SB. A very light breeze was coming in from the ocean, and it was probably about seventy-two degrees. So nice. The pizza was delicious. We had a really good day, and at the end of it, I think that Rose and I had started working our way back toward having trust and fun together.

My friend here in program got a book on the power of positive thinking. I am reading it now. My goal for the next week is to try and focus only on the positive. If I start to get carried away on one of my negative tangents, then I will try to redirect myself. Maybe if I get myself in the habit of thinking positive for this week, I can get myself to a place where I start thinking more positively in life. The book makes a lot of sense to me, so much sense that I think if I can change the way I think, I can change the way I do everything in life. Positive energy and thinking and words all will be manifested and compounded and sent out and come back. Hey, maybe miracles could happen. It could be a revolution of the mind. I'm ready to give it an honest try.

It's not as easy as it sounds. The urge to gossip is huge in a place like this, but that is such a negative thing to do. It's hard to walk away, because I love to hear everybody's dirty laundry. Even if I don't contribute, I know it counts as participation to listen, so I have to walk away. Oh, it's a hard habit to break.

More changes recently. Sunshine now gets to spend every weekend with me, and the weekends are all to be extended weekends. The week will look like this: Friday I go to Santa Barbara to pick up Sunshine from her preschool; then she spends the whole weekend, through Tuesday; then I have to take her back to Santa Barbara, which means that the only days I don't get to see her are Wednesdays and Thursdays. I love this! When I got this news from my social worker, I was so excited that I didn't know what to do. It took all day for it to really sink in. It means that they are finally starting to trust me and that they are really going to give her back to me! All my work is paying off. The worst is over. For every time I gave up in the past, I've finally figured out how to try and try and never give up. I can fight, and when I really do fight, I can win. All I have to do is keep doing exactly what I'm doing, and I will be able to get beyond this. I keep having to say that over and over again. Maybe part of me is trying to convince myself that it is true. Because sometimes it doesn't feel like it will ever happen. Every week in this place goes by so slowly! Now that she is with me so much more, I think time will start to go by more quickly. I think the hardest parts of this are really over.

Another positive thing that has happened is that my final paychecks finally came. I had two uncashed paychecks that were lost, and one that had never been picked up, so that makes three paychecks.

That's about $600, which is like winning the lottery right now. It was great that I didn't have that money until now. It worked out so well, because now I can buy Sunshine good snacks and take us to do fun things during my free time. Most important, I can pay all my remaining rent and be totally ready to graduate when the time comes. You can't graduate unless you are paid up, and now I know I will be.

Part of what I want to buy with the money is a wedding band for Jevon. It's important to me, because the one we got married with was just a band we got there in Vegas, and it made his finger turn green. Not good. He shouldn't have to feel like that. More and more, I feel like the dark cloud that has been encompassing me is dissipating.

I am officially a graduate of the Family Drug Treatment Court! I did everything I had to do, and now all I have to do is move out of this place. What's next for me? I'm looking forward to planning my graduation party. Even though I've already graduated, I get to have a formal graduation party. There will be food, and I get to make a little speech. I think what I will talk about is how we all come into the program feeling like failures. It's hard to pick yourself up when you've fallen down so far and so hard. But we do pick ourselves up. We do it because we know there is no other choice for us without losing our children. So we give up our addictions and put one foot in front of the next, hard as it is. We sacrifice what we have to, and do what they tell us to do. We put our heads down and never give up. The process is grueling and slow, and we are tested. And in the end, some of us succeed. We who succeed are changed forever. We become people who care more about our kids than

217

about ourselves. We become people our families can depend on. We have faced our fears head on and trudged through the horrors of the past and found that we can conquer our demons. We turn our failures into a legacy of love and determination that could never be acknowledged had we not fought the battle in the first place. I will ask everyone in the audience, newcomers to the program as well as fellow graduates, to be grateful for all things, because hidden inside the pain and desperation of losing your kids is the chance to become a role model. It is an opportunity to prove, not only to your kids but to yourself, that you are not "just another drug addict." We are survivors and fighters, and we don't need to believe for one more moment the names we've been called by others or the names we've called ourselves. It's true … It's never too late to turn it all around. All you have to do is to want to badly enough. It's the struggle that makes it beautiful. If it were easy to quit drugs and take on the challenge, a lot more people would do it. The time to make the decision to change is now. As soon as we really decide we are done, the rest of our lives can be lived from a different perspective—one of happiness, freedom, pride, and dignity.

Thinking about it makes me so happy because I know that when I tell my girls I love them, they will know that these are not just words. I have walked the walk. It makes me feel like I can finally start to hold my head up. It feels like my world is coming back into focus, and my self-worth is finally coming back. I feel like even my posture is starting to get better. Life keeps looking brighter all the time.

Right before group this morning, my housemate asked if I would take her to Target so she could get a bathing suit for her little girl. I didn't think the staff would let us, but they said yes! That was great, because while she shopped, I was able to buy things for Sunshine. I got sodas and snacks, juices and fruits, bread and bagels. I was even able to get a couple of movies. This makes me really happy, because now Sunshine will have everything she needs and everything she wants and extra treats to make things more fun. When we don't have things like juice here, it makes me feel terrible, and the shopping schedule never works out. My schedule conflicts with the times they take the other girls. It feels like every time I'm really down about something or need something, it works out. It's like God hears my prayers, even if it is a little prayer like wanting groceries. And somehow, it always works out. If I try to control everything, I can't make it work out in my head, but if I just stop trying so hard to figure out the details, God puts it all together for me. The key is that I should probably just stop worrying so much, and let go. A lot of the people in meetings say, "Let go and let God." This is probably what they mean.

This is my last journal entry before I leave. I finally get to go home. I haven't gotten custody of Sunshine yet, but I am scheduled for the court hearing to get custody twenty days after I move out. All I have to do is go home and wait about three weeks. It's only a matter of time. I did it!

Twenty days after coming home, I got Sunshine back, but they kept my case open to watch me for six more months. By the grace of God, in January 2013, I got custody of Sunshine and my case was finally closed. Some people say they are "awarded" custody. Yes, it is definitely an award. But I say I "earned" custody. I won't say that I ran a perfect program. I didn't. What I did do was try. I tried, and I never lost hope. And I showed myself who I really am. It wasn't easy, and that's what makes it so meaningful. It is, by far, the greatest accomplishment of my life.

Part 9

"So then, if anyone is in Christ, he is a new creation; what is old has passed away. Look, what is new has come!"

—2 Corinthians 5:17

Fall 2012

I had the most amazing experience one morning. First, I was watching Halo go upstairs, so I followed her and caught up with her. She was laughing and happy. She looked beautiful. I sat down on a step, and she got up on my lap. It looked like she had grown since she left, because she looked exactly as old as she should have. Her hair had grown too. It had a nice wave in it. She was able to walk. While I held her on my lap, I told her over and over again that I loved and missed her. She looked up into my eyes, and I could see that her eyes were green. She was so beautiful.

After the dream, I was lying down quietly, happy to have spent some time with my little girl and to see how she has grown. Then I felt the bed move a little. I felt another presence in the room, but I was paralyzed. Suddenly, I projected myself to the ceiling of the room. Lying there, awake but unable to move, I heard the bed creaking with the movement of another energy. I felt a weight on the right side of the bed, but I was stuck, unable to awaken myself. This wasn't the first time this had happened. Sleep paralysis is something I've dealt with for years.

I sensed a negative energy around me, and instead of giving into my fear, I prayed. I called on Jesus. The simple act of saying "Jesus" is so powerful. I called on Him as the Lord of my heart and asked for his protection. I praised Him and expressed my need for Him, because in the battles of the spirit, only He can protect and help me. I prayed with as much faith as I could muster, and in less than ten seconds the dark presence was gone.

I fell back into a sleep, but in this sleep, I was aware that I was asleep and dreaming. Trying to regain my balance, I looked around and saw that I was in a square room with hardwood floors—somewhere I didn't recognize. I felt safe. Then a man approached me. He had a kind energy and put me at ease. The man emitted compassion, patience, and love. He was really tall, seven and a half, maybe eight feet tall. He was the first person I'd met in my sleep/awake place who looked older. His hair was all shades of gray. He was dressed very beautifully in a dark, expensive-looking dress shirt and pants. He told me his name, but it was a in a different language, and I can't remember it now. It was two words. He was explaining things to me. Some of what he said has slipped my mind, but what I remember the most is a circular colored chart. It was like a dial with different sections. The top right section was about spirituality, I'm guessing, because he pointed to an orange-red portion and said, "This is where you got repossessed." Then he pointed to a lavender portion directly to the left side and said, "This is when you united with Jesus." So I knew that the dial read counter-clockwise. I had a picture in my mind of those times. The first place was when I lived with Chuck. The place when I asked Jesus into my heart was down in Perris Valley at U-Turn. I remembered that moment so well.

Next he showed me the section of my chart on the lower right-hand side. He had to tell me what the sections were about, because the chart was in a language I didn't recognize. He said that this was about my kids. I saw three squares going up. Then he took his finger and pointed to a fourth square that looked like it had split in two. I understood that one represented Halo; the other one was the child I would be soon carrying. He walked over to a wooden bench, built into the wall like a window box. While we walked, I asked him when I was going to die. He looked down at me and lovingly said no, and I knew that was a question he would not answer for me. I asked him the next important question on my mind: "When am I going to have another baby?" He looked down at me with kindness in his eyes and hesitated, but not because he didn't know. I had a sense this man knew everything about my past, present, and future. It was as though he was considering whether or not he should tell me.

"When am I going to get pregnant?" I asked again.

"Oh, sometime around the end of last week," he replied.

Then he sat down on the window box and opened his arms to me. I walked over to him and felt safer than I'd ever felt with my own father or any man, for that matter. It was wonderful to feel so loved and accepted. As I climbed onto his lap, I asked him again what his name was. He remained quiet, just holding me, making me feel deeply comforted and peaceful. Tears ran down my face as I allowed myself to be held this way. Happy tears, grateful tears. When I woke up, I cried into my pillow and said "thank you" over and over. What a morning!

It was true. I was pregnant. What does it take to get pregnant? Well, my personal secret is to stop trying. Maybe you've heard that one before. But I really did completely give up. I had to. I needed to protect myself from the constant disappointment of not getting pregnant. I went to the doctor and heard the little heartbeat for the first time. While I was sitting in the waiting room, I realized I was nervous. I remembered the last time I sat in that office. We couldn't get a heartbeat, and we knew the baby was not "viable." I relived that feeling for a bit and then realized how upset I would be if it happened again. I needed my little baby to be okay. Once I saw and heard the beautiful music of a beating heart, my everything changed. I was alive. I finally was being given the gift of life. By the time I was seven weeks along, I was fully in love with my baby. I wasn't too sick but I sure was tired. I was not smoking anymore, and I had improved my eating habits. After all, it was what I'd wanted for so long. Smoking didn't even feel good anymore. By the time I was at nine weeks, I felt really sick and tired. I also had the worst gas anyone had ever had! It was the most wonderful, disgusting thing ever.

We celebrated Halo's second birthday. We ordered her a little cake, and that was difficult because we didn't know what design to put on it. The lady at the bakery asked questions, and we had to explain that it was for a dead girl. You never know what will be hard and, for whatever reason, that was really hard for me. Jevon was there, and it helped to not be alone. He soothed my aching heart by putting his arm around me at just the right time. Sometimes that's all it takes to make me feel better—knowing I'm not alone. I space out when I'm really hurting, and right when I started to do so, he put his arm around my shoulder, and let me lean into him.

Her birthday was good. It was sad and beautiful all at the same time. The beautiful part was that we had a really nice dinner in the living room at the dining table, and we cried together. We hadn't cried together at the same time like that since the funeral. It felt good, very cathartic. The whole day was hard and mournful. We both had Halo T-shirts that I'd had made for a Walk for Babies that we participated in to raise money for the March of Dimes. I was wearing Jevon's because mine didn't fit my chest anymore. At one point I was sitting in my chair, trying to read a book, when I looked down at the shirt. While I was gazing at her fuzzy little head, I remembered her feather-soft hair, and my hands actually ached with the need to touch her again. It was amazing how after all that time, my body still needed to feel her so desperately that I physically hurt.

After thirteen months at Project PREMIE, I finally graduated that program too. That didn't mean that my case was closed, but it did mean I could have a closure. At group, everyone gathered into a circle, and I told my story. There wasn't a dry eye in the room when I finished. It took me an hour, and I cried twice, but I got it all out. It felt really good. Once I had taken care of that, all that was left was random testing. I was down to twice a month.

It was almost Christmas. The previous year, we didn't get a tree. We had no Sunshine, and we were very busy feeling sorry for ourselves, and we couldn't do it. I had been struggling through my first miscarriage at home, and it was right before I checked myself into the in-patient program. It was a crap time of our lives.

In contrast, we were doing pretty well this year. We bought a tree and decorated with the kids. Instead of being consumed with our grief, we acknowledged it and allowed ourselves to laugh and love the kids we still have. Highlights of the night included going to the dollar store to stock up on garland and extra ornaments. Jevon bought a pickle ornament. It ended up being my very favorite thing on the tree. Later, Sunshine danced around the kitchen while I cooked dinner and talked about how excited she was for Santa to come to our house, riding in his "slave." We turned off the house lights, lit up the tree, and ate burritos in the dimly lit living room as a family. What a difference a year makes!

I'm so lucky. Sunshine is such a sweet and generous child. She went into her room while I was napping and picked out presents for her dad, stepbrother, and me from her own toys. I have no idea what she picked for us, but she wrapped these things by herself and put them under the tree. I've never heard of a kid being so thoughtful and adorable in my life.

December 18, 2012

December 18 is my anniversary. I woke up to find a card on my dresser. He remembered! That was pretty cool. He had been very loving, saying sweet things and acting very sweetly toward me. A few nights earlier, when he came home, he told me that he'd missed me. It took me a while to figure out why: just like me, he'd heard about the Sandy Hook School shooting. We talked about it off and on that night. Our eyes welled up thinking about the families of those children: Having to look at the Christmas trees they'd probably already bought. Returning gifts that their children would never open. Staring blank-faced with holes in their souls at the caskets that held their love inside. Trying to celebrate Christmas with their remaining children, if they had them, or the rest of their families. I only have vague memories of the first Christmas after Halo went to heaven. It was so awful, I'm glad I don't remember much of it. December 21, 2012, marked the two-year anniversary of Halo's return Home. Instead of sitting around feeling sorry for ourselves, we got tickets to the *Let's Make a Deal* show. I was so excited. I hoped we would win something but we were not able to scrape together any extra money to buy costumes. Still, it was something fun to do and take our minds off of what we'd lost, at least for a little while.

January 17, 2013

The previous Monday we went to court, and they closed my case. The judge, the workers and other people involved all had very positive things to say. It made me feel really good about myself. I was expecting it, because my worker told me she would recommend a dismissal. But I didn't totally believe it would happen until I heard the judge say the words. Afterward, I felt like a different person. My chest had a spreading feeling of lightness inside, my voice was quieter, and my temper had all but vanished. I was learning what it meant to create my own self-esteem. It felt so good to know that I really did have what it took to conquer the biggest and worst problems that came up in my life. I loved myself. I now knew that I could finish anything I set my mind to. Looking at it all, I give the glory to God. I could have never done it on my own. Never again will I be a prisoner of my own mind.

I have gone back into the courtroom twice, but each time it was to support girls I was sponsoring. It felt good to be there for them. Giving back is something I really wanted to do in my life.

Oh, I almost forgot about my TV debut! Guess what happened? We won! I was called on stage by Wayne Brady himself and asked if I wanted to make a deal! It was so freaking cool! And I won a brand new washer and dryer! The whole drive home, I was in a daze. I couldn't believe it had really happened. The most incredible part of the day was that we only had time to cry once. All day long, I felt my little angel with me, helping me have fun. Wherever she was, whatever she was doing, she didn't want to see her mommy and daddy cry for her. I had a feeling she helped us win. We looked like such a couple of goofs. Auntie Carol and Sophia kept Sunshine for the day, and they also let us borrow a couple of costumes. I dressed as Glenda the Good Witch from *The Wizard of Oz*, and Jevon was a munchkin. He was so great. He even wore striped tights. Watching him stuff his hairy legs into those tights that morning made me fall in love with him even more.

February 22, 2013

I was about six months pregnant and feeling good. After being sick for so long, I was doing better. I could still sleep for half the day though. Then the best thing happened. My parachute *finally* sold. (Remember? I'd sent it to my friend Shawn in New York about two years earlier. At the time, I was pregnant with Halo, and I wanted money for Christmas presents.) I had been praying for money, and then I couldn't sleep at night thinking about my parachute and how long it had been. After getting good and worried about it, I sent Shawn a short e-mail. A week later, a check for $1,100 came.

For the ten days that the money was held by the bank, I compiled a list of things I wanted to get with it. The first thing on the list was Halo's headstone. Other items on the list included the cost of getting Jevon his electrical license, buying him some new shoes, getting Sunshine's ears pierced, paying my late fees at the library, stockpile size 1 diapers, baby wipes, a baby backpack, a new diaper bag, a rug for the living room, a mattress pad for our bed, night gowns for Sunshine and me, and getting my cat fixed. I did all of those things! It was so fun to shop. I also got a few new baby outfits and some clothes for Sunshine. Eventually, I spent the last of the money. I bought a Green Dot card and paid for the first month of life insurance premiums for Jevon. I also paid a huge gas bill that was past due. It had been a cold winter. It was sad to be out of money again, but it felt really good to be fully prepared with everything I'd need in the future—life insurance and diapers! It was great to make a list of things I wanted and then get them all. The cat was fixed, and Sunshine's ears were healing. Best of all, I ordered the headstone, gray granite with an epitaph that read "Where there is faith, there is no loss. Where there is love, there is no separation." Finally, my little darling would have a beautiful stone. It was the last gift I would buy her. It felt really good to do that for her before our next daughter was born.

March 22, 2013

I had a dream that seemed very real: I purged myself of a negative spirit that was clinging to my back. When I was almost asleep, I felt my back tingling and weighted down. I could sense a struggle, and I felt frightened. I allowed myself to fall into a dream. In the dream, I turned around and looked behind me; a young, androgynous girl was clinging to me. Her hair was very short and dark, and her eyes were also dark and stared back at me with anger. My initial reaction to her presence was to get mad back and lash out to try to get her off me. I sensed that she had been spiritually attached to me for a long time, and I wanted to get rid of her. But underneath my fear and anger, I sensed a wiser presence calming me and grounding me with a feeling of love. I crossed myself and repeated the name of Jesus to try to get more grounded. I asked Jesus and the angels to join and help me. The angry girl laughed at me and tried to make me feel foolish for doing this, but I ignored her and eventually realized what I had to do. I gathered myself, faced her, looked into her eyes, and told her she was loved. I told her Jesus was waiting for her with open arms, wanting to embrace her. I asked if she'd be willing to follow me Home. I explained that she would be loved and accepted and once again feel happy. I knew I'd done the right thing when I saw the depth of regret and sadness in her eyes.

Instantly, we traveled to the other side, and right away I called out to Jesus. Immediately, He was there. He smiled, and we approached Him. He recognized her and called her Sarah. There was no hesitation or disappointment in His eyes or body language. There was only love and acceptance. He was completely open and ready to welcome us to be near

229

Him. Shyly, I asked Him for a hug, and He stood up and embraced me. My head nuzzled into the space between His shoulder and neck, and I knew something amazing had just happened. Suddenly, I experienced a deep and profound sense of peace. In that moment, I woke up.

What that dream made me realize was that we are waging battles in the spirit, even if we don't know it. Maybe we can sense it. How do we overcome these spiritual battles? They cannot be won by fighting, either physically or spiritually. The only way we will ever accomplish God's will and carry out God's plan is through love—and not just loving those we like and who are easy to love. The only way to make peace in the place we live is to be peaceful. The only way to experience peace in the darker, lonelier places within ourselves is to love unconditionally. If we interact with those who hurt us or hate us with love in our hearts, they will be unable to perpetuate the battle, and the war will be over. It is easier said than done, but even small acts of love count and are good practice.

My mom helped me learn how to love even when it doesn't feel easy. A few of months ago, she visited with Walter and Payton in Santa Barbara. I know that it was too much to ask to be included; that is the consequence of choices I made in the past. But I would have liked her to tell me what she was doing. Instead, I found out about their visit from my cousin, Sophia, who found out from my grandma. It really hurt me to find out from anyone other than my mom, and what made it worse was that the visit was already over. To me, it felt like all the other times when my mom had neglected to tell me important things until they were over. Again, I felt betrayed. It felt like the times when she'd called Walter and Steve to tell them how badly I was doing. It felt like when she gave me the paperwork terminating my parental rights for Payton after the respond-to date had passed. I knew I needed to talk to her about this. I wanted to move beyond these hurts and tell her that it was important that she trusted me enough to tell me about these things before they happened, not after. I loved my mom, and I was very hurt. But I knew I had to come from a place of love and work this out with her. I wanted a future in which I had a good relationship with my mom. I wanted that not just for my children, but also for me.

Instead of responding to her the way I had in the past, I kept my composure. Instead of yelling, I thought about it. Instead of name calling, I held my tongue. She still didn't apologize. Maybe I didn't handle it as well as I should have. How did I get beyond it? Prayer.

She gave me the silent treatment for a long time, except for the times she asked to see Sunshine. She asked three times in three months for sleepovers. I always said yes. That alone was hard for me. But I knew it was important to be reasonable and not to make things nasty for her with regard to Sunshine. The first visit was fun for Sunshine but frustrating for me; when she brought Sunshine back to my house, she left while I was using the restroom, without even saying goodbye. Then she came back. I was relieved to see her, and asked if she'd come to say good-bye. "No," she said, "I came back because I left my sunglasses." I was so mad, I could barely contain myself, but I said nothing. I kept my mouth shut and walked away. I wondered, *What is my part in this?* I knew my mom wasn't a bad person. I wanted to see what my part was so I could change. I was ready to forgive and forget our ugly past and work toward a future together. I wanted my mom!

The next time she asked to see Sunshine was hardly any better. We met at a halfway point. She wouldn't hug me, which left me bitter and confused. *Surely*, I thought, *I must have done something I don't realize for her to be so cold and withholding.* After a few days, I sent her a text, asking whether I had done anything to hurt or upset her. Her response was, "Heavens no. Have a nice week." I didn't get it.

Our next meeting went surprisingly well. I met with my mom at her request on March 10. She was uncharacteristically nice to me, giving me an easy smile, a real hug, and a block of cheese and an avocado. I was surprised but felt our relationship was finally on the mend. All day long, I thought about her and felt happy in my heart. Sunshine was going to be with her overnight, and I hoped the two of us would get to talk a little bit. Later that day, I spoke with Bruce's son and his wife. They had come for Sunshine's birthday party, but a week early by mistake. While they were outside, Jevon overhead them talking about Sunshine's *two* birthday parties. Jevon told me what he'd heard, and I immediately asked them about it. They confirmed that my mother had hosted a birthday party in Santa Barbara that day. Bruce's daughter-in-law said my mom had told them not to tell me about it, because it was a secret, and I wasn't invited. Wow. That one hurt.

That night, I sent a text asking my mom to tell Sunshine good night for me, adding that I hoped they had a good time at the birthday party. Within five minutes, I got a call from Sunshine. I kept my feelings out of my voice and tried to sound genuinely happy for her. Inside, my blood was boiling, and my heart was breaking. I upset myself into a nice big, fat, ugly cold sore, above the lip line. What was worse was that the party had a Hello Kitty theme, which was exactly what I had planned. My party was scheduled for the following weekend. When Sunshine got back home, I had to order another Hello Kitty cake, even though she'd had one the day before. I felt so unloved and angry at that point. I knew it was best to say nothing to my mom, because I would not be able to hold back mean words.

What I wanted to do was sink to her level, and tell her she wasn't invited to my party and that she couldn't see Sunshine anymore, since she seemed to enjoy using my children to hurt me. She'd known I would find out about the party from Sunshine. If there was one thing Sunshine could do, it was talk. Everyone knew that. So it was a way to hurt me. Try as I might, I couldn't see her perspective on this or her motivation behind it.

To her credit, she did show up to Sunshine's real birthday party and smiled and played nice with me, Sophia, Carol, and Frank. We all felt stress beforehand, but the party went well, and was all about Sunshine, as it should have been.

My next problem was her birthday, coming up in March. Should I acknowledge it? Send a text or a card? It was not an easy decision, but I decided to send a card. I found a perfect one, funny and light-hearted. Inside I wrote:

Dear Mom,

There are a lot of things about you that I don't understand. Some things hurt my feelings. But at the end of the day, you are my mom, and I love you. It wouldn't hurt if I didn't. We'll be okay. I hope for you a year of joy and happiness. God bless you.

Love,
Your daughter

That was the only way I would ever bring it up. After so many years, I realized she would not change. She would not love me the way I needed her to. All I could do was keep my distance and continue to treat her with love when I saw her. After my dream, I was sure that was the only way to handle our relationship without creating more pain for myself and everyone else. I kept praying about it. God can do anything. My job was to focus on the positive and continue loving her no matter what. She had never given up on me through the years. That was one thing my mom consistently gave me: She never accepted that I would be a drug addict for life. She always told me that I was better than that. I wasn't going to give up on her either.

Here's what I need to remember about my mom. She had been through her share of hurts too. Her dad was mean to her as she grew up. Maybe she never felt loved either. She needed to be protected by her mom and never was. She was a really beautiful little girl. It's hard to imagine how mean her dad must have been to hurt such an innocent and sweet child. She went through a lot. Those are her stories to tell. I won't try to tell them for her. But I need to keep things in perspective. Instead of focusing on stuff about my mom I don't understand, I should try to focus on the things I do understand.

When she adopted me, she tried hard. She got real breast milk for me and did this whole set up with hospital tubes and tape and a bag under armpit to keep the milk warm so she could nurse me. She read to me, changed me, did early education stuff for me, and always encouraged me to try harder. She was there for me at all my recitals and school functions. She took me on a train trip all across the United States. She took me to the other side of the world—twice. She bought my grandma's car and gave it to me. She always encouraged me to be the best version of myself. She taught me how to pray. Without my mom, I would be a totally different person. Some of the things I like best about myself are only a part of me because of her. I picture her face, her eyes looking up at me, telling me not to give up on myself. She always said she would never give up on me. Never giving up—I probably got that from her too.

There was no way I could give up on us. We had to get through this together.

April 5, 2013

People should know something about being pregnant in allergy season. If you've already had a child—or, as in my case, four children—and you are planning on having another, don't plan your third trimester in the spring. It can be messy.

Everything stopped when a sneezing attack came on. I'd brace myself. Whether I was standing in the grocery store, or doing dishes, I knew how it was going to be. Sometimes if I crossed my legs really hard and focused all of my energy, I could make sure everything stayed in. Sometimes, there was just no stopping it. I was learning to take the bad with the good in lots of ways.

April 8, 2013

My dad called almost every day. He'd want to go to the bank one day, the store another day, to CVS for some sleeping pills, or the hospital to have his liver drained. His condition was deteriorating quickly. I took him to the hospital, and three days later his abdomen looked like it was swollen and ready to pop again. He was throwing up at night.

We went on some errands, and he left his check book in my car. After my prenatal checkup, I went to his house to return it. I decided to go inside for a few minutes and sit, which was not something I normally did. While I was sitting at the kitchen counter, I noticed some paperwork from his doctor about his diagnosis. It was the results from the MRI I'd taken him to the month before. There was quite a long list of things wrong with him. The thing that stuck out to me was hepatocellular carcinoma. I'm no doctor, but I know that carcinoma means cancer. When I got home, I looked it up on Jevon's phone. Yes, it was cancer—liver cancer to be exact. The Internet gave me a good run down of the situation, no sugar coating or smiling faces with the delivery. The prognosis seemed pretty grim. I could only read so much of it before I felt the gravity of it all. I realized why he hadn't quit drinking. There was an empty, gallon-size vodka container under the counter and a fresh, unopened pint that he'd bought while we were running errands. If a doctor had told me the things I'd read online, I'd probably give up all hope and continue drinking too. I learned that liver cancer is the third-most common type of cancer. It is deadly. If the liver cancer is compounded with cirrhosis—as it was in my dad's case—there is no cure without transplantation. Most patients die within a year.

I was dumbstruck by this information. I knew he was sick, but I hadn't realized he was *that* sick. It was time to write a letter. If I'd been high, I would have had the nerve to look him in the eyes and tell him what I had to say. But if I were high, I wouldn't have the love in my heart to tell him anything at all. Well, I was not going to get high. It simply was not an option for me anymore. I needed to come up with a better means to communicate. Unfortunately, writing was the only way for me to manage it.

I didn't know how to articulate the things in my heart, but I knew that if I didn't write him a letter from a standpoint of love and absolute forgiveness, I would regret it. I asked God to help me with the right words. I'd written a lot of letters in my life, and this was one of the most difficult.

April 11, 2013

Here it is, word for word:

> Dear Dad,
>
> We see each other all the time, but some things are hard to talk about in person. I realize your condition is getting worse fast and that you may not have a lot of time left. The other day you said you aren't afraid to die. That's exactly what I want to talk to you about. I wanted to say something at the time, but I couldn't. It's hard to find the words.
>
> Since Halo died, I have a different perspective on life and death and a deeper relationship with God. During my time alone after she went Home, I searched my soul, and prayed for dreams and gave

it lots of thought. What I discovered is that God isn't angry. God is only *love*. We, as humans, create our own punishments and our own hell. God loved us enough to send His Son. He wouldn't do something like that while at the same time condemning us. If He wanted to get mad, He would have just saved Jesus the effort and pain He went through. None of us are lost or flawed enough to be excluded from His love, acceptance, and forgiveness.

When your time comes to leave your body, please remember that you are not afraid. I don't know what exactly will happen, but I believe that there will be at least one person in spirit who will come and help guide you to heaven. What you will experience is the same unconditional love that God has given you from the time you took your first breath. You will be free from the bondage of a failing body, of regret, and of addiction. There will be no judgment except that which you give yourself.

I do believe that God, in His perfect love for us, always gives us freedom of choice. You can choose to turn away from His love and light, and if you do, you will be stuck in another darkness that is not where you belong. Please accept the beauty that is yours in heaven. You've suffered enough in life, and I know that you can be free from any negativity when you go Home. I cry happy tears when I imagine you feeling embraced in peace, harmony, and connectedness. And maybe someday, when I'm leaving my body, you can be there with me.

Dad, I know I said I would never bring this up again, so I won't go into specifics. Nobody in this world is entirely good or entirely bad. Between you and me, there were some bad things, old things I can't understand. I want you to know that I've put these things to rest and let them go, and that all I have for you is love and forgiveness. That's all I want to say about that.

I remember a lot of good things too, and these are what I choose to hold onto. Like show-you-somethings and camping trips. Cartoons on Saturdays; you bringing me lunch at Laguna Blanca School, Hawaii, and you teaching me to ride a bike. I was really clumsy and would get so mad at myself. I would throw my bike down and want to give up, but you kept on telling me to get back up again. Because of you, I have become a better person. You allowed me to stay with you when I was going to have Sunshine and for a long time after that. You never expressed judgment when I had problems. You always accepted me the way that I was even when I got carried away with drugs. Thank you for that. Nobody else in my life has ever accepted me exactly the way that I was, especially if I was loaded. And so, through you, I learned more about unconditional love. Thank you for your humor. You always made me laugh and helped me not to take everything too seriously. Thank you for your patience. Bike riding wasn't the only thing I learned slowly in life. Thank you for your understanding. Thank you for your many generosities. Both Sunshine and I are lucky to have you in our lives.

I love you, Dad.

April 14, 2013

Dad called to say thank you for the letter. I could tell he really meant it.

April 16, 2013

I took dad to the hospital again. Afterward, Sunshine and I went to her new school to get her enrolled. I couldn't believe she was that big already. I knew I'd miss her little everything.

April 18, 2013

Dad's doctor wanted him to move up his pre-op appointment at Stanford. It had been set for June 25, but the doctor's office called to set up an earlier appointment for him; so it was set for May 13. He had arranged a ride with my mom, because I couldn't drive four hours one-way in June just to turn around and drive four hours back, as I either would be due or would have a brand new baby. She'd agreed to take him on June 25, and I figured she would take him to the earlier appointment too. I thought they had worked it all out. But she couldn't do it. She was going out of town that week. She had plans to go to Utah. Walter invited her to a fundraiser, and she and Bruce were going. She had an opportunity to see Payton and she was going to take it. I was okay with that. Also, she told me before she went up there. What more could I really ask? It was time to start looking at the current situation and not punish her for what used to be. I was happy for her.

What mattered most to me was that I'd be taking my dad after all. What I couldn't understand was why the doctor was still pushing for a liver transplant after my dad was in his office reeking like booze.

April 19, 2013

Halo's headstone was set on this day. We decided we would each cut off a lock of hair, braid the two locks together, and put them underneath the stone. I thought they wouldn't allow us to do that, but they did. The man working at the cemetery remembered us, but I didn't remember him. He was a family friend who went to high school with Auntie Carol. After thinking about it for a minute, I did remember him vaguely. He treated us very nicely. This was also the air date for our *Let's Make a Deal* episode.

After the headstone was set, we went out to lunch. Then we watched the show with Auntie, Uncle and Sophia. We looked as excited and ridiculous as I remembered. It was a good distraction on an otherwise depressing day. Luckily, we had each other. We got through the day together, like we did the funeral. We were really, really together. I remembered what it meant to have an open heart for this man I call my husband. I felt myself loving without reservation, and I realized that I was okay with that again. As I watched him drive or heard him laugh, I'd think to myself how glad I was that we didn't give up. I found myself loving him in a whole new kind of way, and I was grateful for it.

May 13, 2013

I took Dad to Stanford for his initial visit with the doctor to get on the donor list for a new(ish) liver. The drive was about four hours one-way. I had Sunshine sit up front with me so that she wouldn't get car sick. She did really well on the trip, aside from adjusting and readjusting the air conditioning, radio, vents, and volume the whole way.

The trip was physically and emotionally exhausting. My dad was by far in the worst shape out of anyone else in the liver/kidney transplant area. After they took his vitals, the nurse came and got me in the waiting room. That was cool, because Sunshine and I got to go into the other room to wait on the doctor with Dad. The doctor came in after about fifteen minutes, and was very friendly to all three of us. He asked a short list of questions, all of which were answered with lies, lies, and more lies. Not only did Dad say that he'd quit drinking back in September, but he said that he'd only been drinking for a few years, since his wife died. I had never seen that man go one day sober in my entire life. I take that back. Once his health went into a decline, he did try to quit a few times. Every time he tried to quit, he went into seizures on the third day. He simply couldn't quit on his own. It was disheartening to sit there and realize that without honesty from him, it was nearly impossible for the doctors to provide him with the help he so desperately needed. At one point, I had to turn away from the conversation and focus on the wall so that I wouldn't get caught rolling my eyes or making a face.

After a seemingly even longer drive back home, he asked me to go by the Short Stop liquor store. It wasn't for a shot or a half-pint, but a whole pint. It brought tears to my eyes. I just let them fall down my cheeks, grateful that Sunshine was up front with me, and not him. That way, I could cry silent tears of exasperation. I came to realize that every effort and every care I had about his life and health was all for nothing and frigging pointless.

One thing that I was grateful for was going home to a husband who was welcoming, happy to see me, and didn't have alcohol on his breath. I was so happy to see him that I went limp in his arms when he hugged me.

He was not drinking because I was not drinking. It was great that he was supportive this way, because the smell of alcohol was one of my pregnancy no-no smells. It turned my stomach and made me want to throw up. Smelling alcohol on Jevon's lips was like smelling my dad's slow, miserable rotting death, which took away any and all desire to kiss him. The hardest part about this was that, even though it was hard to admit, I still wished I could drink. Regardless of how disturbed, putout, irritated, and disgusted I was over my dad's alcoholism, deep down I wanted to get drunk too. When Jevon was strong and supportive, it helped me get through the night without a drink.

May 17, 2013

We went to a free big sister/big brother class at the hospital. It was hard, but I was able to hold back the tears. I cried for a lot of reasons in those days—sometimes because I saw a cute commercial or I was too tired; at other times because I missed Halo. It was hard to go to a class where Sunshine learned to become a big sister when she had already become a big sister. I felt like I was denying her big-sister role by taking her to the class. The important thing was that she had a great time. We both put on goofy paper hospital hats and plastic gloves as we toured the facilities.

Dad left a voicemail message while I was at the hospital. I usually never let his calls go to voicemail, but I allowed this one exception. His message was just a vague "call me back when you get the chance." I didn't call back. He had been so generous with us, always giving us spending money for this or that. I was grateful for his generosity. I still felt every word of my letter to him. But, at the same time, I kept hearing the words he uttered when the doctor asked why he continued to drink when it was clearly destroying his liver. He said he "just didn't care." For whatever reason, I struggled to let go of those words. I wanted to believe he was going through something emotionally or spiritually and was seeking meaning in life. The reality was he simply didn't care. I needed time to let that sink in. I knew my problem wasn't with him, it was with me. He hadn't changed. I saw only what I wanted to see. The truth was that he couldn't care anymore. My problem was that I needed to accept that and love him exactly where he was. It didn't have to be about me or my feelings. Acceptance was the key, but I just needed a little time to get to that place. I planned to call him back the next day.

May 25, 2013

Guess what he wanted to tell me? He won his case against the phone company he'd been working for. The court sent him paperwork saying that he won more than $900,000, paid in installments for the rest of his life. I guess it really was worth those early morning trips to the courthouse in San Luis Obispo. I was glad that he didn't have to worry about money anymore. He had been incredibly generous. He didn't have that much money, but he was always giving it away. What goes around really goes around. When he told me, I felt a wave of relief. I knew he would live the rest of his life comfortably and never have to worry about losing his house or going without. That made me feel happy and relieved. I hoped he would do something fun for himself.

That weekend, Sunshine and I were home alone. Jevon and Talon went to Lancaster to help Jevon's sister move into her new house. They had planned to go the previous weekend, but the move was postponed, so he was able to take his son. There we were, just her and me. I enjoyed my one-on-one time with Sunshine. We ate ice cream from Baskin Robbins, and then she slept next to me. We woke up in the morning and watched cartoons together. Then I had a little bit of a nesting instinct to sweep, do laundry, dust, and clean the refrigerator. (There were twenty-seven more days until my due date!) Later, we went to the movie theater. We were both excited. She was such a fun, little person to hang out with. She cracked me up both when she tried to be funny and also when she wasn't trying. For instance, she said funny things like "cut me some slats" instead of "cut me some slack," and she loved to help with every chore I was doing. It was endearing how helpful she wanted to be. Most of the time she made the chores more complicated than they had to be, but her heart was always in the right place. She decided she loved ballet. She wanted to start taking classes. Unfortunately, she is about as coordinated as I am, which is to say, not at all. Poor baby. She'd do her turns and stand on her toes and fall down constantly. Yep, that's my girl!

June 7, 2013

I dreamed that I took an elevator to the sixteenth floor of a building. I don't remember much else about the dream, only that I pushed the number sixteen on the wall. That would be a cool day to have little Faith, because it was Father's Day. At that point, my body was so huge that any day would have been a great day to have her.

June 11, 2013

We went to an infant CPR class at Marian Hospital. I wanted us to be prepared this time … just in case. I doubted I would need that lifesaving skill once I actually had it. Still, something inside me said if we took the class, we wouldn't go crazy worrying about the same thing happening again. We were late, which ended up being a good thing, because we missed the introductions. When I looked over the paperwork, I noticed that the introductions included why we wanted to take the class. The last thing I felt like doing was telling a classroom full of strangers that I'd tried to give CPR to my child and failed. *Hi, there! I'm here because I killed my baby.* What a downer.

I was due in a little over a week, and my hormones were making me completely insane. It had been a bad day. When we got to the class, I saw a cart filled with little baby dummies with plastic coverings over their mouths. They were for practice, and they were creepy and grotesque. A video on general household safety was playing. After the video, the instructor passed out the weird practice dummy babies. I made a sour face when I saw ours up close and nudged it toward Jevon so he could go first. Then there was another video about how to perform CPR. Immediately, I started to cry. I cried through the whole class and didn't have any tissues, so I wiped my snot and tears on the sleeve of my shirt. It was dumb and humiliating. The only thing that stopped me from feeling like I was distracting other people is that we were way in the back. Because the lights were down low for video watching, I don't think anyone really noticed.

What I learned was that I'd done some things right, and I'd done some things wrong. I learned how to do CPR and how to deal with choking hazards. I'm glad we went, but I was about as miserable as I'd been in some time. I felt bad all night long, spending parts of it in the bathroom with the door shut and the water running, crying softly into my robe. I kept focusing on the things I'd done wrong and the nagging thought that, maybe, if I had done the pressure right or enough repetitions, she would be alive today.

Part 10

"Therefore, since we have been justified through faith, we have peace with God through our Lord Jesus Christ."

—Romans 5:1

June 2013

Faith was born on Father's Day. She was a gorgeous and perfect creation. I couldn't stop staring at her. God really outdid Himself.

> On a peaceful grassy hilltop, somewhere in Santa Barbara, there are tiny little feet that have withered away to just bones. Here, in my hands, I hold identical feet to those. As I hold her perfect little body in my arms and stare at her feet, soft and warm on my lips, I wonder at the miracle of Faith, and thank God that I am alive in this moment to breathe her in. *This is my baby. I am holding my new baby girl. God answered my prayers.*

That morning, I went into labor. Jevon and his son had a planned a hike with some men from our church.

"Go ahead and go," I told him, "But please, hurry back." We had plans to go to my dad's house. I knew it would be the last Father's Day that my dad would be alive. He'd asked me to take him to Costco to buy pounds of Alaskan king crab legs—my absolute favorite—earlier in the week. If they serve food in heaven, those would be on my menu along with artichokes, fresh bread, and See's Candy.

I knew that my labor pains would produce results later in the day. It was very important to me to be at my dad's house. I couldn't let him down. After Jevon left, I was at home feeling restless and excited and wishing Jevon hadn't left. I always do that. *Go ahead and go. Do what you think is right. I'm okay. No big deal.* But it was a big deal! I needed him there. I was angry at myself for not asking him to stay. I was mad at him for not knowing that I was "trying to be nice" by encouraging him to have fun. Of course I didn't *really* want him to have fun. I wanted him to be at home and miserable with me! I just had to trust God to keep the baby inside long enough for Jevon to get his butt up and down the mountain and for us to make it to my dad's for our visit. I wanted my dad to feel loved.

I showered. I cleaned. I put the clothes and the diaper bag in the car. I took Sunshine to get frozen yogurt for breakfast. When we drove home, things got serious. I could hardly drive anymore. The contractions started to make me double over and rocked my world. I needed Jevon home *immediately!*

He arrived not a minute too late, and we headed straight to Dad's house. My dad looked so happy that day. I can still see him, in my mind's eye, sitting on his chair in the living room and smiling and standing up when he saw me walk in the front gate. I smelled food cooking. Laura was there too. I told everyone that it wouldn't be long.

"We are having a baby today, guys!"

"Really, sweetie?" Dad asked. "Do you have to go?"

"No way, Dad," I assured him. "I wouldn't miss this for anything in the world. The baby can wait. She isn't coming just yet, and I can just sit down when the hard contractions come. I'll be okay. When I'm not okay, we'll leave. It's really important that I am with you today."

He got a big smile on his face and started toward the kitchen, admitting that he had eaten a few crab legs already.

The day was really great. The sun was out and in typical Central Coast fashion, the sky was blue and clear and the weather was temperate. The contractions began to take their toll, and my dad got worried.

"I'm not leaving until I eat some crab!" I tried to talk him out of being overly concerned. Somewhere in his eyes, I could tell that he was pleased I was staying as long as I could. That was it too. I wanted to stay with him on Father's Day until the very last minute.

I wasn't prepared for my mom to show up. But there she was, perky and smiling, walking through the front yard. Part of me was glad, but part of me needed to compose myself.

"Hi," she said and gave me a real hug. It felt good.

"Hi," I said. "I didn't realize you were coming up. I'm having the baby today."

"Wow! That's great! I'm so glad I came up then." I was honestly glad that she had come up too, once I thought about it. My mom had never missed any of my kids being born.

Soon, it was time to go. When I left, I felt really great about the afternoon. Everything had worked out exactly the way that it was supposed to. We'd always look back on that day with a smile.

My mom took Sunshine to Santa Barbara overnight. It was probably best for her to be there. I wanted Jevon's full attention, and Sunshine would have had a hard time watching me go through that much pain. Three hours after I got to the hospital, Faith was born.

July 9, 2013

I had two dreams in which I was wearing black. Soon afterward, my dad died. It was on a Sunday. Laura called and said that they wanted to call an ambulance for him. Right away, I knew. I remembered the dreams. We went over immediately.

What I found when I got there was as tragic and terrible as anything I'd ever seen. It was worse than the child with leprosy in India banging on the car window with his stump. He had fallen down. His whole body was broken. His pallor was troubling, his skin was cold. It was obvious that he'd fallen more than once, because his body was bruised very badly all over, the bruises at different stages in the healing process. Parts of him were still bleeding. He was missing teeth. His head and face were swollen. His jaw was obviously broken.

My heart broke in half when I saw him that way. It was as if somebody had punched me in the stomach, because the wind was knocked out of me. All I wanted to do was put my arms around him and hold him. I wanted to take his pain from him, to love it away. Instead, I watched as he tried to convince me that he was okay. He didn't want me to call for help, but I did. I had to. Once help was on the way, I made sure he was lying down on his bed. I surveyed the room, and there was blood everywhere. He had knocked down shelves and bloodied the floor and walls, apparently falling every time he tried to get up again. The damage to the house was nowhere near the damage to his withered, swollen body. I tried to find a place on his skin that wasn't covered in blood, so I could touch him, rub him, and try to console him. I told him that help was on the way and, more important, that that he wasn't alone and he was loved. They came for him quickly. He went to the hospital in an ambulance. He was there about a half hour before he started to vomit blood.

When he was asked what he needed, he said he wanted ice cream. When the nurse asked if he were in any pain, he said he wasn't. His last words were: "I'm okay." That was so my dad.

And then he was gone.

August 3, 2013

My dad was gone. I'd been able to tell him by letter and in person that I loved him; for that I am so grateful.

The first time I heard from him was about three weeks after he'd left the body. He came through with Elaine, and I could only hear them, not see them. He'd made it Home. It was the exact same way that Halo had come through that first time. Then we visited again, only this time I could see him. We hung out, just the two of us. He looked so much younger and totally content. I'd even call him beautiful. At one point, I told him I loved him and leaned in for a big fat hug and kiss. When I did that, I felt his face. It was warm— quite different from the swollen, yellow, broken, and cold skin I'd touched that last time I saw him at the hospital.

I am so grateful I was able to build a brand new relationship with him. I am so grateful to know that he truly does love me too. August 4 is his birthday. I've heard that it is common for people to die near their birthdays. I will think about him on his birthday as I do every day. I'm so happy that we're still making memories, my dad and me. There is still so much about him that I want to know.

I made him a poster for the memorial we held in his honor. It was really cool, and I hope he got to see it.

August 22, 2013

We had a forty-day-old birthday party for Faith. That was a wonderful day for us, and we shared it with Auntie Carol and Sophia. Halo never made it to forty days, and each day felt like even more of a gift as we watched Faith grow. My fear became unmanageable at times. I'd thought it would decrease, but it didn't. Many times, when we were driving, I'd ask Sunshine to make sure the baby was still breathing. At night I'd have to lie next to her, listening to her breathe, sure that any moment, it could be the last time she inhaled. During the night, I'd startle myself awake until I saw she was alive. Sometimes, by the light of the window at night, I'd hallucinate that she was blue. When she cried, I'd be so full of terror and fear that I'd blow up at everyone around me because my nerves were so frayed. I didn't like myself when I was living in fear like that. I said a lot of prayers, asking God to help me be kinder, more patient, and sweeter, even when inside I was totally freaking out. Some days I thought I was doing better; on other days, I realized I still had a long way to go to become the kind of person I wanted to be.

The previous week, Sunshine started kindergarten. That was a good day. It was hard for me to walk away and leave her at her new table with her new teacher and her new soon-to-be friends. I lingered for a while until it became awkward for me and probably Sunshine too. But when I finally turned to go, I noticed that she too had started to cry. Instead of making me feel better, it made things worse. I was able to get out the door only because one of the other mothers told me I had to go, otherwise I'd just make things worse for Sunshine.

August 23, 2013

I had the best birthday weekend ever. We ate good food, and we had good sex. We overindulged and made each other feel loved. The best part was that Jevon bought me a new tablet— not because he spent way too much money or because my laptop cord stopped working and I really wanted something new to write on, but because he said that his gift was on the one condition that I finish this book. There is no better gift in the world than to know that my husband believes in me.

Things were getting better with my mom all the time. She was the first person I wanted to tell about Jevon's present. I couldn't wait to tell her that I had a new tool to help my writing. She had never given up hope that I would someday write my story and was totally happy for me. The "I love you" at the end of our phone call felt real to me. It has been very satisfying to renew my relationship with her. We don't have to agree about everything or understand each other all the time. The main thing is, she is my mom, and I am her daughter. And I love her.

September 2, 2013

We went to a Labor Day picnic at the park with our church. It was really nice. There were lots of people. I was trying to make new friends. It was hard because all my old friends were gone. I had to let go of any friends who did drugs. I never thought I would be like that, but I had to be. It was not them; mostly it was me. I just couldn't handle it.

I thought about Tara. I'd thought she was my best friend. But it got weird, and it turned out that she wasn't my friend at all. She kept stealing from me. She probably thought I owed her because of the many times she got me loaded. I would have given her anything I had, and in fact I did give her all I had. Just about all the money from the settlement I got after breaking my neck went in her pocket. But what ruined our friendship was when she was at my dad's house, and out of her pocket fell Elaine's diamond cross necklace. I was so disappointed. She acted like it was hers to ease her embarrassment, but we both knew what she had done. Since then, I hadn't made any friends. It was hard to get close to anyone.

September 10, 2013

The tenth was a Tuesday. The previous Wednesday I'd had my tubes tied. Jevon was so supportive and wonderful. He picked up Sunshine from school and had both kids all day. My surgery was around noon, and I went home around five. It was far more painful than I imagined it would be. But I got through it with Jevon's help. On Thursday my mom took Sunshine to school and picked her up. On Friday, she did the same thing. It was the first time I'd felt close to her in a long time. I started to let her in again. Friday morning, while she was with me, we got a call from the New York Police Department.

The message said that there had been an assault involving Rose and her father. I thought that Steve had hit Rose over some typical teenage craziness. What happened was that Rose stabbed her dad. She didn't want to go to school, so she shoved an eight-inch blade into her dad's shoulders and chest, collapsing his lung. She was going to be evaluated in a psych ward. She was on her way to jail. I was so disappointed. I walked around in a fog, almost like I did when Halo died. I couldn't drive or even speak because I was so shocked and stunned. Was my daughter a monster? I didn't know how to move on. I didn't know how to talk about it. How would I recover? My body hurt. My mind hurt. My heart hurt. My daughter hurt.

September 16, 2013

I talked to Rose for the first time since everything happened. Someone at her psychiatric hospital called, saying Rose wanted me to call her, so I did. I was scared as I got ready to call her. I was worried about what to say, thinking she would be angry or blaming or hateful or scared.

When she picked up the phone, I hardly recognized her voice. It was a lot deeper. She almost sounded like a different person. She told me that she'd started her period three days earlier. She talked about happy things. The main thing she wanted to say was how sorry she was she'd missed my birthday. She thought she would get out on October

7, her next court date. She kept asking what I wanted for my birthday. It was so sad. She had no idea about the consequences of her actions. She was looking at attempted murder and would be tried in criminal court as an adult. She didn't have any idea how serious that is. She sounded very loving, which helped me keep the conversation light. She asked if I knew why she was in there. I told her that of course I knew, but we didn't have to talk about it. I just kept telling her I loved her, no matter what.

I told her I would try to send her some books and call her every day. I planned to do my absolute best to keep my word about that. It would be the most I'd talked to her in a long time. She became a little distracted after about twenty minutes; she started talking about a hedgehog outside the window and brought up my birthday again. Then she was called to dinner. When we hung up, it was on a good note, with "I love you" from both sides. I guess it was the best I could expect from her at that time. I felt absolutely sick to my stomach. *I thought I knew her. What happened to my little girl?*

September 20, 2013

I wondered if I had a little postpartum depression. It seemed like I was not normal, even considering the circumstances. Everything felt like such a big deal, and I was not handling things as well as I wanted to. I was driving around crying about my dad. I was so worried about Rose that my digestive system was totally out of whack. I hadn't slept well in four months, and I was so cranky and moody I could hardly stand myself! I wasn't even sure when I I'd last washed my hair.

One thing that was really alarming was my anxiety level. I was very worried about Faith living, actually about her *not* living. I had no cozy- or slow-waking moments. Every time I woke up, it was with a start, in fear, and my hand immediately went to her chest. My every thought was consumed with dread about the many ways she could be in danger. I'd never been one of those kinds of mommies. I was even starting to annoy myself. Luckily for me, boundless joy accompanied these stressful and ugly thoughts.

I love Faith as much as my little heart can handle. I think I might explode because of the intensity of my love for her. She is a beautiful child who smiles and laughs easily. She talks with her eyes just like her daddy. She is perfect.

October 1, 2013

Part of our government shut down, because some members of Congress were against Obama Care. What a weird day. Luckily for us, we didn't have government jobs, but I heard that eight hundred thousand people would be negatively affected by the shutdown. What a sad day. The last time this happened was seventeen years ago, but I couldn't remember it. I would have been eighteen at the time. Maybe I was overseas, or maybe I was too young and self-absorbed to take note. I thought it was too bad that we, as a country, couldn't agree on anything, and that the people in charge were punishing us, the people, instead of themselves. I felt confused and embarrassed by this.

October 22, 2013

Things at home were okay. In all honesty, I couldn't complain. I had everything I'd ever wanted: a loving and thoughtful husband, beautiful daughters, and a warm cozy place to call a home. I loved my life. I loved how I felt about my kids. My heart was full, indeed, it was bursting with the love that I felt inside.

Yet, there were moments in our marriage when things didn't make sense, and we argued about things that weren't really happening. I found myself thinking Jevon didn't love me as much as I loved him, or that he still didn't trust me. It hurt my heart that we had these types of problems. In my mind, they were old problems that we'd conquered, so why were we still not trusting? What was I doing wrong? My identity was built around being a wife and mother, and when there was conflict in my home, I took it very personally.

We needed a little break. So I took the girls up north to my biological dad's house in Redway, which is up in the redwoods by Eureka. It is such a beautiful magical place, and I felt my heart sing when I stared up into those tall trees. Gazing into the majestic trees was wonderful, because I felt like a part of nature. But I also felt small, and so my problems seemed small. The smell, the sounds, the colors were all indescribably beautiful, and though I'd only been there a few times, I felt a strong sense of home. We caught a bus and rode four hours to Hanford, caught a train and went four hours to Martinez, then spent four hours on another bus to Garberville. I hoped it would be a fun trip for the girls and me, and I also hoped five days was long enough for Jevon to begin to miss us.

November 15, 2013

Faith wasn't sleeping through the night. Sometimes I was so tired I thought I was going crazy. And yet my love for her still grew. Her personality was coming through. She smiled with her eyes. There was a sweetness about her that I hadn't seen in the other girls, a gentle nature. We enjoyed each other's company. I would drop Sunshine off at school and bring Faith in from the car for our little bit of alone time. That was my favorite time for snuggles and naps.

We sometimes watched *The Price Is Right*, and sometimes we turned off the TV. We couldn't afford cable TV, so we had only two channels, maybe four, depending on the weather. Somehow there was always something worth watching on during the day. Maybe my standards lowered to match what was available.

One night I was sitting outside smoking—I couldn't believe I'd started smoking again!—and thinking. We may not have had satellite or cable TV, Internet or a home phone, or the bodies we wanted to have, but we had way more than what we needed. The Philippine Islands were hit with a terrible hurricane, and we watched people being rescued from the rubble. We saw dead people wrapped in rugs on the sides of the roads. Meanwhile, we had walls around us and food in our bellies. We may have lost our one, but we still had these two (sometimes three, counting Jevon's boy) there at home with us. How grateful and lucky we were to have each other in this silly little neighborhood on the Central Coast, in this home with its quirks and weeds, and our cat that occasionally got fleas. How sweet was our life that every morning we woke up with the sunshine and kissed each other good-bye, knowing we would see one another again that night and have a dinner together on our TV trays, watching one of the two (maybe four) channels.

Faith has fallen asleep on my lap, her little diaper butt sticking out, and her soft-haired head pointing up toward me, mouth open. Her breath smells so yummy, like the sweet scent of heaven. She radiates warmth and perfection. And I am the happiest person in the world.

December 13, 2013

I am trying to get my girls some Christmas presents. My last day to safely order for delivery by Christmas Eve is today. It is so hard. How do I order great gifts for a nine-year-old I don't know anything about, and a fifteen-year-old who is serving time for a violent crime? I don't even know my babies anymore. It breaks my heart. I'm worried they're going to think I'm lame. I'm sending Payton a "best-selling" locking journal from Amazon.com. Still looking for what I'm going to send Rose. When I started to cry, I decided to take a break and do what I'm trying to introduce to Payton ... journal. Okay, back to business. I can do this!

I did it! Finally! After toiling for what felt like forever, I got presents for both the girls. For Rose, I got some "Reasons I Love You" stones. Some examples are: Because of your smile. Because you are beautiful. Because I do. They say what I want to say, and I hope she will know they are from my heart. I cried before I found them, and I cried after I found them. Being a mother is so incredibly great and so unbearably hard at times too. What would I be without the experience of motherhood? I love it so much.

December 2013

Over Christmas, we went to Hawaii. My biological brother flew Jevon, Sunshine, Faith, and me to Kona for six days. Last year on Halo's death day, we went on *Let's Make a Deal*. This year on her death day, we were flying over the Pacific. It was a fantastic, once-in-a-lifetime trip. My biological dad and his wife met us there. When I was nine, my dad took me on a trip there, and it was so much fun. Over the years, I've looked back on that time with him as one of the greatest we ever had together. As an adult, I must say, the islands seemed even better! This gift was so beyond generous, I didn't know how to handle it. We slept at a house they rented, cooking dinners together and getting to know each other better. They had been there for a little while, so they knew the fun places to go to during the day. It was amazing. We went snorkeling, and I got to swim with big sea turtles! I saw two of them up close. You're not supposed to touch them, but I didn't know that until it was too late. That was incredible, so great that

I'll be telling the story to my grandkids years from now. We also went zip-lining. Sunshine was too little to go by herself, but she was able to go tandem. She has a lot of guts, let me tell you! I couldn't believe it. What a wonderful gift. We had never taken a honeymoon, so this was really special to us, something that our whole family will never forget. Life is good!

January 2, 2014

I've been thinking about getting my story out there, assuming anyone will consider publishing it. The thought has always been in my mind, although it sounds kind of fanciful, like "yeah, I'm working on a book." But maybe I'll actually try to make it happen.

Complicated issues have made me question whether I want to tell my entire life story. *What would people think? Would I make more problems for myself? What if nobody cared? What was my ultimate purpose? What if it were too hard or I was not smart enough?* Ultimately, this isn't a story about just me. This is a love story, a love story about God and me. I realized that I must not only include God in my story, I have to make the whole story revolve around Him. This isn't a sob story, but one about redemption, hope, and never giving up.

I want to make sure I include the bad things I've done so that my account is balanced and fair. Writing a memoir is bound to seem self-absorbed, but I want to point the focus away from what I did and make it more about what God does. Without God in my life, I know without a doubt that I would have failed. I am not any good without God. I have found a hundred ways to fail in my life. When I try to do things on my own, and before I had a solid relationship with Jesus, I did fail. Only after I asked

God into my heart was I ever able to do anything worthwhile.

Who is God? To me, God is a perfect, all-knowing force of love. I believe God's divine spark is in every single living thing in this universe. I believe in Jesus as the Son of God, a beautiful, perfect, and selfless man who came here to show us what being a Christian should look like. Everything I've ever experienced firsthand or read about Jesus is a message of unconditional love, healing, and inclusion of all who are sick, rejected, hurting or in need of being saved. I think that is everyone. That's what I need to write about.

Is it taboo to write about God? I watched a movie that proposed "it is not intellectual suicide to claim there is a Creator behind the Creation." I am a thinking person who lived much of her life without knowing God. As a child, I blindly believed in God, because my mother told me about Him. But I hadn't yet fallen in love with Him. As I grew up, I overthought things, picked apart the details of God, and I lost my faith. I read science books and believed science was undeniable. Then I had my experiences with God and realized that God was also undeniable.

I came to understand that God and science exist simultaneously. God is in science. If you understand science, you don't have to stop believing in God. Science is not the opposite of God. It's not God *or* science; it is God *and* science. I've seen the little fish bumper stickers with feet so many times. They are supposed to mock the fish stickers that represent God. Remember, though, that Darwin never figured out how life started on Earth. He merely theorized that life evolves. Yes, of course we evolve. I personally have evolved. We are always changing. It is how we survive.

I don't want to lose my Christian readers. I'm no scientist, and I won't claim to be that smart. What I'm trying to say is this: God created life. If you have rejected the beauty of God because you know all that smart science stuff, maybe you can give it a little more thought. I heard on a news broadcast that scientists have proven the big bang theory, based on some wave patterns in the ocean. The big bang theory is exactly what we read about when we open the Bible and read the first book of Genesis.

In time, I began to believe in God for real. Then I went through a time when I rejected religion. I didn't go to church. I found reasons to pick apart religion based on a few major issues. But you don't have to be religious to open your heart to God. Believing in God is the first step in having a spiritual life. It's one thing to believe in God; it's another thing to love God.

One of my hang-ups is war. I can't understand how people fight wars in the name of God. I don't want to be grouped with a bunch of people who believe in doing that. I think war in the name of God is the worst form of blasphemy ever imagined. What I've realized is that all churches don't condone wars. Humans killing one another certainly isn't something we condone at my church. God is love and life. I once saw a bumper sticker that read "who would Jesus bomb?" That summed it up for me.

Then I got offended by the word *sinner*. For some reason, it raised my hackles: *Who are you to call me a sinner? Have you never made mistakes? You think you're better than I am?* I didn't want to feel judged by the people I met at church, so I stayed away.

I will tell you this: If you feel judged by everyone at church, or they act like they are better than you are, you are probably going to the wrong church.

I have never felt chastised at my church. We are a family at our church, and we all strive to love and accept each other the way Jesus asked us to. People are nice to me whether or not my tattoos show or my child throws a big tantrum in front of everybody after a baptism and it's obvious that my parenting skills are less than perfect. In my quest to get it right, I sometimes fall short. Okay, I often fall short. We all accept that we're not as good as we want to be. We lift each other up; we do not put each other down.

The word *sinner* is just a word. What it reveals is that we all screw up sometimes. The important thing is to try to do better next time. We all have felt weak, lame, insufficient, confused, lost, broken, or alone. I truly believe that God is always right there with us, loving us, waiting for us to love Him back. God isn't some angry old guy on a cloud with a lightning bolt in his hands, ready to strike anyone who swears or whatever. He doesn't want any of us to go to hell. It breaks God's heart when we turn away from Him. I can tell you with absolute certainty that it is never too late to open your heart to God. He always accepts us the way we are and exactly where we are in life.

My final hang-up regarding religion is judgment, which is at the center of bigotry and hatred. Many pious people have decided certain people don't fit the mold and are not good enough to receive God's love. That is an absolute lie. None of us were good enough. That's why Jesus died for us; because of His gift of love, every single human being *is* good enough. Nobody has the right to judge another human being. That job is for God, and God alone. In Jesus's day, it was even worse. Jesus called those who judge other people hypocrites. He saw into the hearts of people. He knew we all needed grace and mercy. Jesus made it a point to show love to those who were chastised by society. Jesus was an equal-rights activist.

It breaks my heart to see the stigmas that have been attached to Christianity. Jesus died with a message of forgiveness on His lips. One of the last things He said was, "Forgive them, for they know not what they do." He was speaking to God about the very men who had tortured Him and nailed Him to a cross. Can we then forgive one another? Can we accept and love those who look differently than we do? Can we accept and love someone who is gay, lesbian, bisexual, or transgender? Can we accept and love those who have different political views or cultural backgrounds?

I want to be the kind of Christian who does what Christ did. I want to speak words of love and acceptance and harmony. We each have a divine spark of light inside of us that connects us to God. We are all connected to one another. God is infused in the very cells of our bodies. We see Him in the microscopic miracle of our DNA. We feel His magnificence when we watch the sunset or look up into the night sky, humbled by the grandeur of all that is or ever was. It is amazing to me that He has created such a vast universe and still cares about our little lives.

God has been misrepresented as mean and cruel. Let me say again that God loves you. That is not just a meaningless platitude. It is the truth that is at the center of every good thing in my life. No matter what you have done, God loves you. No matter who you love, God loves you. God loves you if you are a lumberjack. God loves you if you are a hippie. God loves you if you watch reality TV. God loves you regardless of whether you are a

Republican or a Democrat. If you have contributed in any way to make God look hateful to anyone, ostracizing the person and turning his or her heart away from God, don't worry. God loves you too. (But please stop making that sad, heartbreaking mistake.)

Perhaps it's time to stop worrying what denominations we belong to. I doubt those details matter to God. What I think matters to God is if He is asked into our hearts. It's time for us to stop focusing on our differences, and to embrace our similarities. The darkness knows that in order to defeat us, it will have to divide us. That mission is accomplished when we fight amongst ourselves. I have no idea how much time we have left, but I do know that there is little hope for our future unless those who know the truth stand united.

Maybe you're wondering how I can believe so strongly. Here's what I did. After giving it a lot of thought, I decided I had to know for sure. So I prayed: "God, if you are real, please show me." What happened was beautiful, profound, and unique to me. God reveals Himself in a special way to everyone. Trying to explain it here would be pointless, because it was my experience, tailored for me by a God who knows my heart and mind.

Here's the last thing I'll say about God (for now). I hear people question how a loving God can allow such suffering. Life hurts, I know. Bad things happen to good people. Many people are searching for the meaning in life. Why are we here? We are all here to learn. We come into this life with a set of lessons we helped choose for ourselves. How do we learn? We learn through experience. (Personally, I never learn anything the easy way.) First, we learn what *not* to do. Then, we learn what *to* do. Simply put, I think it's all about learning to love. Be kind to one another. Ellen

DeGeneres says it at the end of every show. I love it! It is so fundamental. It is so awesome. Yes, be kind to one another. I start with me. You can start with you.

January 8, 2014

I went to Santa Barbara to pick up Sunshine from Auntie's house. She'd wanted to spend the night, so Auntie Carol came up yesterday and picked her up. She is such a dear. While she was here, she went to court for some dad stuff with me, helped me with the kids, fed Faith some big girl applesauce, went to get fresh bagels, watched the kids again so I could mop, helped with the laundry, went to lunch with us, and even brought some leftover pasta so I didn't have to cook dinner. What a Godsend! When I went to pick up Sunshine, I stopped by to see Grandma Mae. It was so wonderful that my grandma was still alive. Seeing her so old was sad in a way, because I knew that she hurt. But she always looked beautiful to me.

February 3, 2014

We saw a movie called *The Lone Survivor*, based on a true story about four navy men who went into Afghanistan on a mission. Only one of them lived to tell the story. Watching the movie made me unbelievably sad. It was a really good movie, and I love anything based on real-life events. What made me sad was the killing. That sounds naïve, I'm sure. What did I expect from a movie about the war? We watched it at the drive-in; I was in the backseat, so I could nurse Faith without making Talon feel weird. The best part about sitting back there was that I could cry as much as I wanted without being noticed. Violence in movies usually doesn't bother me much. This time, it did. I'd recently seen an interview with the real-life lone survivor, Marcus Luttrell. What I saw on the movie screen was what he actually had to live through.

I imagined him sitting in a room somewhere, remembering the details, and someone else listening and jotting down his story. I pictured him recalling the head of another man being blown off or seeing a bullet hole in the head one of his dying brothers. I wondered what God felt on that day in Marcus's life. I felt absolutely broken-hearted.

We are all God's babies, even those of us who don't choose to believe in Him. He loves us, regardless of religion. I never backed the war, but once it got started, I always supported our brave troops. It put things in perspective for me, because I thought about my silly little life in Santa Maria, California. There I was, worried constantly about being a letdown. I was always thinking that God must be getting tired of my worries and my trials. Every day when I prayed, I asked for something else, always needing to change because I was tired or weak. *I'm not the mom I want to be. I'm not the wife I want to be. I need so much improvement!* As I watched the men die in the movie, and knowing that people die every single day, I realized that God probably doesn't think I'm that bad. My issues are pretty small compared to what is really going on in the world. I'm sure He hasn't gotten completely tired of my prayers or my needs just yet. Overall, I'm probably doing just fine.

February 4, 2014

Something amazing happened. After all these years, Walter finally wrote me an email. I didn't have Internet access, so it was there for five whole days before I read it.

> Hey,
>
> I hope you are well. I hear about you from your parents when I see them, and they tell me you are doing well and working toward building a solid life for you and your family. I'm happy and proud of you

for this. It seems like you and I should begin some sort of communication. Let me know your thoughts.

Love, Walter

My response was dated February 5, 2014.

Hey Walter,

Your e-mail makes me very happy. My life has never and will never be complete until Payton is in it. Please let me know what I can do. My only hope is for her to know she has a mommy who truly loves her.

I couldn't believe this was happening! I thought I'd have to wait until she was eighteen to contact her again. I was over the moon and planned to write more after I called him. I was sure the process would be slow going, but this was the first step. Then I got a card from Payton.

Dear Mom,

I really hope we can see each other soon. I really want to meet Sunshine and Faith. I miss you a lot.

I LOVE YOU!

Love, Payton

While I was happy that she was thinking about me and loving me, it broke my heart that she had to miss me. I knew that at the root of her love for me, there had to be pain. She probably felt rejected by me. She should not have grown up without a mom. On top of it, she had a dad who told her that I'd "left them." That's what he'd said to me on the phone when I called: "when you left us." She probably had no idea I'd taken her with me. It broke my heart to think about my little girl hurting. It angered me that she did not know the truth. Of course, I never left her. She was one of the great loves of my life. I loved her before she was ever born. I will love her every day of her life. I needed her and would never accept things the way they were. Unfortunately, her dad ran the show, and I had no legal leg to stand on. If I showed up there, he would have turned me away or called the police. I had to work my way back into Payton's life. He was in control, and there was nothing I could do about it. What he didn't realize was that by punishing me for leaving him, he had punished her. Her self-esteem and self-worth would never be as good as they would have been if he'd have allowed me to see or at least talk to her.

Dear Payton,

Thank you for the card! I love that your dad made cards out of a picture that you drew. What a great idea! I think your art is amazing. I still have a picture you drew me two years ago on my fridge. It is of all us girls and says "family" on it. It's my favorite. Payton, I want to see you so much. Every day that goes by, I miss you. I dream about you all the time, which means I even miss you in my sleep. I'm sorry that I live so far away. It is so hard to not be able to see you. I am doing everything to make sure that I will be able to see you again. Your sisters are kind-hearted and loving. I know you will really like them. Sunshine is going to turn six soon. Faith is pulling herself up to a stand now and has two teeth. Sunshine is a reader like you. We read every day. When you were a baby, I read *Goodnight Moon* to you every single night. I'm glad you love reading. I do too. I am always reading a book. I am also working on writing a book. You are a big part of it, Payton. Without my love for you, it wouldn't be as good of a story at all.

Love,
Always & Forever,
Mom

There are some ouchies that can never be kissed better. Even if she knew the real truth of it, the damage already would have been done. She still will have grown up without a mother. When I thought about it, tears welled up in my eyes, and my throat tightened. I wanted to wrap my arms around my little girl, look her in her eyes, and tell her I love her over and over until she believed me.

Walter could give Payton everything I couldn't in terms of money and opportunity. But nothing could take the place of a mother's love.

February 7, 2014

On *Good Morning* there was an expert giving men Valentine's Day tips. The advice was really great. First, get a card, and write in it. Say that she is beautiful, that you love her, and, finally, why you love her. How do some men not know these things? To me, this stuff is so basic. I wondered what basic things men need that some women don't know to do.

I knew, for example, that Jevon needed to feel I was listening to him. Even if he told a story in the longest way possible and paused throughout to search for the right words, I had to listen without interrupting. He had to feel like he was being helpful with the baby. In my mind, I thought I was being a good wife by taking care of everything so that when he got home, all he had to do was shower, eat the dinner I made, and relax. I thought he would prefer not having to work after he got home, but I was wrong. He enjoyed taking care of Faith and feeling like he was needed in that way. While he didn't get up at night with her—and she woke up as many as six times a night—that was because I was still nursing. I thought I was the perfect wife because I did everything, but it didn't make him happy. I guess you never can know what a person wants, no matter how much you think you know them. It's all about being open to change, and being able to talk about things.

I was becoming the kind of wife and mother I'd always wanted to be—*becoming* being the operative word. I had more patience and more inner contentment, which translated to kindness and compassion. I focused on what I had in life, instead of missing what I didn't. My fuse used to be so short. One time when Sunshine's room was really messy, I yelled at her, and then I put myself on a time-out in my room. I felt so miserable about yelling at her that I cried. At the time, I was pregnant and moody, but it was no excuse. That wasn't the kind of mother I wanted to be. I wanted to be a mommy. I wanted my children to be happy, feel totally and unconditionally loved, and know that they were safe with me. I wept and prayed to change, yet I didn't see a change. What I did feel after that, though, was a nudge inside my heart right before I yelled. But I'd yell anyway and feel even lousier for having yelled, for pushing past the feeling inside.

Eventually when I had that feeling inside me, it would shut my mouth. I would say whatever I needed to in a normal tone and walk away, and the feeling would pass. I was not where I wanted to be. But at the end of the day, I could close my eyes and sleep in peace, knowing that my girls had gone to sleep knowing that they were loved. No matter how frustrated I got, I was finally behaving like a grown-up.

Being a mommy has been the most challenging and wonderful experience in my life. Over the years, it is the one thing that has forced me to grow and taught me how to love the most. I would be nothing without my beautiful and special daughters. They have given me so much more than I could ever give them. All I can do at this point is show, every day that I live, how grateful I am to have them.

February 11, 2014

Sunshine was sick. Her left ear had been infected the previous week. Now her right ear was infected. Poor baby. We made a really fun day out of it, though. We watched a cartoon, played Chutes and Ladders, and went outside and blew bubbles. Faith loved the bubbles. We played dominoes. Then we got ready to have lunch. This was what normal felt like. I loved and appreciated my calm little life.

February 13, 2014

Everything is hashtag this and hashtag that, but I still don't have a Twitter account. Heck, I don't have Internet or cable television service!

Last night, I was up a lot, and it wasn't even the baby's fault. She woke up three times to eat. Mostly, it was Jevon's snoring that was keeping me up, so I lay in bed, staring at the wall and thinking. Finally, I went into Sunshine's room and slept with Faith on the bottom bunk of the bed. She tosses and turns quite a bit in her sleep, and the cat likes to sleep on the bed too, so I hardly got any rest in there either. That gave me even more time to think. Sometimes, I'd have deep thoughts of self-reflection or spirituality on sleepless nights. Last night, I had no interesting revelations. The one thought that meant anything to me was that I am getting old. I feel old because the new generation of people was all about the hashtag, and I'll never be able to think of it as anything but a pound sign. That is a silly thing to lie in bed thinking about, but it consumed my thoughts because of how different I've become from the youth around me. I can see myself as a fuddy-duddy someday, still saying "pound sign" and watching people's eyes glaze over as they wonder what the heck I'm talking about.

Last month I found out that I am going to be a grandmother. Julia is having a child. She is in her twenties and married. They have been trying for a while to have a baby. This is really wonderful news, and what makes it even more amazing is that she wants me to be in the hospital room when she delivers her baby. I am so honored and grateful for this that I don't even have the words. Her due date is September 18. What an exciting and wonderful time.

In other news, Rose got into a fight. She had been seeing a girl in the place where she is serving her time. After they broke up, she and another girl "attacked" the girl whom she had been seeing. They are calling it an attack because the other girl didn't fight back. They held this poor girl down and beat her. Because of this, they will either move Rose to a different detention center or extend her sentence. Either way, I'm sad that Rose is still unable to manage her emotions and make better choices. I am worried about the rage she is exhibiting and concerned that she isn't learning how to control herself.

Rose had no reason to do this. Her excuse was that she was sick of hearing the other girl sing. It breaks my heart to imagine her being so mean. It wasn't shocking to hear she did this. Nothing could shock me after hearing what she did to her dad. It still felt disappointing, because she is now being medicated and is supposed to be making progress. I guess with all of us, progress isn't as clear or quick as we would like it to be. Two steps forward, one step back. My hope is that she will learn how to manage her anger before she tries to make a life for herself out in the world. Otherwise, she may end up seriously hurting or even killing another person. That is my worst fear. I would never want to be responsible for bringing someone who takes another human life into the world. What happened to the beautiful, happy child I nursed, who fell asleep on my chest? *Where did my baby go? What did I do? What can I do now? Where do we go from here?*

On a lighter note, Faith is finally crawling. If I put her down, she can get her little self anywhere she wants to go. It may take a while, but she can get there. Right now, in fact, she is inches away from my keyboard. She is very smart and interested in everything I do. She is so adorable. She has the biggest smile on her face right now. She has the most beautiful little angel face in the whole wide world. After Halo died, I imagined holding her again. I imagined it so much and with such emotional intensity that it made my skin ache. Even my hands ached with the emptiness of not holding her. Now, as I spend my alone time in the morning with my little baby Faith, I appreciate it much more than I could have ever appreciated it had Halo lived. It is pure bliss to watch her, smell her, and touch her, in the quietness of the morning, in my cozy little room with my curtains drawn. There's nothing like our special time together, as I nurse her and watch her snuggle in and close her eyes to take a little cat nap.

February 14, 2014

Today is Valentine's Day and we're planning on dinner out. One of my favorite gifts for Christmas is restaurant gift cards, and Jevon's nephews are always really good about that. This year we have two gift cards, and I plan on using one tonight.

Tomorrow, we're going to Santa Barbara. My mom wants to spend some time together and go through some old pictures she says she hasn't looked through in over twenty years. In a way, I'm looking forward to it, but I'd say the prevailing emotion when I think about doing this is dread. She knows that I'm writing down my story. Maybe these things will trigger some memories and allow me to present a more complete project. We'll see how it goes.

I talked to Rose. We did our usual small talk, which comes somewhat easily now; then we talked about God. She always gets quiet when I talk about God. Since I don't do it very often, I'm not sure if she is ignoring me and rolling her eyes, or listening intently. Either way, I felt it in my heart to tell her that it is perfectly normal to wonder if God is real. I admitted that I too dissected and dismissed many of my childhood ideas about God. "In order to get beyond that," I told her, "what you have to do is ask God to show Himself to you." She was quiet. *Wrap this up quickly*, I thought. "Tell God that if He is real, you need Him to show you," I continued. "If you pray honestly, and are willing to wait for Him to answer you, He will show you in a very personal and real way that He is there." I know it to be the absolute truth, and I know that it works, so now I will wait and see what happens.

February 23, 2014

What I learned from looking at the old pictures was simply this: for every sadness and pain I ever experienced, there were a hundred joys and smiles. There are so many memories of days and moments that were happy, times that were good, and these are far more important and fun to remember. Who out there has had a perfect childhood? Whose family life is ideal? Whose life has been only rainbows and sunshine? My life led me to where I am, and I am grateful for every single day of it. My life, when remembered with an open heart, has been mostly good. I love my dad, I love my mom, and I love my past. If it weren't for that exact path, I would not be who I am today, and I really love who I am. Then the most surprising thing happened. I realized I am, and always have been, okay.

Epilogue

"I can do all things through Christ who gives me strength."

—Philippians 4:13

That verse is my mantra. Everything I thought I couldn't do, including writing this book, has been accomplished because I relied on God. Many biblical verses mean something to me, but this one best fits my life story. It is only because of Him that I have gotten through it all and still have joy. We all go through stuff. I've been through some things, just like everyone else. Do we allow these things to define us and drag us down? How do we turn our pain into positive things from which we can learn? How do we let go of the emotional chains that bind us to our past? The answer is so simple: God.

Faith turned one. SIDS is the leading cause of death in children between the age of one month and one year. I had been anxiously waiting for her to turn a year old so I could sleep, breathe, live. Finally, I felt like we got to keep her.

We were all in the car together, and we went through a fast-food drive-through. Jevon was driving, and the kids were in the back. We were laughing about something. It was a carefree moment in our lives, and it made me feel happy. We are so lucky. We do things together. We eat together. We play together. We listen to each other. We make choices together. We enjoy each other. I could ask for nothing more. I feel happy.

We are moving from our home on Sunset Avenue. Moving has been harder on me than on Jevon, who wanted to move right after Halo died. But I couldn't walk away from the house. All the memories I have of her life are there. It is also the place that cradled me back to life after she went Home. Within those walls I learned how to live again after falling to pieces on drugs. In that bedroom I felt safe enough to remember how to love again. I knew, after she died, that wherever we ran to, we would be exactly the same—just miserable living somewhere else. It was like that saying, *wherever you go, there you are.* I had spent my whole youth running away. I had to stay and make my peace with the house. Now, I think I finally have, so we have decided to move on.

My relationship with my mom has been restored. It may be even better than it was when I was a child. Getting to know her as an adult has been great. Having a relationship with her is a wonderful and unexpected treat. It isn't forced, and it isn't hard. It is nice, fun, and enjoyable. I look forward to seeing her. I love her, quirks and all. She loves me, despite how weird I am at times. Our relationship is better than I ever thought it could be, and I am very grateful for her.

God continues to work on my heart. My understanding and appreciation are developing inside me as I cultivate love with my beautiful little family. My anger, frustration, guilt, and shame are still healing. I am still wonderfully human, but my willingness to listen in the quiet moments brings me peace. I love being with my family, and I love any little bit of solitude I can get. I find myself spending more time in prayer and meditation. What I am discovering is an ultimate gratitude for everything, whether it is a trial or not. I truly feel that God has worked some kind of miracle on my mind. Drugs are dead to me. Now I just wait on Him, seeing what the next chapter in my life will bring.

There are still some unresolved and painful areas of my life. I wonder if or when Payton will ever come back to me. I love her and miss her terribly. I can't stand that she is out there, most likely feeling rejected by me. It breaks my heart for her. I must wait on God to bring her back to me. The situation is so out of my control that I know I must, for my own sanity, let go and trust God. I can't make Walter let me talk to her or see her. This is another opportunity for me to develop my faith. I know he can't keep her away from me forever. And my number one girl, Rose, is still, as of today, in an institution. We talk at every opportunity. She has her good days and her bad days, just like we all do. I think her emotions are almost bigger than what she is capable of tolerating. I don't know where her life will lead her. I wish I could do the normal teenage stuff with her, like teaching her to drive or helping her with relationship problems. There are hundreds of things we've all had to let go because of what happened a year ago. As of now, they still haven't given her a real diagnosis. They throw out terms like autism, bipolar disorder, suicidal/homicidal ideation, personality disorder, and hormonal imbalance. They've thoroughly medicated her. All I can do is love her, support her, and trust that God will carry her through just as He has carried me. What I hope for her is simply this: a normal life. What I hope for all my children, those away from me and those living with me is this: a close relationship with God and to know that they are unconditionally loved. This is my constant prayer for all of them. I look back and think that if I had only felt unconditionally loved that I would have been better off. But hey, I am still okay. Always okay. Even better than that, I am alive and love my life.

The whole point of my book is joy, no matter what. It's not just about being a survivor. Yes, we survive the hardships.

What other choice do we have? We can't curl up and die, though we may want to. It's about using that pain to create inside of ourselves some kind of platform from which to take flight. It's about self-reflection: owning your mistakes, forgiving others for their mistakes, and taking God's hand. I believe that forgiveness is the key to freedom. That includes forgiving yourself. When you let go of the past and approach failures with understanding and compassion, then you can learn to love. The kind of love I feel is bigger than any pain I've ever had. I am filled to capacity and overflowing with love for everyone in my life, including me. Do I feel pain still? Sure. PTSD and depression haven't become strangers to me. Some days are still very hard, but I get up. I stay up. I never give up. In the back of my mind, I know that tomorrow will be better, and if it isn't, the next day will be. So I keep living. I keep remembering what I do have in life.

Is there another soul who has looked in the mirror and not recognized herself? Is there another lost human being in this world who has trudged through life with PTSD wondering how she can wake up and continue fighting to barely survive the day? Is there another broken parent out there reading this who has buried her beautiful, perfect little child? Yes, I know you are out there. I know you are hurting. These pains don't go away. My heart aches for you. Please allow me to help you in the only way I know how.

Life goes on. Life after life goes on. You are not dead yet. There is no such thing as death. All there is to do is something so simple and easy: ask for help. God is right there, waiting. All you have to do is ask Him inside your heart. He is right there, waiting to lift you up and show you the way. All it takes is the willingness to let Him in. Just pray, quietly, inside your own mind or out loud. How happy are you now? What do you have to lose? You have *everything* to gain.

God, I need you in my life. I acknowledge you, and I want to learn more about you. I invite you into my heart and my life. Please show yourself to me, and guide me closer to you from this day forward. I accept you and want to know you more. Amen.

Acknowledgements

First and foremost, I thank God. Without God, I would have lived a self-centered, wasteful life and had an embarrassing, pitiful death. Everything I am and everything I have is because of God.

I thank my husband, "Jevon," for his love and patience. Thank you for marrying me. Thank you for believing in me. Thank you for being the generous and loving father you are to all of our children. Thank you for always kissing me good-bye when you go to work, even if you are mad at me. Thank you for holding down the fort while I was in program. Thank you for how hard you work for our family. Thank you for getting clean and sober with me. It wasn't easy but we did it together. I'm so proud of you. Thank you for making me a better person.

I thank my mom for always believing in me and for encouraging me to write. Without you, there would be no book. Thank you for wanting me when I was born. Thank you for not giving up on me, for always trying to get me back on track, and for never turning me away when I would show up at your house, wanting to get clean, time after time. Thank you for your reaction when I told you I had finally finished the book. Thank you for opening up to me and for rebuilding a relationship with me that is better than I ever could have imagined it would be.

I thank my first daughter, "Rose," for teaching me how to be a mom. You are still my number-one girl and you always will be. I will never stop believing in you. Thank you for being so loving and understanding. You have no idea how beautiful you are, but I hope that someday, you can see yourself the way I see you. Then you will realize you are perfect, exactly the way you are. I am so lucky to have you as my daughter.

I thank my daughter "Payton" for teaching me how to love more deeply than I ever thought I could. Please forgive me, my love. I know I haven't been there for you. Hopefully, someday I will have the opportunity to give you all the love you deserve.

I thank my daughter "Sunshine" for teaching me how to dig deep and never give up. Because of you, I fought, and I won. You are such an open-hearted and special girl. Thank you for making me laugh every single day and for your forgiveness. You were my only reason to get up and keep trying during the hardest part of my life. You are my sunshine and you make me happy when skies are gray.

I thank my daughter "Halo" for teaching me how to love God. If all I could have was thirty-nine days with you, then it was still worth it. You gave so much in so little time. I loved every minute of our life together, and I can't wait to hold you in my arms again. Someday, my angel. Please forgive me.

I thank my daughter "Faith" for bringing me back to life after my heart was broken. You are so precious. I said a million prayers, asking God to give me a baby. And then He gave me you. My life wouldn't have ever been complete without you.

I thank my grandma for unconditional love. You always made me feel safe, special, and wanted. Every kid should have a grandma as beautiful and loving as you are.

Thank you to my biological dad, "Harold," and his wife, "Ivy." You have been so kind and generous to me. Getting to know you has been so much fun. Thank you for treating me like I have been in your lives forever. Thank you for believing in me even when I was a wreck. Thank you for your positivity and encouragement. You love me for better or for worse, and I have desperately needed that. I appreciate you both very much.

I thank Auntie "Carol" for helping me through my grief. Thank you for loving me and my kids and for helping me as often as you do. Your generosity and humor have helped me more than you realize.

I thank my cousin, "Sophia" for all the help and support you have given me with this project. Your willingness to help me made me feel inspired and motivated, and I appreciate everything you've done. You are loyal, generous, and thoughtful and I am lucky to have you as a cousin and best friend. You are the best fairy godmother in the whole world.

Layne, I want you to know that I haven't forgotten you or the gift that you gave me. What you did for me changed my life forever. Had it not been for your compassion I would not have been able to do any of this. Not a day goes by that I don't appreciate you. When I prayed for mercy, God gave me you. Thank you. I owe you my life.

I thank "Jodi" for trying to get me away from what's-his-name. Thank you for putting up with me over the years, even when I let you down. You have always remained open-hearted and kind, no matter what ridiculous thing I was going through. You are a beautiful human being.

Thank you to everyone who donated money to help me with this project. I appreciate the help from my husband, my dad and my mom, my aunts, uncles, cousin and dear friend, Julia. Thank you so much for helping me make my dream a reality.

Thank you, Scott. Your positive feedback, help, and encouragement motivated me to continue on the road to completion. Finding out I was getting published by a Penguin Random House company was one of the best moments of my life! Thank you, Jane. The job you did editing my manuscript was truly incredible. The work you put into it was beyond anything I could have hoped for. When I got the file back and saw all the work you did, I was moved to tears.

Thank you, Pastor Paul and Lucy Berry and our church family at Calvary Chapel Santa Maria. You are wonderful role models. You helped us find God again when we were in a world of hurt. Thank you for your guidance and kindness. I want to be you when I grow up! You lead by example and have shown me how great it really is to be a follower of Jesus Christ.